LIVING THIS LIFE FULLY

Living This Life Fully

Stories and Teachings of Munindra

Mirka Knaster
In collaboration with Robert Pryor

Foreword by Joseph Goldstein

SHAMBHALA
BOSTON & LONDON
2010

Shambhala Publications, Inc.
Horticultural Hall
300 Massachusetts Avenue
Boston, Massachusetts 02115
www.shambhala.com

© 2010 by Mirka Knaster

The author's proceeds from the sale of this book will be donated to establish a scholarship fund at the Barre Center for Buddhist Studies to honor Munindra's memory. All rights reserved. No part of this book may be reproduced in any form or by any means, electronic or mechanical, including photocopying, recording, or by any information storage and retrieval system, without permission in writing from the publisher.

9 8 7 6 5 4 3

Printed in U.S.A.

♾ This edition is printed on acid-free paper that meets the American National Standards Institute z39.48 Standard.
♻ Shambhala makes every effort to print on recycled paper. For more information please visit www.shambhala.com.
Distributed in the United States by Random House, Inc., and in Canada by Random House of Canada Ltd
Designed by Gopa & Ted2, Inc.

Library of Congress Cataloging-in-Publication Data

Knaster, Mirka.
Living this life fully: stories and teachings of Munindra/ Mirka Knaster in collaboration with C. Robert Pryor; foreword by Joseph Goldstein.
p. cm.
Includes bibliographical references.
ISBN 978-1-59030-674-1 (pbk.: alk. paper)
1. Munindra, Anagarika, 1915–2003—Teachings.
2. Dharma (Buddhism) I. Pryor, C. Robert. II. Title.
BQ972.U64K63 2010
294.3'5—dc22
2010022447

Contents

Foreword	vii
Anāgārika Munindra: A Brief Biography	ix
Introduction	xix

1. Be Simple and Easy, Just Rest in Awareness
   Sati (Mindfulness) — 1

2. If You're Not Happy In Body, You're Not Happy Out of Body
   Samādhi (One-Pointedness of Mind) — 17

3. It's Really Possible to Wake Up
   Saddhā (Conviction) — 29

4. Give Everything with an Open Heart
   Dāna (Generosity) — 47

5. Take Care of Dharma and Dharma Takes Care of You
   Sīla (Virtuous Conduct) — 63

6. Say What You Mean and Mean What You Say
   Sacca (Truthfulness, Integrity) — 79

7. I Made Up My Mind
   Adhiṭṭhāna (Determination, Resolve) — 93

8. Slow and Steady Wins the Race
   Viriya (Energy, Vigor) — 109

9. When the Fruit Is Ripe, It Will Fall from the Tree
   Khanti (Patience, Forbearance)   119

10. If You Love Your Enemies, Then You Will Have No Enemies
    Mettā (Loving-Kindness)   129

11. Can I Help You?
    Karunā (Compassion)   147

12. There's No Pizza in Nirvāna—Are You Still Interested in It?
    Nekkhamma (Relinquishment, Renunciation)   159

13. Joy Is a Factor of Awakening
    Pīti (Delight)   171

14. Come and See for Yourself
    Dhamma-vicaya (Investigation, Curiosity)   181

15. No I, No Me, No Mine
    Paññā (Wisdom, Discernment)   195

16. It's All a Passing Show
    Upekkhā (Equanimity)   211

Acknowledgments   225

Notes   229

Glossary   231

Contributors   239

The Munindra Memorial Scholarship and Archives   253

Foreword
Joseph Goldstein

I first met Munindra in 1967. I had been introduced to Buddhism as a Peace Corps volunteer in Thailand two years earlier, but when I returned home and tried to practice meditation on my own, it didn't take long to realize that I needed a teacher to help cut through the confusion in my mind. In those years, the Buddha's teachings were relatively unknown in the West, and I decided to return to Asia in search of someone who could guide me on the path.

Through what Tibetan meditation master Trungpa Rinpoche so aptly called "the pretense of accident," I ended up in Bodh Gaya, the extraordinary place of the Buddha's enlightenment. While sitting in one of the tea shops across from the great Mahabodhi Temple, I heard about a teacher who had just returned from nine years in Burma and who had begun teaching vipassanā meditation. I soon went to meet him, beginning what would become a lifelong relationship with Anāgārika Sri Munindra, a classical meditation master and scholar and a uniquely iconoclastic *kalyāṇamitta,* a spiritual friend.

One of the first things that Munindra said to me when we met was that if I wanted to understand the mind, I should sit down and observe it. The great simplicity and pragmatism of this advice struck a very resonant chord within me. There was no dogma to believe, no rituals to observe; rather, there was the understanding that liberating wisdom can grow from one's own systematic and sustained investigation.

This, indeed, was the outstanding quality of Munindra's life. He always wanted to test the truth of things for himself, to see things firsthand and not simply believe what others had said. And it was this very quality that he encouraged in all of his students. Given the great diversity of Buddhist lineages and traditions, methods and techniques, Munindra's openness of mind became a powerful influence in all of our own unfolding dharma journeys.

Living This Life Fully: Stories and Teachings of Munindra is both an insightful introduction to and a wonderful remembrance of this unusual teacher. Mirka Knaster has woven together recollections from many of Munindra's students, highlighting his great warmth and curiosity, his incisive wisdom and compassion. These stories are a dharma teaching in themselves, revealing how a great teacher takes every circumstance of life as a vehicle for deepening understanding. This book is a testament to a life fully lived.

Anāgārika Munindra
A Brief Biography
Robert Pryor

Anāgārika Munindra was a Bengali Buddhist master and scholar who became one of the most inspiring and influential vipassanā teachers of the twentieth century. For many who met Munindra, even if only briefly, the encounter could resonate years or decades later as a pivotal point in their spiritual life. The power of his presence resided in his single-minded focus on Dharma as a path to realization and awakening. He fully embodied the principles of Dharma and was, for his students, a powerful example of "living the life fully," as Munindra himself would put it. Munindra invited his students to let their practice and life unfold in a natural way. He delivered this advice in an urgent, simple, and very personal way that was the hallmark of his teaching style.

Anāgārika Munindra was a key force in the transmission of Buddhism to the West. He, like Thomas Merton or Alan Watts, was active in the twentieth century as a teacher who linked the traditions of the East and the West, forming bridges between these two complex cultural areas. While Thomas Merton and Alan Watts were Western contemplatives who explored the religious traditions of Buddhism, Anāgārika Munindra was born a Buddhist in India and became a meditation master who was able to convey his teachings in a way that deeply transformed his students in Asia and the West.

Speaking in English, he was able to create a link between the vipassanā tradition of Burma, where he trained with Ven. Mahāsi Sayādaw, and the inquisitive European, North American, Australian, and other Western students whom he inspired and guided in meditation. While Merton and

Watts were Westerners who wrote widely about their spiritual experiments, Munindra was an Easterner whose impact on the world has been felt primarily through the work of his many outstanding students.

Because Munindra taught in a traditional style, person-to-person, rather than through writing, we have been largely in ignorance of the profound effect that he has had and continues to have on the transmission of Dharma to the West. This book brings his message and skillful intuitive style to life for a wider public who did not have the opportunity to practice meditation with him in person during his years of teaching in India and the West.

The following brief biography will clarify how the circumstances of Munindra's life led to his becoming the teacher of so many significant figures in the movement of Buddhism to the West during the twentieth century. There were three major influences that contributed to his success as a teacher of vipassanā meditation: his Buddhist family background, his work with the Mahabodhi Society, and his training in Burma. When combined with his natural intelligence, curiosity, enthusiasm, and goodwill, these experiences prepared him to be one of the most effective vipassanā teachers of the twentieth century and a vital link between the tradition of vipassanā as taught in Burma and the Buddhism that is now taking root in the West.

The Early Years: 1915–36

Munindra was born in a small village near Chittagong in Bengal (located today in Bangladesh) on an auspicious full moon day in June 1915. He was brought up in a Buddhist family that was a part of the Barua clan, a Bengali-speaking Buddhist community that traces its roots to the time of Shākyamuni Buddha. His family was aware from his birth that he was a special child who the astrologers said would be a gifted teacher and not a householder. His father was educated and imparted to him a love of learning and books, as well as a tolerant attitude toward their neighbors in nearby villages who were Muslim and Hindu. While Munindra was still living at home, his father became a monk, and this gave him a personal model for a life that was devoted to Dharma but still in touch with the everyday world.

The influence of his loving and supportive family environment was profound, as was his parents' willingness to let him pursue a life of learning. He attended local schools, where he studied English as well as Bengali and explored various religious traditions through reading. He had a strong love of books from an early age and demonstrated both a single-minded focus and great curiosity. Although he was the top student in his high school class, he chose not to compete in the final exam and receive a graduation certificate, feeling that the pursuit of formal education and certificates had become a distraction from his effort to deeply study Dharma. Nevertheless, he was invited to teach in the local school, and did so for a time, as his intellectual talent was already recognized.

In his Bengali background and early education, it is possible to see the character of Munindra emerge as a humble, intelligent, curious, and open-minded teacher who was respected and supported by his community.

The Mahabodhi Society Years: 1936–57

In 1936, Munindra moved from his village to Calcutta, which was the intellectual capital of India at the time. He was invited to stay at the Bengal Buddhist Association and teach English to the monks there. During this period, he also studied Pāli (the language used in the canonical texts of his Theravāda Buddhist lineage) and the Abhidhamma, an early compilation of Buddhist philosophy and psychology. His curiosity drew him to lectures at the Mahabodhi Society, an organization founded in 1891 to revitalize Buddhism in India and revive pilgrimage sites associated with the life of Shākyamuni Buddha. He gradually became more involved with this organization, adopting the lifestyle of an *anāgārika* (literally, homeless one), an intermediate role between a lay practitioner and monk popularized by Anāgārika Dhammapala, the organization's founder. Although invited to ordain as a Buddhist monk at this early stage of his life, Munindra chose instead the lifestyle of an *anāgārika* because he knew that it would be less restrictive and permit him more time to pursue his studies.

In 1938, he was invited to serve with the Mahabodhi Society in Sarnath, where he spent the next ten years. At that time, both Sarnath and nearby Varanasi were centers of activity for Buddhist, Theosophist, and Hindu teachers, including Krishnamurti, Lama Govinda, and Ānandamayee Ma. Munindra's open-minded nature allowed him to learn from all of these traditions and also to closely observe the various teachers. His personal style continued to be a humble one. Eschewing the formality of some of the gurus he met, we can see the beginning of his own teaching approach as a simple spiritual friend, or *kalyāṇamitta*.

During his time in Sarnath, Munindra's responsibilities included supervising the bookshop at the new Mahabodhi Society temple and answering the many questions of visitors to the temple. On one occasion, Mahatma Gandhi visited, and Munindra sat with him on the cool stone floor, explaining the elegant wall paintings that depicted scenes from the life of the Buddha.

From 1948 to 1951, Munindra accompanied various Mahabodhi Society delegations that took Buddhist relics to Burma, Nepal, Sikkim, and Tibet. These experiences broadened his sense of the Buddhist world and introduced him to many important dignitaries. The relics were conveyed from place to place with great honor and ceremony, while large crowds came to pay their respects along the way. In early 1951, after a demanding trek from Gangtok in Sikkim, the delegation reached the Chumbi Valley in southern Tibet, where the Dalai Lama was in residence. During the delegation's stay there, Munindra met with the Dalai Lama several times. Through this as well as later meetings in Bodh Gaya, Munindra and the Dalai Lama developed a friendship that lasted for decades.

On the journey to Burma, the relics were conveyed on an Indian navy ship, and the delegation was met at the quay with great ceremony. During his long stay in Burma, Munindra had the opportunity to meet U Nu, the Burmese prime minister, as well as many outstanding Buddhist teachers and scholars.

From 1953 to 1957, Munindra was the superintendent of the Mahabodhi Temple in Bodh Gaya, where the Buddha reached enlightenment under the Bodhi Tree. As the first Buddhist superintendent since the twelfth century, he had the important and delicate job of converting the ritual practices at the temple from Hindu to Buddhist, while maintaining the goodwill of the local people.

During these years, he often hosted important visitors to the Mahabodhi Temple, including Prime Minister Nehru as well as many notable Buddhist leaders. In 1956, he was part of the Buddha Jayanti celebration on the 2,500th anniversary of the Buddha's passing away, or *parinibbāna*. At this time, many political leaders visited Bodh Gaya, and Munindra was invited by U Nu to travel to Burma for the purpose of learning vipassanā meditation. The practice of vipassanā had disappeared in India centuries earlier when Buddhism died out in most of the country; however, it had been preserved in Burma. Munindra understood that mastering vipassanā would allow him to directly experience Dharma, and so he welcomed this invitation with enthusiasm.

During the years from 1936 to 1957, the Mahabodhi Society had become the second major influence on Munindra's thinking and character. Working with the society enabled him to pursue his interests in studying Pāli, Abhidhamma, Theosophy, and Yoga, while learning Hindi and improving his English. He continued to evidence his early character traits—humility, intelligence, curiosity, and open-mindedness in these new situations.

Throughout this period, Munindra continued to value learning and books above worldly concerns, even though he was actively involved in helping the Mahabodhi Society. Finally, when offered the chance to learn vipassanā in Burma, he unhesitatingly accepted the opportunity to deepen his understanding of Dharma.

Dharma Practice and Study in Burma: 1957–66

During his years in Burma, vipassanā meditation became the third major influence on Munindra and the focus of his life from that time forward. After his arrival, he first spent several months at Sasana Yeiktha meditation center in Rangoon practicing under the guidance of Ven. Mahāsi Sayādaw, one of the greatest Burmese meditation masters of the time. Munindra reached high levels of spiritual accomplishment due to his previous preparation and single-minded dedication to the practice. Despite considerable pain in his body, he sat for long hours of continuous practice and achieved remarkable progress relatively quickly. It was here that he developed his devotion to the lineage of his teacher, who instructed him in personal interviews throughout his training. In later years, he would always carry a simple square of cloth given to him by Mahāsi Sayādaw as a cover for his meditation cushion. With great deference, he would gently place it on his seat before beginning his practice, thus honoring his teacher each time that he sat to practice or give a dharma talk.

After this initial period of practice, Munindra spent five years in intensive study of the Pāli Canon under the guidance of U Maung Maung, a highly respected Theravāda scholar, eventually becoming a master of the intellectual as well as the experiential aspects of vipassanā meditation. Every day during these years, he studied from dawn to dusk with enthusiasm, and he later remarked that understanding the Pāli texts was easy once one had direct experience of the Dharma through meditation.

When he had completed his studies, he returned to the meditation center of Mahāsi Sayādaw, where he trained as a meditation teacher and was valued as a spiritual guide by members of the Bengali Buddhist community living in Rangoon. He even trained some of his Bengali students in concentration, or *jhāna,* practice and the development of psychic powers in order to prove that this could still be done by following the classic texts. He verified that some of his students were able to see into the future, visit other realms of existence, or even appear suddenly at a distant place. The most skilled of these meditators was Dipa Ma (Nani Bala Barua), who later became an influential vipassanā teacher after returning to Calcutta and was highly respected in the United States as well.

After mastering both the theory and practice of vipassanā as taught at Sasana Yeiktha meditation center, he requested permission from Mahāsi Sayādaw to receive training in several other methods of vipassanā so that he could understand the full range of techniques then available in Burma. Munindra then spent several months visiting other meditation centers and acquainting himself with their methods of vipassanā training. Thus he came to realize the wide variety of methods that could be employed in the service of directly experiencing Dharma. During his last year in Burma, Munindra was ordained as a Buddhist monk. However, when he decided to return to India, he determined that it would be more effective to teach there as an *anāgārika*. So he gave up his monk's robes in favor of the simple white clothes that became familiar to his later students.

The vipassanā movement in Burma that shaped Munindra holds that the principal goal of meditation practice is liberation or awakening rather than simply the reduction of suffering or stress. This movement developed in the late nineteenth and early twentieth centuries as part of a revitalization of Buddhism in the face of the challenges of European colonialism and the introduction of Christianity. Burmese teachers such as Ledi Sayādaw and Mahāsi Sayādaw felt the need to emphasize the personal realization of Dharma in one's present life, and vipassanā meditation was the key to this transformation. This approach tended to put less stress on the importance of ritual practices. Therefore, the vipassanā that Munindra learned was not dependent on traditional Buddhist rituals or beliefs that were unassociated with the pursuit of realization through meditation practice.

The form of vipassanā practice that Munindra studied in Burma would later appeal to his Western students in Bodh Gaya. At Mahāsi Sayādaw's center in Rangoon, vipassanā meditation was taught in personal interviews rather than large lectures. Each practitioner would work at his or her own speed, according to the teacher's advice and supervision. Although there was great respect for the lineage of the teacher, there was not a sense of the infallibility of the guru, but rather the teacher was looked on as a spiritual friend.

This would be the model of instruction that Munindra later followed and with which he was always most comfortable.

Realization or enlightenment is said to occur in four successive stages that are recognizable to the teacher. These stages are *sotāpanna, sakadāgāmī, anāgāmī,* and finally *arahant*. At each stage, some of one's impurities are eliminated, but removal of all negative character traits is not reached until the fourth and final stage of *arahant*. To be an effective vipassanā teacher, it is not considered necessary to have reached that final stage. There is an implicit recognition that teachers are human and fallible and that one's personality remains even after attaining realization. Munindra became a living example of the expression of enlightenment through a distinctive personality. Years later, his students would comment on how he embodied Dharma through his unique style and perspective.

When Munindra departed for India in 1966, after nearly nine years in Rangoon, he took with him twenty-six crates of Buddhist books as well as the blessings of the vipassanā community. He was, in fact, fulfilling a Burmese Buddhist prophecy that anticipated a resurgence of Buddhism and vipassanā meditation 2,500 years after the Buddha. This helps to explain not only why Munindra felt called to return to India and teach vipassanā where it had been unavailable for so many centuries but also the reason why hundreds of Burmese came to the wharf to bid him farewell when his ship set sail. His action was seen by all involved as the fulfillment of a historic prediction, the beginning of the movement of Buddhist practice back to the land of its origin and then onward to the rest of the world. Munindra was uniquely prepared to carry these hopes, as he was a fully qualified vipassanā teacher who had thoroughly mastered the Pāli Canon and was fluent in Bengali, Hindi, and English.

The Bodh Gaya Years: 1966–85

On returning to India, the natural place for Munindra to settle was Bodh Gaya, where the Buddha had attained enlightenment under the Bodhi Tree. He never went back to being superintendent of the temple but simply lived in Bodh Gaya and was available for teaching. As he began to offer instruction in vipassanā, all the strands of his background finally came together. His knowledge, experience, language abilities, and humble style attracted more and more students. He was a model of integrating the practice in daily life, and his open-minded approach was particularly attractive to young

Westerners. He did not hesitate to send his students to other meditation teachers, and Hindu gurus, such as Neem Karoli Baba, often sent their students to him.

Munindra became a key resource and teacher to many Westerners who are now important teachers and writers in the movement of Buddhism to the West. His love of books, knowledge of Buddhist philosophy and psychology, familiarity with a wide variety of traditions, and fluency in English enabled him to inspire a generation of Westerners who had eclectic interests and a deep curiosity about meditation. The teaching style he used was an informal interview that put people at ease and allowed them to ask as many questions as needed. As so many of his students report, he taught as much by his actions and advice in the bazaar as through his formal meditation instruction. His simple and committed lifestyle was an inspiration to his students, who saw him as an embodiment of Dharma.

From 1966 to 1977, he remained in Bodh Gaya, but beginning in 1977, he was invited by his students to travel and teach in North America, Europe, and Australia. From 1962 until the 1980s, Burma was closed to outside visitors who wished to practice meditation; therefore, Munindra became one of the few qualified teachers available who could teach vipassanā in English at that time. During those years, he lived very simply at Samanvaya, the Gandhi ashram, or the Burmese Vihar. Anyone with an interest could ask him for instruction, and he would give individual advice based on the person's questions and level of experience. Munindra was generous with his time and would often spend hours each day with whoever wanted to see him.

The years 1977 to 1985 found Munindra particularly busy with many teaching tours to Western countries, as well as time spent teaching in Bodh Gaya and Calcutta. This was a period of expansion and experimentation for the vipassanā movement, which was new in the West. In 1976, several of Munindra's students, including Joseph Goldstein and Sharon Salzberg, founded the Insight Meditation Society in Barre, Massachusetts, which has since become one of the most important centers for vipassanā training in North America. Munindra was invited to teach at this and other centers that his students had founded. Although he enjoyed traveling in the West, his heart always remained in India.

Munindra's Western students were impressed by his level of energy when traveling, as well as his insatiable curiosity for all that was new and strange to him. Between meditation retreats, he was always happy to explore the local sights with his students, and he often had more energy than they did even though he was much older. However, after 1984, Munindra largely remained in India, as his health was often not good enough to travel and he preferred to live in India.

The Later Years: 1985–2003

In 1985, Munindra had surgery in Calcutta that was not successful and led to poor health for the next few years. After a second surgery in 1988, he spent several months recuperating in Hawai'i at the home of his student Kamala Masters, who later became a vipassanā teacher herself. Fully recovered, he returned to India and was invited by S. N. Goenka, the influential lay teacher of vipassanā, to stay at Goenka's meditation center at Igatpuri, near Bombay, where the climate would be better for his health. Goenka and Munindra had been friends since Munindra's time in Burma. When Goenka began to teach vipassanā in India, Munindra encouraged him and sent many of his students to practice with him. From 1991 until his death, Munindra spent the majority of his time at Igatpuri, where he lived in retirement but was consulted on matters relating to the Pāli Canon. He occupied a simple meditation hut that was frequented by visitors when he was not in retreat.

Starting in 1979, Munindra began to teach vipassanā annually to a group of American university students in the Antioch Education Abroad Buddhist Studies Program. Throughout his retirement, Munindra faithfully kept this commitment and taught for three weeks in Bodh Gaya each September. He also spent some time each fall in Calcutta, where he visited family, friends, and students before returning to Igatpuri for the remainder of the year.

In this final period of his life, Munindra continued to inspire the students who practiced with him through his enthusiasm for Dharma and his example of what it means to lead a life in Dharma. As the years passed, his teeth began to fail, but he refused to get false teeth, as he insisted that he wanted to experience the natural changes of aging. He would often remark that his body was failing, but his mind was quite fine.

Munindra's love of books and learning persisted, as did his open-minded approach to Dharma. Although he was a living example of the power of meditation to reduce stress, he continued to insist that the purpose of vipassanā practice is to attain liberation and that it is possible to do so in this life. His single-minded focus on enlightenment and the path to realization was conveyed with an urgent conviction to those he met. Even as he lay ill and dying at his family home in Calcutta, Munindra was still able to inspire his visitors with the clarity of his vision of Dharma and the power of his loving-kindness.

Introduction

Mirka Knaster

Diminutive yet striking in his signature white robes and white hat, Munindra was an enthusiastic, energetic, and immensely inquisitive Bengali meditation master who had a profound impact on people everywhere he went, even on many who never met him. Those whose lives he touched remember him not only for his erudition and expert guidance but, most importantly, for his embodiment of Dharma—he lived what he taught. Through his presence and actions, Munindra made otherwise abstract ideals come alive.

Like his fellow countryman Mahatma Gandhi, Munindra was one of those rare individuals who demonstrate seamless integration, rather than conflicted separation, between daily life and spiritual practice. Through his attitudes and behavior, he held out the potential of what is attainable: to be at home in this body, in this place, in this time, under these conditions; happy and at peace with oneself and in harmony with others.

Munindra was also an illustration of what neuroscientists are now able to confirm through sophisticated technology: By training the mind, one can change the brain so that positive emotions become enduring character traits, rather than just occasional states. Based on his personal knowledge, Munindra was convinced that even nowadays people are capable of tasting what the Buddha and his disciples experienced more than 2,500 years ago. What may seem out of the ordinary or even impossible is actually within reach of those who make the effort. Yet Munindra never pretended to be extraordinary, exceptional, or perfect. He was simply a flourishing human being, not a saint. With all his idiosyncrasies and fallibility, he walked the path and enabled others to walk it too.

For Munindra, spiritual life was not limited to meditating in silence, living in a monastery, or attending intensive retreats. Nor did a life steeped in Dharma have anything to do with arcane and esoteric doctrines or ritualistic and exclusionary practices. Munindra made Dharma highly accessible and himself widely available. His easygoing, outside-the-box, nonsectarian openness, as well as a no-frills, no-airs attitude, had great appeal. According to Munindra, Dharma was all about "living the life fully."

A Surprising Start

The idea for this book came unexpectedly and inexplicably. In May 2004, I was sitting and minding my own breath in the meditation hall at the Forest Refuge, in Barre, Massachusetts, when a thought arose out of nowhere. It was as though someone suddenly asked out loud, "Who is honoring Munindra-ji's* life and legacy in the *Dhamma*?" But, of course, there was complete silence in the hall.

Later, in my room, I jotted down the question and then let it go. Perplexed as to why it had arisen in my mind, once my month-long retreat was over, I decided to inquire among several individuals who had been close to Munindra (who had passed away the previous October). Kamala Masters suggested that I contact Robert Pryor, who had known Munindra since 1972. When I reached Robert, I learned that in 2000 he had conducted twenty-one hours of interviews with Munindra and also had received permission to use photographs from Munindra's extensive collection in any future book about his life. After some discussion, Robert and I decided that since our intentions were similar—to pay tribute to an important dharma teacher and pass on his wisdom—we would collaborate on the project and, in the spirit of *dana*, any proceeds would be donated to a scholarship fund at the Barre Center for Buddhist Studies in memory of Munindra.

So I set aside two other writing projects and began to search for people around the world who had known Munindra. One person led to another and, in turn, to another. After listening to hundreds of down-to-earth, poignant, humorous, and instructive stories, I became determined to find a way to share those personal experiences as well as Munindra's direct teachings. I sensed that, when woven together, they would provide a panorama of his life and service and, simultaneously, inspire and encourage readers on their own voyages of transformation.

---

* In India, adding *ji* to someone's name or title is a sign of affection and respect.

Yet Another Surprise

The question that arose during my retreat was not the only mystery that presented itself. There was also a curious incident that occurred in Asia.

In addition to interviewing most people by phone and some via e-mail, I went to India to meet Munindra's family in Calcutta, to visit some of his old haunts both there and in Bodh Gaya, and to interview local people who had known him. Then I did the same in Burma, which was Munindra's spiritual home in many ways. It was in Rangoon that something completely unanticipated happened. When I was introduced to Daw Than Myint, she handed me a simple school notebook that Munindra had entrusted to her a few days before returning to India in 1966. In it, he had written a short autobiography.

Unbeknownst to anyone, this record of Munindra's life had been sitting in a bookcase in Daw Than Myint's family home for four decades. Amazingly, it had escaped destruction by the moisture, heat, and insects common to a tropical climate. Other books in the bookcase had succumbed to silverfish, and hundreds of books stored in trunks had been eaten by termites. Yet, somehow, this inexpensive notebook had remained intact and unblemished. Daw Than Myint said to me, "I have been waiting forty years for someone to come and use this," and I felt the hairs on my arms stand up.

About the Book

Living This Life Fully is divided into sixteen chapters. Each one is devoted to a different quality of awakened mind and heart and to how Munindra embodied and taught that particular quality. There are many qualities to cultivate on a spiritual path, but I focus specifically on these sixteen because they represent various schemata in the Buddha's teaching. I derived them as follows.

The *bodhipakkhiyā-dhammā* are the thirty-seven qualities conducive to awakening or enlightenment. They are divided into seven sets: the four foundations of mindfulness (*satipaṭṭhāna*); the four right efforts (*padhāna*); the four roads to power (*iddhi-pāda*); the seven factors of awakening (*bojjhaṅga*); the five spiritual faculties (*indriya*); the five spiritual powers (*bala*); and the Eightfold Path (*aṭṭhaṅgika-magga*). I made a chart of these thirty-seven qualities, then added the ten perfections (*pāramī*) and the four divine abodes (*brahma-vihāra*), and observed quite a bit of overlap. From these lists, I distilled seventeen discrete qualities. However, in the process of writing, I eliminated a chapter on calm or tranquility (*passaddhi*) because the quality appears within so many stories throughout the book.

Each chapter focuses on a specific quality, but deciding where to situate a particular story often provoked a debate in my mind as I wondered which quality it best exemplifies. For example, one particular anecdote someone shared was not exclusively about loving-kindness (*mettā*), as it also clearly exemplified mindfulness (*sati*) and effort (*viriya*). Thus, placing it in the chapter on *mettā* was somewhat arbitrary.

No one quality functions in isolation. The Buddha's path is not a linear progression from A to Z. Bringing any characteristic to fulfillment is a matter of bringing them all to fruition, for everything on the path operates by way of mutual support, reciprocity, and interdependence.

Living This Life Fully begins with mindfulness and ends with equanimity (*upekkhā*). It could have as easily opened with generosity (*dāna*) and closed with wisdom (*paññā*). You can move from chapter 1 to chapter 16 or read whichever chapter appeals to you randomly. In the same way, when you choose a quality to cultivate, you may soon notice that, perforce, others come into play to complement and reinforce it.

If you are interested in a greater explanation of a quality, at the end of each chapter I have given a detailed definition set off from the body of the chapter. At the opening of each chapter, you will find a brief one- or two-word definition of the quality. However, translating a Pāli term into only one English word is a challenge because there are shades of meaning that are lost. Take *saddhā,* which is usually rendered as "faith," a word that conveys something quite different in Christianity than it does in the Buddha's teaching and, thus, could be misinterpreted. The definitions at the end of each chapter provide some understanding of the origin and nuances of the terms. These definitions are not from Munindra, but are based on my own research and have been checked by dharma teachers and scholars. In combining personal anecdotes with this information, my intention is to honor Munindra's own way of being in the world and teaching—everyday experience partnered with scholarship.

Direct Quotations

Each chapter opens with one of Munindra's pithy utterances, while a quote from the Pāli Canon, generally from the Buddha, concludes it. Within the text itself, indented paragraphs are direct statements from Munindra, taken from talks recorded by David Johnson in the late 1970s and from a series of interviews that Robert Pryor conducted with Munindra in 2000. Other quotes attributed to Munindra (those not set off as extracts) vary in tone or idiom because they are paraphrased or based on what people remember hearing him say. Variations also may be due to the fact that English is not the first language for some of the people I interviewed.

Foreign Terms and Conventions

I have included Pāli terms throughout the book to reflect how Munindra communicated: He incorporated the ancient scriptural language into his dharma talks and conversations. I hope they will arouse your interest, stimulate further exploration, and help expand your practice of Dharma.

Munindra most often referred to the Pāli rather than Sanskrit version of a name or term: Gotama rather than Gautama Buddha, Dhamma rather than Dharma, Abhidhamma rather than Abhidharma, *kamma* rather than karma, *nibbāna* rather than nirvāna. I did not alter direct quotes to make them uniform, but left them as I heard them, to reflect how Munindra or another person spoke. When Pāli and other foreign terms (Hindi, Sanskrit, and Burmese) occur in the text for the first time, they bear a brief definition that is usually not repeated but can be located in the glossary at the back.

Sanskrit terms that are familiar and appear in English dictionaries are not in italics; for example, karma, nirvāna, sūtra, and Dharma. All Pāli terms are in italics, except for Dhamma and vipassanā. Since these words are so frequently used, they are italicized only the first time they occur. I have included diacritics because, otherwise, certain names and terms might have not only a different pronunciation but also another meaning. However, I have chosen not to use diacritical marks in the names of geographical places and institutions because these names are easily recognizable without them. Although some place names in Asia have changed, I have kept those that Munindra was accustomed to: Calcutta instead of Kolkata, Rangoon and Burma instead of Yangon and Myanmar, Varanasi instead of Benares.

Contributors

Living This Life Fully is a project built entirely on generosity (*dāna*). More than two hundred people helped to make this book possible by contributing leads, interviews, recordings, scholarly expertise, photographs, letters and other memorabilia, hospitality, and much more. While everyone is recognized in the acknowledgments, only those individuals who are directly quoted in the text are briefly described in a list of contributors at the back of the book. This was done simply to avoid the awkwardness of repeatedly identifying a person. These succinct descriptions are based on information provided by the people themselves.

Abbreviations

Quotations from the following texts that compose the Pāli Canon were taken from a variety of translations in published works (see bibliography) as well as from the website accesstoinsight.org. In a few instances, Munindra translated Pāli passages directly while speaking, in a dharma talk or an interview.

Texts from the Pāli Canon:

AN	Aṅguttara Nikāya (Numerical Discourses)
BV	Buddhavaṃsa
DN	Dīgha Nikāya (Long Discourses)
Dhp	Dhammapada
It	Itivuttaka
Khp	Khuddakapāṭha
MN	Majjhima Nikāya (Middle-Length Discourses)
SN	Saṃyutta Nikāya (Connected Discourses)
Sn	Sutta Nipāta
Ud	Udāna

OTHER ABBREVIATIONS

BCBS   Barre Center for Buddhist Studies
IMS   Insight Meditation Society
SRMC   Spirit Rock Meditation Center

Final Note

Researching and writing *Living This Life Fully* afforded me an illuminating experience of great satisfaction that I could never have anticipated that day in May at the Forest Refuge. It has been a privilege and an honor to be moved to tears and amused into laughter by the many people who were willing to reflect on Munindra's influence and impact. I am deeply gratified by how much I have learned and how much that has affected my own practice. May Munindra's life and the stories of those who knew him also provide a source of deep inspiration and encouragement as you journey toward peace, happiness, and freedom.

1

Be Simple and Easy, Just Rest in Awareness

Sati (Mindfulness)

When mindfulness is there, all the beautiful qualities are nearby.
—MUNINDRA

The practice of mindfulness, of nonjudgmental awareness, lies at the heart of the Buddhist path. For Munindra, mindfulness was not a mystical state but a mundane act that anyone could and should do in any moment. He emphasized this to his students:

> Everything is meditation in this practice, even while eating, drinking, dressing, seeing, hearing, smelling, tasting, touching, thinking. Whatever you are doing, everything should be done mindfully, dynamically, with totality, completeness, thoroughness. Then it becomes meditation, meaningful, purposeful. It is not thinking, but experiencing from moment to moment, living from moment to moment, without clinging, without condemning, without judging, without evaluating, without comparing, without selecting, without criticizing—choiceless awareness.
>
> Meditation is not only sitting; it is a way of living. It should be integrated with our whole life. It is actually an education in how to see, how to hear, how to smell, how to eat, how to drink, how to walk with full awareness. To develop mindfulness is the most important factor in the process of awakening.

For many students, Munindra's best teachings took place outside the meditation hall. "One of the nice things about him was he was just very ordinary in how he taught you," says Daniel Goleman. "You would walk into the bazaar with him and go to the post office. He was the epitome of mindfulness all the time."

This afforded Akasa Levi a model of what it means to be an elder in the Dharma, to be a full human being. "He was always pointing out details," says Akasa. "At the bazaar he would say, 'Notice how the lemons are stacked. See how the vendor does that, where he puts the bad ones and keeps the ripe ones.' We'd be walking along, and my mind would be running, and he would say, 'Oh, look! See the little flower!' He would bend to look at it and say, 'See, it grows like this.' He would lightly touch it, taking me out of my head and back to the earth, back to what was right there. You could say he distracted me back to the present moment. He was very good and very soft with that. Munindra would say, 'Pay attention. Be mindful of all the details.' He would stick the word *mindfully* into just about every other sentence he uttered."

When Ginny Morgan wants to bring to mind a paradigm of how to move through the world, she too recalls her time with Munindra: "To wander around in a flea market and have someone buying something on one hand and then turning it into a dharma talk, going back and forth, and have it all be of one fabric, was really powerful for me."

Michael Liebenson Grady, who was Munindra's attendant at Insight Meditation Society (IMS) for a time, adds, "Munindra had the ability to see the Dharma everywhere, in everything, including all the ordinary experiences of daily life. This attitude is helpful to lay practitioners. Some of my most vivid memories are mealtimes with him. I used to watch him eat. He had a healthy appetite and was so mindful and present when eating."

Mind and Mindfulness

"Mind and mindfulness are two different things," Munindra used to explain.

> Mind by nature has no color. When it is colored with greed, we call it "greedy mind." When anger arises, at that moment, it is called "angry man" or "angry mind." If there is no mindfulness, mind is influenced by this anger. Anger has the nature to pollute the mind; it creates poison. But mind is not anger; anger is not mind. Mind is not greed; greed is not mind. Please remember

this. Mind has no nature of liking or disliking. "Mind" means "knowing faculty," "cognizing faculty."

Munindra would then describe *sati:*

> Mindfulness is a different thing: alertness, awareness, remembering, heedfulness. It means not to forget, just to be aware, to be mindful of what is going on. When you are asked to walk on a [narrow] one-bamboo bridge over the river, you have to be so careful on every step. Once you forget, there is every possibility of falling down. If you lose your mindfulness, you will hurt yourself or kill yourself. So, in reality, mindfulness means not to forget what is going on at the present moment—in thought, in word, in deed.

Munindra noted that though the mind is "always there, always working," we are not always mindful. He said, "Many times you will see that mind is not with you, you are not with the mind. Mind is somewhere else, thinking something else, while [the] eating process is going on mechanically, unmindfully." According to Munindra, there is only one way to conduct all activities—with moment-to-moment awareness.

The Practice Is Simple

Munindra highlighted simplicity and ease. Joseph Goldstein says he must have repeated thousands of times, "Be simple and easy. Take things as they come." Still, that is a challenge, especially early in one's practice. As Munindra once mildly chided Michael Stein, "The practice is simple, and you make it complicated."

Sometimes students misunderstood Munindra's use of "simple." When they saw him bargaining intensely, even for a bag of peanuts, they questioned his action and reminded him, "You said to be simple and easy. What are you doing?" He would pause, then respond, "I said to be simple, not a simpleton." As Roy Bonney understands this, "Essentially, what I took from it is that it's really important to have a practice and recognize the truth of the world, but don't be a fool in the world."

Munindra taught that true meditation can have a refreshing or relaxing effect:

> When mind comes to a silent state, then we recoup our energy again. Meditation is not forcing, not straining oneself. It is harmonious work with the whole being, not fighting. If we understand the process of meditation, it is so simple. As long as we do not understand, it is an extraordinarily difficult task because our mind is not trained not to cling, not to condemn, not to judge, just to be with what is at the moment. But once you understand the Law [Dharma], then it is the most simple thing—it is a way of life. As one develops mindfulness, after some time it takes care of itself; it becomes effortless, automatic.

His words were a balm for Larry Rosenberg: "His instructions were so simple and natural and ordinary: Just be aware of what's happening. But I was in tears. It was his emphasis on awareness, which for me is the whole thing. He knew that the bottom line was finally, 'Are you awake or aren't you?' I had been with Zen teachers and Tibetan teachers and there was a huge amount of culture, and he didn't bring much cultural baggage at all. Awareness was awareness, and it was open to anyone."

This "amazing awareness" is what Matthias Barth found so special about Munindra, for it was evident in the most commonplace circumstances. "In his presence, even the arrival of a train at a London tube station became an event. The sound of the train, at first hardly noticeable, growing ever more with its approach, the wind being pushed before it, the movement of the waiting crowd—all this came alive in the field of his infectious mindfulness. Being with Munindra was a living practice of moment-to-moment awareness, awake and open in the here and now."

No One Way to Be Mindful

Among the many methods of *vipassanā* (insight meditation), Munindra never designated "the right one." Jack Engler says, "Whether it was mindfulness of sensation or mindfulness of another class of objects at any one of the sense doors made little difference to him, as long as it was mindfulness."

"I didn't feel any sectarianism from him at all, or 'you gotta sign up for something' or 'you shouldn't sign up for something,'" Eric Kupers says with a laugh. "It was just very much about the living truth of the teachings in the moment in a very down-to-earth way."

Munindra's acceptance of various ways to practice was due to his receptive nature and to his experiences in Burma. After intensive training with Mahāsi Sayādaw, and with his permission, Munindra studied with local teachers who taught different forms of insight meditation. He stated,

> I found all these trainings complementary, not contradictory. All these methods are for the development of *Dhamma*. They are a means, not the end. If one trains one's mind in one way and thoroughly understands, then other methods are not difficult. Whatever sect or school one may belong to, it is always helpful if you keep the mind open, because there is nothing to cling to.

Munindra kept his mind open, urging mindfulness even in those activities he did not subscribe to. Mirko Frýba (now Ven. Āyukusala Thera) learned this when he first arrived in Bodh Gaya in 1967. After visiting the Mahabodhi Temple, he sat down in a small tearoom next to the stairs leading to the temple entrance and caught sight of a bald monk clad in bright yellow and smoking a cigarette. "What does your guru say to your smoking?" Mirko twitted him. The monk replied, "My guru says, 'Bring the cigarette to your lips mindfully, then mindfully notice the touch sensation, then mindfully inhale, then mindfully notice the feeling. . . .'" Mirko asked him for an introduction, and the monk took him to see Munindra.

The Bigger Picture

Munindra never encouraged frivolity in practice, but his open-mindedness impressed and inspired his students. Appreciating Munindra's free-form approach, Sharon Salzberg says, "His view of meditation was very big—live mindfully—it's OK if you go to the bazaar for a cup of *chai* [tea]. He kept broadening my sense of what the Dharma is and what the path is. He left me with a very big sense of, as he put it, 'living the life,' of not being so prescribed and formalistic or stylized about practice, but really understanding its roots in transforming one's mind."

Lama Surya Das agrees, "What always comes up for me is how sitting meditation is not the end-all and be-all. Walking meditation, mindfulness in daily life, and so forth, were also extremely important. He really exemplified that and took away the total emphasis on just silent, closed-eyed meditation. He helped me understand more about what living Dharma and mindfulness practice and real awareness are. He was a great teacher of integrating

Dharma in daily life, how to be mindful in daily life." Or, as Saibal Talukbar expresses it, "Life and Dhamma are always to be connected."

The major impact Munindra had on Grahame White was helping him see that practice becomes a holistic way of living. "What he was able to do was show me that the ten-day retreat syndrome wasn't really where it was at, that it really had to be an ongoing part of your life," he says. As Munindra used to repeat, "You can practice any time." Grahame adds, "That was the thing that eased all my tensions, and I was able to relax much more with my understanding. It took me a while to get it, but once I learned it and became independent in my mind, that was the greatest thing—to not think that meditation practice had to take a particular form, to be restricted to retreats. As long as you learn to be mindful in whatever situation you're in, you're OK."

Jack Kornfield puts it succinctly: "He didn't divide life from meditation." And that is why he was such a vital model for people East and West.

Mindfulness for Householders

Kamala Masters greatly benefited from Munindra's approach to mindfulness in everyday life. As a young mother struggling to raise three children, she was unable to dedicate time to formal sitting practice and retreats. Munindra did not let her family circumstances be an obstacle. When he found out that she spent a lot of time washing dishes, he immediately seized the opportunity to teach her *sati* at the kitchen sink. He instructed her to have a general awareness of washing the dishes: the movement of her hands, the warmth or coolness of the water, picking a dish up, soaping it, rinsing it, putting it down. "Nothing else is happening now—just washing the dishes," he said. Then he told her to experience her posture. He did not insist on her moving slowly or observing every detail of every moment. Instead, she was to exercise general mindfulness of whatever was occurring as she cleaned the dishes.

Standing next to her, Munindra would occasionally inquire, "What's happening now?" When she replied, "I'm worried about paying the mortgage," he would suggest, "Just notice 'worried,' and bring your attention back to washing the dishes." When she told him, "I'm planning what to cook for dinner," he repeated, "Just notice 'planning,' because that's what is in the present moment, and then return to just washing the dishes."

Munindra guided Kamala with as much seriousness as though on a formal retreat. By practicing diligently, she soon realized its advantages. "Doing this ordinary task with intentional mindfulness has helped me to notice and experience many things more clearly," says Kamala. "The changing physical sensations, the flow of thoughts and emotions, and my surrounding environment are all much more alive. This practice helped collect my mind so that it was not so scattered. It has required me to develop more perseverance, patience, humility, clear intention, and honesty with myself. These are no small things. Just from washing the dishes! The resulting enjoyment of being more fully present with life is a rare treasure in this world."

Instructing Kamala in how to wash dishes mindfully was only one part of the training. Munindra also noticed that she passed through the hallway from her bedroom to the living room many times each day, so he suggested it as an ideal place for walking meditation. From the threshold of her bedroom door, he directed, "Every time you step into this hallway, see if you can use the time as an opportunity to be present with the simple fact of walking. Just walking. Not thinking about your mother or about the children . . . just experiencing the body walking. It might help you to make a silent mental notation of every step. With each step, very quietly in your mind you can note, 'stepping, stepping, stepping.' This will help you keep your attention connected to your intention of 'just walking.' If the mind wanders to something else, as soon as you notice that it has wandered, make the silent mental note, 'wandering mind.' Do this without judging, condemning, or criticizing. In a simple and easy way, bring your attention back to just the walking. Your practice in this hallway will be a wonderful training for you. It will also benefit those around you because you will feel more refreshed."

Kamala recalls that it did not seem like much of a spiritual practice, but every day as she walked back and forth through that hallway on her way to do something, she had a few moments of clear presence of mind—unhurried, unworried, at ease with life for those precious ten steps. And she extended mindfulness practice to all the household chores—washing clothes, ironing, wiping counters. This was her main practice for several years.[1]

Slowly and Quickly

Just as Munindra's perspective on mindfulness had nothing to do with being in a special place, it also did not require a slow pace. That he moved quickly, but always mindfully, expanded a student's comprehension of practice. "He seemed to be more of an explorer in motion than in stillness," says Erik Knud-Hansen. "I think he did his sitting practice privately in the early mornings—he did the stillness part on his own time. During the day, he was out and about. Watching him, I learned that the speed of your body doesn't have to detract from an emphasis on the mind seeing the truth. In the last twenty years or so of teaching Dharma, I've appreciated the need for the seeing of the truth to not be related to some particular bodily attitude or even mental attitude—truth is truth every moment. I think that he understood that some people wanted to get stuck in slowness."

Erik continues, "He was reflecting an area of practice that some people would respond to by saying, 'That's not practice; that's just being alive.' Somebody who is living Dharma is not making that distinction, whether sitting down, standing up, talking, walking through Disney World, or walking in a meditation hall. Munindra's example and teaching was seeing the truth not so much based on a specific practice, but seeing the truth of mind itself. He taught the freedom to be alive and to see things that are right in front of your face."

The Benefits of Seeing the Truth of Each Moment

Munindra's message, says Robert Sharf, is "Basically, it doesn't matter what style of practice you're doing. Either you're doing it mindfully or you're not. And if you're doing it mindfully, there will be benefits; if you're not doing it mindfully, there won't." Munindra said,

> People can do things better when they are mindful. It is not only beneficial on a spiritual level, it is also beneficial on a physical level. It is a process of purification too. When mind is purified, many psychophysical diseases are cured automatically. People understand their own anger, hatred, jealousy—all these unwholesome factors which arise in the mind and which we do not understand generally. So many psychophysical diseases, which we accumulate unconsciously or by reflex action emotionally, [can] come under restraint, but not by suppressing. By coming close to and seeing them, people become free from many physical ailments, many mental ailments. They become more sweet, more loving.

For Maggie Ward McGervey, the benefits of mindfulness are obvious. From Munindra's teachings and her experience of vipassanā has come a greater appreciation for the body and the mind. "He spent a lot of time focusing on the senses, whether it was noticing a tickling sensation on your hand, or the feeling in your throat. It grounded me in my body in a way that was really important," she recalls. "I can still remember how he would coach us to simply notice and label the thoughts and sensations that came up for us during meditation. He would repeat the labels twice: 'thinking, thinking' or 'itching, itching.' He would say, 'Just watch the sensation.' That's fused into me now. If I feel panicky because I'm late for something or feel annoyed, then I can simply go back and realize that it's just a thought. It affects my life a lot less. If I stub my toe and feel the pain, I immediately go to realizing that it's just nerves and sensation. I can cut out all the ripple effect of the anger and frustration and see the emptiness of it."

Munindra explained how this works:

> Unpleasant feelings are most prominent to us because, when we experience pleasant feelings, we don't mind. But when we experience the unpleasant feeling, we don't like it and we condemn. We have to observe it. We have to penetrate it. We have to pierce through it. We have to understand it. When you keep the mind there, then you will see that it is not static; it is a process, and afterward, it disappears. But don't expect it to come or to go. If you expect, then you have to be aware of the expecting mind. Not clinging, not condemning, not hoping. Whatever comes up, see the thing as it is, at this moment, without liking or disliking. If you like it, you feed it with greed; if you dislike it, you feed it with hatred. Both ways, the mind is unbalanced, unhealthy, unsound. [The] object itself is neither good nor bad. It is our mind which attributes the color—it is good or it is bad. We are influenced by that and then reaction comes. Be gentle with everything that comes up. Keep the mind in a balanced state. We are following the middle path. Be fully alert.

Heather Stoddard says that learning to be fully alert "was so simple and direct—with no ritual, no frills at all. You just went in there and did this awareness practice twenty-four hours a day." She adds, "It's like learning to ride a bicycle or to swim. Unless you actually experience it yourself, you don't know anything about it. And once you've experienced it—the perception of the functioning of the mind—there's no way that you can forget it or that it doesn't influence your life at every moment. Following the daily vipassanā practice of strict and continuous observance of body, mind, and breathing, I felt that I had not learned so much in all my eighteen years, at home or at school, as I had during those three weeks with Munindra-ji in Bodh Gaya."

Munindra repeatedly conveyed that mindfulness was about the truth of any given moment. He told Oren Sofer, "What is happening is the truth. If your mind is distracted, in this moment, that is the truth. Accept it." Such advice enabled Giselle Wiederhielm to deal with deep back pain on a retreat. In a dharma talk one night, Munindra stated that one can even use pain as a focus and live with it. "I really learned by facing it," says Giselle. "Sometimes we don't face up to what's going on, but by facing it, it's not just pain anymore and it's a way to resolve it. It took me three days, but it went away. That was incredible because I spent the next week free of pain."

Another gain derived from mindfulness is having more energy available because attention is not divided. According to Gregg Galbraith, when Munindra was involved in something, he was fully into it: "When Munindra was eating, his attention would be totally with that. When he was talking, he would talk. But you didn't really see him spreading his attention to a lot of different things. He had this quality of just being there in the moment. If you were going to buy him a ticket to travel to Europe, he would get very engaged in it: 'What's it cost? Where do you stop? How long will it be?' He wanted to know every little detail. And when it was done, he would put it out of his mind."

Gregg once asked Munindra, "How can you always be in the moment when there are things to take care of in the world? You have to think of the future. If you're going to go to a school, you've got to enroll and do this and that." Munindra told him that you simply do whatever it is—plan a trip, eat dinner—but once you are finished, you do not spend time thinking about it. You go on to the next thing.

The Freshness of Each Moment

Mindfulness is an opportunity to experience everything anew. Michael Liebenson Grady remembers a particular phase during a three-month retreat when "things seemed so flat and uninteresting. My motivation was beginning to lag, and my mind began to wander more. Munindra suggested that I pay attention to the breath as though it were my first breath and my last. For some, this might not be good advice but, for me, it was perfect. From this suggestion, I saw how important it was to bring a quality of freshness to the present moment, a quality that I saw in Munindra all the time."

Sharon Salzberg found this instruction helpful as well, especially early in her practice in India, and not just with each breath. "I was to be with each step, each sound, each taste just this way," she writes in *A Heart as Wide as the World*. "Practicing in this spirit allowed me to bring a fullness and an immediacy of attention to each moment of my meditation. The fragmented aspects of my self came together. I was no longer so tempted to compare the present to what had happened in the past, because where was the past, if this was my first breath? And if this were my last breath, I certainly could not postpone giving it my full attention, lost in the hope that something better might happen later on. I was not so inclined to experience the present with judgment, because how could I judge what I was going through without bringing in the past or the future? It is a beautiful and powerful way to practice—as well as a beautiful way to live and die."[2]

Thought of Your Mother Is Not Your Mother

Munindra frequently reminded his students that thinking and meditation are not the same. He would inquire, "Do you want to think or do you want to meditate?" He made the distinction by speaking of two worlds: one of concept, the other of reality. "Mostly you're living in the world of thoughts," he said. "Dhamma and meditation practice is living in the world of experience." For Oren Sofer, this admonition meant that "life is so short—what we can actually experience from moment to moment is so brief and fleeting—that to spend time being lost in thoughts and ideas about what is happening is insane, leading us away from the Truth."

Munindra asked his students,

> If you observe your mind, what will you find? We find that our mind is constantly thinking of something of the past or planning for [the] future. The past is not real; it has gone. [The] future also is not real; it has not come. Real reality is the present state. We are living in the present moment only. The present moment is true. So we have to live the life fully, being alive, seeing things as they are at this moment.
>
> This thinking mind cannot meditate. As long as mind does

not stop thinking, one cannot meditate. Meditation is not thinking; it's not imagining. Meditation is the process of silencing the mind. Unless mind is silent, there is no experience, there is no meditation.

To help students better understand what he meant, he gave this example:

> A thought of your mother appears in the mind. You never invited the thought. It just came, and you become aware of it. But [the] thought is not [your] mother; it is just [a] thought or [an] image of mother. It is like a dream. In the dream, you feel hungry and food is offered to you and you take it. When you wake up, you see that it was a dream, not real. You ate food in the dream, tasted it. It appeared to you as real at the time of dreaming, but when you wake up, you see it was not real.

Mindfulness at the Core

Munindra was unambiguous that *sati* is absolutely crucial to dharma practice—the linchpin. "For forty-five years, Buddha taught Dhamma in different parts of India, under different circumstances, to different people, at different levels," he affirmed. "He gave about 84,000 discourses. All the teachings can be summarized in one word—*appamāda:* mindfulness, heedfulness, nonforgetfulness." *Appamāda* is a synonym for *sati*.

This message would emerge "like clockwork," says Danny Taylor, who at times wondered why Munindra was "rambling all over the place" in his talks: "He would always come back to the same thing. Right on the dot of the hour, he'd say something like, 'If you have trouble with any of this, it doesn't really matter. There's only one thing you've got to remember, there's only one duty, and that is to be mindful.' He'd always finish with this."

Danny says that what he learned from Munindra was that "if we analyze too much, we'll just get ourselves caught in knots. At the end of the day, the thing that will reconcile everything is to keep being mindful. You don't need to worry about all this intellectual stuff. Just be mindful."

Mindfulness Is Always Useful

In stressing the magnitude of mindfulness, Munindra would quote the Buddha: "*Sati sabbatthikā*" (SN 46.53). [Mindfulness is beneficial in all cases.] For example, Munindra said,

> There should be balance between heart and brain, between emotion and intellect, between faith and wisdom. So how to do it? This *sati*, mindfulness, brings balance between the two. Both are necessary. Also, too much effort makes a person restless; too much *samādhi* [concentration] makes a person sleepy. How to know how much effort is necessary, how much *samādhi* is necessary? It is the function of mindfulness. When mindfulness is there, then it has the nature to bring balance between effort and concentration.

Sati not only performs a fundamental role in harmonizing opposites, it also provides the brilliance of a lamp in shadowy places. "Where there is light, there cannot be any darkness," Munindra used to say. "*Sati* is always wholesome, always an illuminating factor." He described how:

> All the dirt accumulated in our unconscious, subconscious, we are just following life after life. So when you observe silence, all kinds of thoughts come up on the surface. It is not somebody sending it to us; it is part of our life. You get caught up with the thought because, say, somebody scolded you in the past but you suppressed it. But when the mind is silent, not talking, not busy, anything can come up. At that time, you see things because of awareness. You are asked to develop mindfulness because *sati* illuminates [the] whole mental field. As soon as things come, you see them as they are. When they come in darkness, they get fed; when there is light, they get dissolved, they remain unfed, unnourished. Our duty is just to observe. Passive observer: You have nothing to do. When you are running after this sight or this sound or this thought, you are wasting your energy, no? Mind becomes exhausted. But when you are a passive observer, if anything comes up, you see it in the light of mindfulness and it dissolves.

Mindfulness, thus, also has the function to protect, "guarding the mind from impurities, defilements, negativities," Munindra said.

> By watching all six sense doors, you will not get involved. But when you condemn, you recondition; when you cling, you recondition. When you experience and [do] not identify, when there is no clinging, no condemning, it is called cleansing, deconditioning. [A] process of purification is going on, [a] process of unfolding. Mindfulness is the main factor that eliminates the three root evils—greed, hatred, delusion.

Kamala Masters once asked Munindra whether he got angry. He told her,

> Yes, anger comes, but there is a sign, a signal. There is a feeling; it's uncomfortable. So when there is that sign, do not let it [anger] come out of your mouth, do not let it go into your actions. You just let it pass. Be mindful—watch it, [noting to yourself,] "anger, anger, anger."

Munindra also made clear that anger is not an unchanging block of emotion. Caitriona Reed paraphrases his advice to someone who talked about repeatedly getting angry: "Notice the anger, and notice it's not the same anger. You say you keep getting angry, but just notice carefully and you'll see that every time it's a different anger."

Because mindfulness has the nature to penetrate through all psychic layers into the depth of mind, it affords the opportunity to deal with the past, present, and future in a new way. Munindra said,

> By constant practice, our whole inner being comes into the conscious level—nothing remains hidden. It is the process of self-discovery. As you go deeper and deeper, then those impressions that accumulate in our daily lives by action and reaction will come up on the surface level, and they are washed away. In every moment—sometimes happiness, sometimes unhappiness, sometimes good, sometimes bad, sometimes disturbed, sometimes concentrated—one's duty is just to be mindful, not to be stuck to any phenomena, and not to react. The Buddha always said to be

mindful and equanimous. Awareness and equanimity, these two factors go together.

Just Remember This

Munindra's simple instructions still have the power to support his students. Erica Falkenstein remarks, "In times of stress, I always hear Munindra-ji saying, 'Moment to moment,' and it helps me focus." A similar thing happens for Max Schorr: "He was such an amazing teacher that whenever you'd be in contact with him, he would bring you to more mindfulness. Just seeing him walk, the way he was so deliberate and caring and overtly compassionate and mindful himself, had a powerful effect on me. Now, whenever I even think of him, it brings a little bit more mindfulness." What prompts Oren Sofer is recalling Munindra's exhortation before leaving the room after a talk: "Just remember this—everything should be done mindfully."

For Munindra, mindfulness illuminated a clear direction to *nibbāna*:

> If we know how to live at this present moment, mindfully and clean [i.e., with *sīla* (virtue)], then the next moment comes all right and we build our future. Working in this way, walking on the middle path, leads you toward liberation, total freedom from the cycle of birth and death.

This is the direct path for the purification of beings, for the surmounting of sorrow and lamentation, for the disappearance of pain and grief, for the attainment of the true way, for the realization of nibbāna— namely, the foundations of mindfulness.

— THE BUDDHA, MN 10.2

sati: from *smr* or *sar* (to remember, to have in mind). Most frequently, *sati* is translated as "mindfulness," but also as "recollection," "wakefulness of mind," "attentiveness," "the state of not forgetting," and "nonconfusion." When considered synonymous with *appamāda*, *sati* is "watchfulness" or "vigilance," a presence of mind that guards it from what is unskillful or unwholesome. Combined with *sampajañña*, it is "clear comprehension" or "clarity of consciousness" or "alertness."

Because its chief characteristic is "not floating away" (*apilāpanatā*), *sati* stays with an object. It is direct and objective knowing of all mental and physical activities, uncolored by misrepresentation or judgment. For that reason, the *satipaṭṭhāna* (four foundations, or establishings, of mindfulness: body, feelings, mind, and mind-objects) are a primary practice for developing both insight and concentration, as well as for living daily life. They do not foster memory in the Western sense of the past. Rather, they promote "proper" remembering (i.e., "keeping in mind") with wisdom (*paññā*), which sees things as they truly are: impersonal processes or phenomena that are impermanent, unsatisfactory, and not-self. Such insight leads eventually to the uprooting of all defilements, to liberation.

Sati appears several times in the thirty-seven requisites of awakening: as the seventh link (*sammā-sati*) of the Eightfold Path, as one of five spiritual faculties (*indriya*) or powers (*bala*), and as one of seven factors of awakening (*bojjhaṅga*). It plays a central role in balancing the other factors.

2

If You're Not Happy In Body, You're Not Happy Out of Body

Samādhi (One-Pointedness of Mind)

These miraculous powers are not important; liberation is important.
—MUNINDRA

Be an Ordinary Person

In the late 1970s, when Munindra first began to tour and teach in the West, an invitation from Gregg Galbraith brought him to Columbia, Missouri, where he stayed with Ginny Morgan. Ever eager to share Dharma, Munindra suggested that she gather some Buddhists to ask him questions. At that time there were no practice groups or *sanghas* in the area. However, at Ginny's request, a community radio station announced that a spiritual teacher would be at her house and people could come for an hour to talk with him.

"Sure enough, some people showed up," Ginny recalls. "One of them was a sixteen-year-old boy who had a Carlos Castaneda book under his arm. He was just the sweetest, most open human being. The others were kind of intimidated by Munindra, but this boy could not get enough of him. He sat as close as he could get. When Munindra asked, 'Does anyone have questions?' this boy said, 'Yes. I want to know how to leave my body.'"

Munindra looked at the boy and said, "You want to leave your body?" And the kid said, "Yes. You see, I'm not happy. My whole life is miserable, and I just can't stand it another minute. I want to leave." (Ginny comments that this was amazing because the boy's demeanor was not miserable; he seemed interested, joyful, and energetic.) Munindra looked at him, patted him on the knee, and said, "If you're not happy in body, you're not happy out of body."

The boy gasped and said, "Oh, well, Carlos Castaneda says..." Munindra patted him on the knee again and said, "I know of this man. He's not happy either. Please, if you can listen to me, I will save you many steps. Yes, these kinds of mystical things are possible, but you will get caught in this power and you'll go around and around many lifetimes. Please, listen to me now, and I will save you many steps. Be an ordinary person: Get married, have children, cook breakfast. Be present in your life."

Learning to Fly

Fascination with so-called magical powers that can arise from intense *samādhi* prompted people to inquire about them. In the early 1980s, when Maharishi Mahesh Yogi (the founder of Transcendental Meditation) was teaching students to fly, Marvel Logan (then known as Mahesh but now Bhante Vimalaraṃsi) asked Munindra what he thought about this. Munindra wanted to know how much the course cost. When Marvel told him it was about two thousand dollars, Munindra quipped, "I can fly around the world for two thousand dollars." "OK," said Marvel, "I guess I know what you think about that then."

Munindra was not only being practical about money, he was also saying that ultimately such abilities are inconsequential. Asked whether he could teach his students to fly, Munindra said, "Oh, yes, I could teach you that. But it would be easier to buy a plane ticket."

It is not that Munindra thought that *samādhi*, the basis of these sorts of magical powers, was useless or unnecessary. He taught that *samādhi* is a means, not an end. Denise Till comments, "He never wanted to talk about past lives or future lives. He wasn't into all this psychic business or clairvoyance. He said, 'That's just part of the path on the way. You drop all that. You let go of the *samādhis* you go into. The essence of the path is attaining liberation.'"

Understanding Samādhi

In studying the Pāli Canon, Munindra found that the Buddha spoke of and taught two kinds of meditation: concentration development and insight development. He explained,

To start with, concentration is necessary. We are beings of the sensual plane (*kāma-loka*). Our mind is generally diffused, scattered. Constantly we are coming in contact with six kinds of objects—sight, sound, smell, taste, touch, and thought. Our mind is wandering from one object to another moment to moment. *Samatha-bhāvanā* (concentration development) is a means for calming the mind. Buddha has mentioned there are many methods for it, such as visualization and chanting. From the wandering state of mind, we are trying to fix bare attention on a particular object, ignoring all other objects. Attention means to be with the object. This also goes with one-pointedness, but they are two different things. Supposing one gives attention toward fighting, killing, robbing. It is called improper attention; it is wrong *samādhi*. As soon as mindfulness joins with the mind, then all the factors become purified because mindfulness is always wholesome, always an illuminating factor.

As human beings, we have the potentiality to attain all kinds of happiness, all kinds of higher experiences. But as long as we are in the world of senses and concepts, certain forces pull us down. Those forces are called *nīvarana* (hindrances)—sensual desire, ill will, sloth and torpor, restlessness and worry, and doubt. As soon as we try to practice meditation, to collect our mind, these hindrances come on the way. When concentration is highly cultivated, one comes to the *jhānic* plane, experiencing absorptions, a state of stillness, a blissful state. Then the five mental hindrances are suppressed, go down to the bottom.

Munindra described the five *jhānic* factors that have the power to block *nīvarana*: Mindfulness stops the wandering mind; rapture stops irritation; happiness stops worry and anxiety; sustained thought stops doubt; and applied thought stops laziness (sloth and torpor).

What are these *jhānas*? They can go higher and higher but they are all conditioned, mundane, not supramundane, not beyond. But these absorptions are helpful to collect and compose the mind, to suppress all these negative forces that come on the way.

To help students better understand, Munindra made the following comparison:

> If we want to throw something upward, it comes down because of the gravitational pull of the universe. But the tremendous force of a rocket surpasses [that] and becomes weightless—gravity cannot bring it down. If you go higher, then forces of a higher planet pull you toward that. In the same way, as long as we are in this ordinary level, we don't feel the gravity of the hindrances. But as soon as we try to concentrate our mind, then these negative forces come. Constant effort, constant mindfulness [remembering to bring the mind back to the object], makes the mind very powerful and sharp. Then these hindrances are suppressed. The *jhāna* factors of absorption cause the mind to surpass this state. They come to a higher level and become prominent, and they make the mind strong. Interest is there. Enthusiasm is there. Mind becomes easier.

Nevertheless, Munindra cautioned his students about such altered states of consciousness:

> This *jhāna* itself is not enlightenment. It is liberation only in the sense that one has transcended negative forces, the hindrances. A human being is now in a position to experience incredible bliss, but it is not sensual happiness—it is not dependent on pleasant sensual objects—it is mental happiness. Even higher *jhāna,* where one can experience infinite consciousness, is also not enlightenment.

When he gave dharma talks, Munindra distinguished between *sati* (mindfulness) and *samādhi* (concentration) as two different but complementary methods, supporting each other for the purpose of gaining insight (vipassanā) and wisdom (*paññā*) toward attaining liberation. *Samādhi* or *samatha* can ease the way. Munindra identified three ways to awaken: First do *samatha* practice and apply the calm and collected mind for vipassanā; or else practice *samatha* and vipassanā together; or practice only vipassanā. He said,

> Supposing you want to cross a big river. You can cross by swimming, but you can use [a] boat also. A boat is much easier, more

pleasant. If you have *samatha-vipassanā*—when you know both—you have the boat and can quickly cross this river. But if you do not know *samatha*, you have to use [your] hands and feet. Without *samatha* practice, it is called *sukkha-vipassanā* (dry vipassanā). It is good to know both.

Deep Concentration and Supernormal States

During his long teaching career, Munindra, like the Buddha, did not encourage cultivation of the "magical powers" that can result from deep states of concentration. The Buddha banned his disciples from exhibiting in front of laypeople the various *iddhis* or *siddhis*—ranging from clairvoyance, clairaudience, invisibility, and teleportation to accessing memories from past lives. He also prohibited using such powers unless one was fully awakened. The Buddha himself possessed all the supernormal abilities, but he employed them as an aid in reaching people and bringing them to Dharma, rather than for show. Only those who experience a level of realization can be trusted with *siddhis,* because, as Munindra noted, "*Samatha* can be misused. By thought force, you can kill, you can rob—you can do many wrongs. *Samatha* purifies the mind temporarily. It is very useful for developing vipassanā, for developing anything good."

While Munindra was in training in Burma, Mahāsi Sayādaw, recognizing his attainment and sincerity, suggested that he learn these supernormal perceptual states before returning to India, the land of *siddhis*. However, because Sayādaw had already assigned him to teach meditation to Bengalis, Nepalis, and other Asians living in Rangoon who came to the center, Munindra did not have the time and seclusion necessary for *samatha-bhāvanā*. He did, however, decide to experiment with his most advanced students.

Munindra wanted to challenge the conventional thinking of his time that said, "We cannot learn those things; they have disappeared now; we have to wait for the next Buddha to come." Such doubt aroused his interest in finding out what was true, just as it had during his childhood, when people said no one had attained or could attain awakening since the Buddha's era.

> When I studied Dhamma thoroughly, when I experienced it for myself, I found that this idea was not correct. Buddha said anybody who practices Dhamma in this way can experience Dhamma anytime. Because people do not study Dhamma thoroughly, and

also most of the time they do not practice thoroughly, they say something else. They talk mostly about *dāna* and *sīla,* not very much about the practice.

Such views regarding obstacles to awakening in contemporary times were quite common until the latter half of the twentieth century. Munindra had a hand in changing them, starting with an experiment. He chose certain students for their purity of heart. He said that people must fully know Dhamma first, because if they were not deeply rooted in it, they might go astray and become overly fascinated with what he called "miraculous powers." He felt no concern that these particular students would get addicted to such states and inflate their ego.

Despite the potential for abuse, Munindra said,

> Understanding *samatha*—what it is, how it is—is not a bad thing. Buddha [had] all these [powers]. You can play with your mind. From first *jhāna,* you can go to second *jhāna;* from second *jhāna,* you can go to eighth *jhāna;* from eighth *jhāna,* you can come to first *jhāna.* You can play with your mind! It is a blessing. But *samatha* is done only to understand vipassanā thoroughly. *Jhāna* cannot eliminate defilements, negativities—all kinds of greed and hate and delusion. Whatever we did in the past, it remains. That cannot be cleaned by *samādhi* or by *sīla;* only by vipassanā it can be cleaned. When mind is silent, they [the defilements] come up on the surface. As soon as they come up, you see them as they are—the factors of darkness. But if your mind is illuminated, as soon as they come, they don't get fed and they die out. So, in this way, all the past is cleaned.

Munindra described some of the results of training a few students in *samatha-bhāvanā*. He basically followed part two of the *Visuddhimagga* (The Path to Purity), a fifth-century Theravāda commentary by Buddhaghosa. Depending on the *jhāna* entered, the meditators were able to visit other realms or other times, because "the mind can travel anywhere and see anything" or do any number of things. "When mind is absorbed in a deep *jhānic* state, then you are gone beyond physical consciousness," Munindra clarified. "If anybody pierces you, you do not feel pain. You do not hear any sound."

Dipa Ma was one of the students Munindra guided in accessing eight classical *jhānic* states and the *siddhis*. According to an interview Jack Engler conducted with her, she once resolved to enter and remain in the eighth *jhāna* for three days, eight hours, three minutes, and twenty seconds. Precisely at the end of that period, she came out of it. She was able to perform the five supernatural yet mundane powers. For example, from his room at the Mahāsi Sayādaw center, Sasana Yeiktha in Rangoon, Munindra noticed her in the air near the tops of the trees, playing in a room she had built in the sky by transforming the air element into the earth element. On other occasions, she and her sister Hema Prabha Barua spontaneously appeared in his room for interviews. Dipa Ma could also leave by going through the closed door or the nearest wall. She learned to cook by making the fire element emerge from her hands, and she duplicated her body in order to have someone accompany her if she had to walk alone at night.

To verify these human capacities and dispel the doubts of a highly skeptical professor of Ancient Indian history at Magadh University in Bodh Gaya, Munindra set up a simple trial. The professor stationed a graduate student in Munindra's room at Samanvaya, the Gandhi ashram, to watch Dipa Ma in meditation. Though she never got up and left, she showed up at the professor's office miles away and conversed with him.

Munindra also tested her power to move back and forth through time. For example, when he knew that U Thant, the Burmese diplomat, was scheduled to give a speech at the United Nations accepting his appointment as secretary-general, he asked Dipa Ma to go into the future and remember his words. Munindra wrote down what she said and later, after U Thant spoke, he compared it with the speech. They were identical.

Dipa Ma was able to do all this and much more. Yet, she told Jack Engler that none of it is important because it does not purify or liberate; it does not generate understanding or end suffering. And that is what Munindra emphasized to Sharda Rogell decades later when she wanted to know more about concentration practice and to understand how Dipa Ma had psychic powers. He told her,

> This really isn't so important. It's not the best way for you to spend your time. When I came back to India, many students who had done *jhānas* and had some miraculous power said, "This power has gone. I cannot do it." Dipa Ma only had psychic powers when she was in retreat, in deep states of concentration, but she

couldn't sustain those powers outside. I said, "You learned that those things can be done, that people can be trained in *abhiññā* [the six higher powers or psychic abilities], but don't bother for all those things."

Munindra elucidated the limitations of the *jhāna* experience:

> Our hindrances are suppressed, but they are not eliminated from the inner mind, from the unconscious level. As long as you remain in *jhāna,* you are free from these negative forces, but you are not totally free. As a human being, you cannot stay there long because your body belongs to the physical plane, so you have to come back. When [we] come back and come in contact with the sense objects, then we get attached to sense pleasures; we cling, we condemn. Irritation comes, anger comes, hatred comes, or greed comes. There is every possibility of falling from the *jhāna* again if there is no understanding, no wisdom. Then we feel sad.

Munindra pointed out that, unlike *jhāna,* insight meditation (vipassanā) does have the power to eliminate, step-by-step, all the inherent, dormant forces such as fetters, defilements, and hindrances, and to entirely uproot them from the unconscious level.

Helping Others to Concentrate

Munindra himself never went through a course of training in intensive *samādhi* practice. His main practice focused on insight throughout his life. Nonetheless, he experienced great concentration in meditation, being able to sit for many hours, and he applied it in daily life. "By living with him, you could really learn to appreciate the power and benefits of just plain meditative concentration," says Uffe Damborg. Munindra explained, "You can develop *samādhi* in day-to-day life by cultivating mindfulness."

Tapas Kumar Barua comments that, as an academic student, he felt overwhelmed by everyday worries, and they interfered with his daily activities. His uncle, Munindra, provided him with a simple solution: "It's quite possible that you are trying to do a lot in just a single frame of mind, so half the mind is there and half is here. Try to concentrate your mind on one thing because you will find the benefit instantly. Start doing it."

The memory of Munindra's guidance has also helped others with concentration. On retreat in 1980 at Sasana Yeiktha, in Rangoon, Ven. Khippapañño found that when he was not fully aware of the rising and falling of the abdomen, he did not achieve complete concentration. Recalling Munindra's instruction to focus on the abdomen transformed his meditation. "Then I go deep into *samādhi* and there is no wandering, no thinking," he says. "So when I am sitting in meditation and my meditation is not good, I think of Munindra's words from the first time I met him [in Bodh Gaya, 1967]. Then meditation comes quickly, automatically, similar to the engine of the car. I turn the key and my concentration comes."

Seemingly Psychic

Though Munindra did not exhibit the same powers as Dipa Ma, his own level of concentration was such that he appeared to sense acutely what was going on with his students. Ginny Morgan recounts an uncanny experience she had in a car with Munindra. She was in the backseat, and the driver was saying things that she found insensitive. "I was sitting back there thinking, 'Ugh, this man is just rude.' Munindra turned around and looked at me and said, 'Ginny, what are you thinking?' I looked at him and smiled. Then he held his hand out and said, 'No, don't answer. Just know that there is suffering in your mind; it is not happening in anyone else's mind, only in yours.' I thought, 'Dang! Caught in the act.' I just laughed, and so did he."

Although Munindra never claimed to communicate telepathically, there are people whose experiences made them wonder. Daw Than Myint and her mother Hema Prabha Barua made a habit of visiting him every evening at Sasana Yeiktha, not far from their house. She remembers, "On some days, when I was feeling tired or it seemed there was nothing new to report, I would tell my mother, 'Today we won't go. I'll go early in the morning.' But then sometimes my mother and I could not stay at home. She wouldn't say anything, but I'd ask her, 'How about going today?' 'I'm ready to go,' she'd say. Then we'd leave and find him walking at the top of the hill, waiting for us. Maybe in his mind he was calling us. After a few times, my mother and I suspected this, so we asked him, 'Munindra-ji, did you call us? We decided not to come today and suddenly we had to come.' He wouldn't deny it or confirm it. He would say, 'Oh, it's just your faith, your *saddhā*.'"

Daw Than Myint notes that this happened to other people as well. On one occasion, when Munindra found some difficulty in translation, he was very eager to consult with an Indian man who could translate from Bengali to Burmese. But the man lived nine miles from the center. Since Munindra was in retreat, he could not leave to look for him, and there was no phone contact. Yet early the next day, the man came knocking at his door and said, "I just wanted to come."

Ordinary and Extraordinary

Munindra eschewed talking about past lives or future lives, perhaps because it was a hot topic and bandied about without discretion, but some of his Asian students could see such lives and were convinced they had shared an earlier lifetime with him. Munindra was open to other worlds and different dimensions of reality. Recalling the early years in Bodh Gaya, John Travis says, "I listened to him go into great detail, sometimes for two hours. There was this incredible excitement about the Buddhist cosmology. You felt like you were surrounded by *devas* and all kinds of unseen things, in some way. He had that twinkle in his eye about the unseen. It was not just a belief system for him."

Yet, in his inclination and recommendation toward ordinariness—his goal was insight not magic—and his ability to concentrate deeply, he was still extraordinary. As Roy Bonney puts it, "Munindra's gift was his ordinariness as an expression of his extraordinary experience."

Some of his old students comment that when certain teachers walked into a room, they sent a palpable wave of powerful energy, but when Munindra passed by, nothing special happened. Yet, therein was the appeal. "That's what I liked about Munindra, that he was normal," says Grahame White. "It's one of the reasons why he didn't attract a lot of people—he had a very simple sort of persona. Like the Dalai Lama says, 'I'm just a simple monk.' That's what Munindra was like."

> *This holy life does not have gain, honor, and renown for its benefit . . . or the attainment of concentration for its benefit. . . . But it is this unshakable deliverance of mind that is the goal of this holy life, its heartwood, and its end.*
>
> —THE BUDDHA, MN 30.23

samādhi: from *sam* (together) + *ā* (toward) + *dhā* (to get, to hold), a coming together rather than a scattering apart; or from *samā* (even) + *dhi* (intellect), a state of complete equilibrium of a detached intellect. *Samādhi* is generally understood as the fixing of the mind on a single object—unification or one-pointedness of mind (*ekaggatā*). The mind remains steady, unmoved, unperturbed, and undistracted by sense objects.

Samādhi ranges in intensity from "preparatory concentration" at the beginning of the mental exercise, to "neighborhood concentration" nearing the first *jhāna*, and to "attainment concentration" during absorption. When *samādhi* is present at the four noble path- and fruition-moments (*magga phala*), with *nibbāna* as the object, it is associated with the supramundane. All other kinds of concentration, no matter how blissful, are mundane. An important role of the teacher is clarification of this distinction.

Since *samādhi* helps settle the mind and inhibit the five hindrances (*nīvarana*), it affords the space in which to see clearly and penetrate to insight. Concentration is also the basis for the six *abhiññā* (supernormal knowledges), including magical powers (*iddhis* or *siddhis*). Because some powers can be misused, traditionally they are considered a distraction from the ultimate goal of complete freedom from suffering.

The second of the Eightfold Path's three divisions is *samādhi* (*sīla* is the first and *paññā* is the third), which consists of right effort, right mindfulness, and right concentration. As *sammā-samādhi* (right concentration), it is the path's last link, defined as the four meditative absorptions (*jhāna*), and associated with karmically wholesome consciousness. It is one of seven factors of awakening (*bojjhaṅga*) and one of five spiritual faculties (*indriya*) or powers (*bala*).

3

It's Really Possible to Wake Up

Saddhā (Conviction)

I don't believe in not possible.
—MUNINDRA

For Theravādin Buddhists during a good part of the twentieth century, the idea that one could awaken was generally considered the stuff of myths. Although the Pāli Canon recounts one episode after another of disciples "falling into the stream" (the noble attainment of stream-entry or *sotāpatti*, the first of the four transcendent stages on the path to *nibbāna*), most people assumed that such feats belonged to ancient times, not contemporary ones. By the middle of the 1800s in Burma, a revival of vipassanā emerged in reaction to colonialism and began to alter that attitude. Munindra benefited from this movement. While he had a strong foundation of traditional family faith, he sensed something was missing. He finally found it in Burma in 1957.

Family Faith Becomes Utter Confidence

Munindra's devoutly Buddhist parents cultivated his earliest beliefs in the Triple Gem (Buddha, Dharma, *Sangha*) through family practice. At dawn, his mother freshened their mud house with water, set a bowl of water at the altar, and burned some incense in the fire to create a nice scent. After washing up, Munindra and his brothers would go out to their small garden and pluck flowers for the altar. Then parents and children would sit together to chant. Once they all finished reciting prayers and sūtras, the boys would bow to their elders to show respect and receive their blessings. In the afternoon, they repeated this ritual upon returning from school.

When Munindra was about eight, his father introduced him to Dhammasaṅgaṇī, the first section of the Abhidhamma *piṭaka* (the third division of the Pāli Canon), translated into Bengali by a relative. At such a young age, he did not understand the material, but was quite interested and loved the book.

Although Munindra believed in the Buddha's awakening when he was just a boy, unshakable confidence (*saddhā*) in the Three Jewels did not ripen until his forties. Before Burma, some uncertainties about Dharma still lingered in his mind because he had not yet experienced those aspects himself. That changed with his first breakthrough in meditation while training with Mahāsi Sayādaw. "When I tasted Dhamma for the first time—I could see the truth as it is—my mind overflowed with enthusiasm, with *saddhā*, with faith in Dhamma," he said. "This Dhamma cleared many doubts which I had."

For the rest of his life, Munindra inspired and guided others to follow Dharma. For him, *saddhā* was never a simple belief in a particular tradition, but the utmost confidence in the purifying and liberating value of the Buddha's path. He knew from direct experience what was doable. David Johnson says, "Munindra would tell anybody who would listen about the three signs of existence—*anicca, dukkha,* and *anattā*. He was like a scientist who had just made a discovery and had to tell everyone what a wonderful thing he had found and how they could find it themselves."

Why Not Now?

Munindra insisted that if it was possible to awaken in the Buddha's era, why not now as well? He was so eager in his dedication that he was able to encourage laypeople—in Asia and the West—to practice and realize Dharma even in the midst of ordinary daily life. In turn, some of them went on to assist yet others to do the same. For instance, Dipa Ma's influence spread through a group of housewives in Calcutta—even though they had no opportunity to enjoy the peaceful environment of a retreat center—and also among Western students.

"Munindra-ji instilled in me that you didn't have to do it a particular way to get to *nibbāna*," Kamala Masters explains. "He would give me examples of people experiencing it [*nibbāna*] in the middle of eating or brushing teeth—at any time. I always had a sense of possibility beyond form or format. I've seen yogis do that without ever going to Asia, housewives who don't go on to become teachers." He also inspired his niece Subhra Barua through stories about such people: "He told me that in this world, nowadays, it is possible to realize Dhamma and to get rid of suffering. He always encouraged me to do so [i.e., to meditate] because it is possible."

Munindra countered skepticism about the possibility of awakening whenever anyone asked him whether there are some people who have reached the levels of *sotāpanna* (stream-winner), *sakadāgāmī* (once-returner), and *anāgāmī* (nonreturner) in the current era. He told them that, indeed, such people exist, but there are no signs or marks, no tail or halo to indicate realization. This spurred on many practitioners to persevere.

In the late 1960s and early 1970s, when Joseph Goldstein first practiced with Munindra in Bodh Gaya, they used to walk together through the village. Joseph remembers Munindra pointing out simple residents who had been his students, many of whom had attained different stages of awakening. "Seeing these people encouraged me, because judging from outward appearances, you would never guess their spiritual attainments," says Joseph. "They looked like simple village folk going about their business. I came to appreciate, firsthand, the often-stated truth that realization does not depend on social or educational background." Because Munindra spoke a lot about those stages and, in particular, about Dipa Ma and her attainments, Joseph says, "It kept the highest aspirations very alive. It all really seemed possible."

Uffe Damborg concurs, "This is where I believe I'm heading, *nibbāna* or awakening. Maybe not in this life, but I have great confidence that my life has direction, and that this goal is attainable. This confidence comes from the sort of psychological, spiritual intimacy I experienced in my relationship with Munindra."

Presence Imbues Confidence

Munindra's simple presence itself—permeated with unswerving faith in Dharma—was all some people needed. David Gelles calls it "real, nourishing encouragement." On Munindra's recommendation, he went to sit a retreat at Dhamma Giri (a meditation center established by S. N. Goenka in Igatpuri, India, where Munindra was in residence at the time). "Munindra walked me around the grounds, talking about all the future plans for Igatpuri," David recalls. "He was resoundingly optimistic and forward-thinking."

David found the retreat tough and went through some terrible days of physical and emotional pain, yet he says, "Coming out of that retreat was one of the happiest days of my life. I don't know why. I didn't reach any great plateau that I've remained at since then. It was just committing to it and doing it, and having him there—having him personally bookend that experience for me, kind of holding my hand as I went in and as I came out."

Although Peter Martin was a student of S. N. Goenka and one of his assistant teachers, Munindra's presence at Dhamma Giri served as a kind of touchstone for him. It especially comforted him during "bumpy" times on long retreats. "He was such a presence—so grounded, so practical," says Peter. "I would walk by his *kuṭi* [meditation hut] and there would be a few pairs of slippers outside or sometimes his white robes would be out on the line. His lights were on as I'd go off to meditate at four o'clock in the morning, or as I'd come back, late at night. It always felt very reassuring to me that he was there." He continues, "Sometimes these long courses were pretty bumpy, as they can be. During bumpy periods I would walk by and just take reassurance from the fact that here was this being, undoubtedly doing his meditation, practicing *mettā,* sending his good thoughts and good wishes to all that were around there—I know he did that all the time. To be in that environment with a person like him, and that person in particular, was really reassuring."

Munindra provided a link of faith to the tradition. "He was an embodiment of the Dhamma and a representation of the qualities toward which I was working and the path I have chosen to walk on," Peter adds. "He was a teacher not by what he said—I never heard him give discourses—but by the way he was with people, the way he carried himself, the way he talked. He embodied these qualities of trustworthiness, honesty, renunciation, self-sacrifice, compassion—all of these things that, for me, are so important and that I work toward. He had developed them through his own work."

Kamala Masters also found that Munindra invigorated her faith in being able to follow the path to its ultimate end because his "words were not just from a book, but he really and truly exemplified what he was teaching. Respect, kindness, generosity, compassion, inner quiet, and profound wisdom were clearly evident in him." She says, "As far as I could tell, he was 'walking his talk.' When we see the teachings embodied in someone, that living reality infuses us with faith that we have the same potential. And that faith holds us together through our practice. . . . Munindra's example awoke in me the confidence and determination to realize my own spiritual aspirations. This is how I recognized Munindra as a true spiritual teacher for me."[1]

Manisha Talukbar remarks, "Preaching is easy; anyone can do [it]. But he was an embodiment of the Dhamma—how to live the life, how to progress according to the right path. He was a source of inspiration to us. Whenever I'm in a problem, I think of him and then get some courage, strength to face the problem. He always made everything so simple, and we believed that, yes, it is possible to live the life of Dhamma."

"He always took students toward this confidence of 'yes, yes, it is here and now; it is not somewhere very far,'" says Itamar Sofer.

How Far We Can Go

As Rebecca Kushins tells it, she learned from Munindra that "if I really wanted to look at every detail of my life and understand what it is to be alive, what is going on in this mystery—to understand my mind—I could really do it. In his presence, I found that I really wanted to. I felt my own sincerity, and I felt only encouragement from him. I never doubted it when he said it was really possible for me to wake up. Whatever law of physics it is—when you get something rolling that has inertia, it just keeps going—I feel like he gave me a big push, and I'm still going."

Munindra's message is that we *can* go the distance. Danny Taylor says of Munindra, "He represents progress in the Dharma. He embodies the sense of how far we can go. This wonder about the Dharma, it's endless—stay open to the next bit." He elaborates on his understanding of Munindra's influence, noting, "If you feel seen by a person, even if for a moment, there's a sense that they've got you on their radar. That's quite profound in terms of giving you confidence. I got a lot of that from him, and got it in the letters that he wrote to me. My experience with Munindra built resilience that I didn't even know was being built."

Danny goes on to say, "It's a bit like in a bicycle race when cyclists get into a formation called a peloton, where one guy goes first, taking up the windbreak, and all the others get in behind and away they go. It's a lot easier to ride behind that one cyclist because there's a slipstream. Munindra provided the slipstream for people, so you felt like you could go forward but your experience was weightless."

Heather Stoddard remembers getting "pulled in" on her first trip to Bodh Gaya in 1966. She was already quite interested in and reading about

Buddhism before she sat down under the Bodhi Tree to meditate in her own way. She recalls, "Then, after some time, this man walked up, all dressed in white, with a white towel folded on his head. He said, 'Come with me.' So I got up and went. It was as simple as that. I went and talked to him for a very short time. He said, 'You should enter a three-week retreat.' So I said, 'Yes, OK.'" She laughs and notes, "You don't normally just follow a man that you don't know in India. But it was such a spontaneous and natural thing to follow him. It was without obstructions of any kind. The retreat went very smoothly. I learned more in those three weeks than in my whole life. After that I never met him again, but it was terribly important and marvelous to be guided by him."

Wanting to Know

Many people were intrigued to know what Munindra knew. What made him so joyful, calm, and loving? He had felt a similar curiosity about the Buddha since childhood. Oren Sofer was one of many inquisitive Westerners who wondered, "Is he enlightened? Has he really experienced this? Is this something that's for real?" One day, Oren asked Munindra directly if he was enlightened. Munindra leaned forward, made eye contact with him, and told him that even if he had awakened, "How could I possibly tell you?" Oren remembers, "I just got this sense of affirmation inside that this was something real, that there was no doubt in his mind about it. It was like his way of telling me, 'Yes—and I can't tell you. You need to find out for yourself. Enlightenment can happen at any moment.' There was such a sense of possibility. That was so inspiring for me."

Sometimes yogis, as meditators are often called on retreat, thought that they knew what awakening was, only to find out otherwise from Munindra. Jeffrey Tipp got a taste of what spiritual confidence means when he discussed with Munindra a meditation experience he had had at IMS. After describing it to him, Jeffrey asked, "Was that a real opening, Munindra-ji? Was that a glimpse of Buddha-nature?" And Munindra replied, "No, no, that's not it."

For Jeffrey, that proved to be a turning point. "He was that brief, just passing it off as another experience, but it was with such clarity and certainty in a kindly manner. It really taught me something: It cut my attachment to the kind of phenomenon that had happened and made me appreciate the depth of what I was trying to cultivate, that it was beyond my grasp in terms of any experience I'd ever had. It raised the bar. I began to realize, 'Oh, I really do have to practice hard and dedicate myself because this is beyond what I'd imagined it was.'"

Jeffrey says that this simple response from Munindra was like a transmission: "Before he said this to me, I had a definite idea of what enlightenment was, what an enlightened person was, and what an experience of Buddha-nature was. I'd done a lot of reading. I had been practicing six or eight years and, before that, I'd been a TM [Transcendental Meditation] teacher and a Christian monk. I felt I had a lot of practice under my belt and knew where I was headed. This experience showed me that I really didn't have a clue, and I needed to rely on a realized teacher."

Jeffrey continues, "It was almost a split second in our exchange, but he was coming from a place of no doubt and complete confidence, just speaking directly from experience. It's just like when you drink water and you know it's cold. It's that kind of knowing, and it conveyed so much trustworthiness in what he was saying. He zeroed right in on what I was talking about. He knew about that mind state, and he knew that it was something really previous to anything of any substance. That was when I started to have another take on the role of the teacher, that it's not just someone who can give a dharma talk and lead the retreat, but [it's also someone who] can actually guide you in an inner way. There's guidance there that's not written in books—it's the living Dharma."

Faith as Passion for Dharma

Munindra's faith was passionate and contagious. Sara Schedler says his total dedication to Dharma—"not in any kind of pompous or disingenuous or overblown way, just so simple"—challenged her conditioning. "Faith is such a tricky thing, particularly in my family," she explains, "because my father left a very orthodox Christian tradition at a young age. Munindra would talk about *devas* or different realms of existence, and he'd say, 'It's true, but don't take my word for it.' There was a real lightness about it. It wasn't the kind of faith I was familiar with, which was heavy, fire and brimstone. It was nothing like that."

Munindra's intense love of Dharma could keep his talks rolling for hours. Some students found that listening to him tried their patience, but

Matthias Barth says, "It was beautiful and liberating to listen to. He could start spontaneously just about anywhere and, within a short time, would be in the middle of a wide-ranging yet precise exploration of the Buddha's teaching. Each one in the room felt he was being addressed individually. His confidence in the Buddha, the Dhamma, and the *Sangha* affected his listeners."

Robert Beatty thinks of Munindra's exuberance as "good modeling." He remembers a particular statement that burst forth from Munindra many times with great fervor: "The light broke out in Bodh Gaya and spread around the world."

Howard Cohn says, "What most comes through is Munindra's embodiment of Buddha-Dharma; his love, inspiration, encouragement, and clarity, and, at the same time, his living this life of simplicity. His love of Dharma was more impactful than any particular teaching—and the fact that he was part of my root lineage in vipassanā practice. I think of him that way and feel very blessed to have studied with him and to feel like I'm part of that. It's given me a sense of security and confidence."

The Big Picture

Munindra's conviction in Dharma also translated into a much bigger picture of it than simply sitting in meditation. When Jack Engler once asked him, "Munindra-ji, what is the Dhamma?" he did not hesitate to respond, in his Indian English, "The Dhamma is living the life fully."

David Brody describes how Munindra's sense of Dharma's vastness triggered a shift in himself in Bodh Gaya: "I remember him talking about going into these states where the mind would stop. Here he was as old as my grandfather, and he was sitting these retreats that I, twenty years old, wasn't capable of for many different reasons. It just taught me that there's a lot out there, much more than I thought. The possibility in Buddhism was as big as I could imagine."

David continues, "He was really inspiring: the joy that he lived life with and just the lightness of being that was clearly evident from the beginning of interaction with him. Being around him showed me that living a life based on the Dhamma is a noble path, and people have been doing this for thousands of years and will keep doing it because it's based on true principles."

David recalls Munindra saying, "Once you fully accept the first noble truth of suffering, you can't go back." He adds, "In other words, anybody who's had a real experience with the Dharma can't go back to not knowing. Even if you move away from it, you can't go back to pretending like you never knew it."

The Dharma Doesn't Suffer from Comparison

Munindra's broad vision deepened following his training with Mahāsi Sayādaw. With his teacher's permission, he visited many vipassanā centers in Burma, each of which taught a different approach. As a result of being familiar with at least four dozen techniques of insight meditation, Munindra knew that Dharma was not restricted to only one way of practice. He trusted that all the methods, at their core, could lead to insight. Perhaps that is why he was not competitive and never evinced anxiety about losing students to other teachers or traditions.

As Sharon Salzberg notes, when Western seekers started arriving in India in the late 1960s, the country was (and still is) abundant with gurus and spiritual paths of every stripe and hue. The plethora of choices could cause uncertainty and conflict in some seekers, pushing them to keep looking, hoping for someone or something that would finally answer their search. Students would tell Munindra that they were interested in going off to meet another teacher or explore practices other than vipassanā. Yet, he consistently remained open and encouraging. Often astounded by this response, they asked him why he was so easygoing. In his calm and quiet way, Munindra would say, with boundless confidence in its power to transform one's life, "Dhamma doesn't suffer from comparison." Dharma and dharma teachers do not have to be possessive about anything or anyone. As he once told Oren Sofer, "This is not Munindra-Dhamma. This is Buddha-Dhamma. I do not teach Munindra-Dhamma. It's one Dhamma."

Gregg Galbraith says, "If there was someone else that he felt had potential, he wanted to look them up and then would tell people, 'Go see what they have to say.' Rather than feel territorial about the teachings or that you must learn this way or that way, Munindra was the opposite. He really tried to raise the boats of the whole Dharma in the West. Even though he strongly taught the Mahāsi [Sayādaw] method, he didn't believe in getting hooked into a method. He really believed that, whether you're doing Zen or Tibetan or whatever, if you understand the essence of Dharma, then the teachings are the same everywhere, so not to get confused by the different vehicles that bring you the Dharma." Joseph Goldstein, who later wrote *One Dharma* about this very issue, says he learned from Munindra that "all the techniques are really skillful means."

Munindra had learned this from his teacher. When he asked his permission to go to other practice centers in Burma, Mahāsi Sayādaw told him, "Once you understand the nature of mind, the nature of Dhamma, it is not difficult for you. You should go meet all the teachers. It is good to know Dhamma from different angles."

Gregg Galbraith says, "One of the things I got from Munindra is that you have to look within yourself and find the Dharma. That's why he always sent people to go learn anywhere and everywhere and not to get tied up in stereotypes or preconditioned things. For me, that was a big help because, like most students, I was looking to find the answer, the correct way, and usually looking for the answer is wrapped up in tradition and ritual and dogma. Munindra taught me that we can learn from all that, but that isn't it. Like the Buddha said, 'Be a light unto yourself.' Munindra taught that directly and informally so well, because he brought the light out, he brought the good out in people. It was hard to be around him and not feel better about yourself, because he wasn't condescending, he wasn't judgmental."

Confidence in Unfolding

Munindra also manifested his conviction in Dharma through the unselfconscious way he behaved among others. Erik Knud-Hansen clarifies this point: "I didn't see him acting out being a 'spiritual person.'" He keenly felt Munindra's influence "as a freedom to have faith in the Dharma, to have the right kind of faith in practice. It's a movement of liberation, not hindered by what something outside of yourself is saying—'Oh, you're supposed to contain yourself; you're supposed to act right.' I had a lot of respect for Munindra in that regard. He just wasn't censoring things around him but moving spontaneously."

For Erik, Munindra was "an example of somebody who was not afraid to talk about Dharma." And he did it even when people became impatient with his long talks: "His faith was that if that's what people are going to go through, OK. He allowed himself to serve the need without trying to make it comfortable for people." Erik laughs when he says that, for Munindra, "to hear more Dharma is better."

"In his own simple, innocent way, he had tremendous courage," James Baraz adds. "He was not deterred by what other people thought, because he just had confidence in the Dharma, more than confidence in any one person. He had great respect for other people—wherever you find truth, this is the Dharma."

Confidence in Others

Munindra also demonstrated his conviction in the power of Dharma by believing in his students' abilities, even when they lacked confidence in themselves. Peter Meehan recalls that Munindra would come out to talk to him when he was in private retreat at the International Meditation Centre in Bodh Gaya at the end of 1979: "I'd say something like, 'I don't know about this,' and he'd say, 'Don't worry about that. This is a good thing for you. Keep going.' He didn't always give me explanations, like other teachers do in the West, but that confidence made me go on."

Then, one day, while Karen Sirker and Peter were sitting with Munindra in his room at the Burmese Vihar (a monastic residence), Munindra swept them up with his fervor. Having received a letter from one of his Western students who was at Mahāsi Sayādaw's meditation center in Rangoon, he turned to Peter and Karen and, out of the blue, said, "You should go to Burma." Taken aback, Peter replied, "Munindra-ji, have you forgotten that I've just started my sitting practice? What am I going to Burma for?" Ever undaunted, Munindra said, "No, this is it! This is a great opportunity! You should go! I know this can happen!" Peter says, "We were naive enough and, gosh, he's so easy to trust, so we said, 'Maybe we should go to Burma. . . . Yeah, we're going to Burma!' He had that kind of infectious enthusiasm."

Munindra's encouragement accompanied Peter to Burma. "I felt so woefully novice," he admits. He would report to a monk that his knees were "on fire" and he could not sit for the entire period. Then he would overhear other yogis report about "four-hour standing meditations." But he would remember Munindra's smile and confidence and hear him saying, "It'll all be fine. Just keep going with it. Don't worry about those things." When Peter and Karen returned to Bodh Gaya, Munindra was excited for them, especially because they had stayed the course in Burma. As Gregory Pai remarks, "He had this wonderful ability to simply cut right through any kind of reservations, doubts, questions, or barriers that one might have."

Kamala Masters explains that it is not so much that Munindra dispelled doubts in others but that he instilled so much confidence through his own unwavering certainty: "They were riding on the coattails of his faith even when they didn't understand intellectually what he was talking about. It gave them time to discover for themselves."

Pushing Forward

Munindra expressed his confidence in students not only by gently encouraging them to keep going but also by suddenly placing them in a position to speak publicly. Fred von Allmen remembers how Munindra ran some retreats in the early 1970s in Bodh Gaya: He would start a one-month or six-week retreat and then, after two or three days, he would say, "Now, if you have a question, you can ask Joseph [Goldstein]." Fred continues, "So that's how, in a way, Joseph started to teach more officially or publicly. It's where I heard Joseph's first talks on bare attention and things like that." If Munindra had not done this, Grahame White notes, Joseph probably would not have taught until much later.

When Alan Clements came from Burma to Calcutta as a monk in 1980, Munindra invited him to an event one morning where they would be given *dāna* (in this case, lunch). Alan relates what happened when they entered the venue: "I've seen a lot of devotion in Asia, but it was mind-blowing to see five hundred people there, throwing down flower petals. He was honored in the realm of the gods. Then we sat and food was offered. At the end of it, when it's customary for the presiding senior to give some form of dharma talk, he looks at me and says, 'Time to give the dharma talk.'"

Alan says that he had never before given a dharma talk. "I think I broke out in hives, sweating nails. I said, 'Munindra-ji, beyond the obvious, that I don't speak Bengali . . .' And he said, pointing to himself with a smile, 'No better translator.' And so, thank you, Munindra-ji, for the opportunity to do the impossible. I have to say, it was one of the most anxiety-ridden experiences, just breaking a threshold that I hadn't touched in two years of intensive practice in Burma. Whatever stage I thought I had attained, it was nothing like breaking through this fear barrier. I don't know whether it was planned, or whether he felt it was an important thing, but I attribute my first dharma talk to Munindra-ji."

Munindra demonstrated the same confidence in female practitioners. As

Christina Feldman notes, he was "completely evenhanded in his approach." Robin Sunbeam adds, "I never felt second-rate around Munindra-ji. He treated me like a promising yogi." In fact, his two closest Indian disciples were women: Dipa Ma, a highly accomplished and beloved teacher in her own right, and Krishna Barua, who traveled and cotaught with him from 1979 to 1989.

Spreading the Dharma

Munindra's impassioned conviction in and reverence for Dharma led him to travel widely in the world in order to share the Buddha's teaching. He sincerely believed it could help everyone and did not hesitate to speak to anyone, regardless of religious upbringing. Through confidence in his students, he promoted them to help propagate Dharma too, be it through teaching, setting up monastic training centers, or establishing lay retreat centers.

Erik Knud-Hansen comments, "It's clear that students of Munindra—Joseph Goldstein, Sharon Salzberg—have had a big impact on interesting others in the topic. A good deal of that came from Munindra's enthusiasm of aiding and abetting this movement, of getting people who had found him in India to go back and share it with others and stir up interest. He was devoted to the Dharma, and people naturally got devoted to him as well as to the Dharma. For him, the Dharma was the important part; getting devoted to him as a teacher was not important."

Dispelling Doubts

Because Munindra had managed, by dint of his own effort, to attain insight, he was confident that others could come out of confusion too. Michael Liebenson Grady remembers how Munindra was instrumental in dispelling his own reservations: "I was a classic striver. This created tension in so many ways and also quite a bit of doubt, since my experiences on the cushion were so different from what my experience of my life was off the cushion. In many ways, there was quite a bit of fragmentation on my spiritual path. My work with Munindra-ji (at IMS around 1983) helped turn this around and inspired renewed faith in the Dharma. Even though Munindra taught within the Mahāsi [Sayādaw] method, his approach to the practice and life was so much more relaxed, which is just what I needed at the time."

Munindra stressed clarity: "You should be very clear about the practice and why you're doing it. If there are ever any questions about the practice and what you're doing, *that* you should clarify. There should be no doubt about the practice in your mind."

Of Course It's Possible

"I don't believe in not possible," Munindra said. "Because I tried many things of Buddha-Dhamma, in many aspects, I found it is true, it [awakening] happens. If you're really enthusiastic, if you want to experience Dhamma, there is a way. It's possible in this very life. This is a relearning, reeducation. Buddha said everything for the path is so clear, there's nothing to be in doubt about."

There was an unmistakable sense of spiritual urgency (*saṁvega*) in Munindra's encouragement, particularly in the last years of his life. He knew, from experience, the truth of Buddha's words: "Those who have faith in the Noble Eightfold Path have faith in the best; and for those who have confidence in the best, the best result will be theirs" (AN 4.34). So he was fervid about his intentions for himself and for others:

> I want a person who is really practicing, who is serious—they must experience Dhamma! They come on track. Life becomes very easy, simple, and wonderful—an asset for the world. That's what I want. If they follow the teachings, within a short time it can happen. There is no time limit; every step takes you nearer the goal. They must understand how to live in the moment. They should take advantage of this. They should not spoil this life, not miss the opportunity. Human life is very precious. Once they go backward, it is very difficult to come ahead. That's why they must make best use of the time they have in this life.

Karmic Connections

Karma and its repercussions in many lifetimes might be hard for Westerners to swallow, but such concepts did not prove difficult for Munindra—they were part of the air he breathed. Nor did his Asian students with a family background in Buddhism harbor the skepticism that Westerners did.

Dhammaruwan Chandrasiri says, "He had a very strong belief about us being friends in a previous life. He didn't have a doubt; I didn't have a doubt." As a child in Sri Lanka, Dhammaruwan told his parents there was someone who had been his friend in a past life but now was living in India, near the Bodhi Tree, and dressed all in white. His father went to Bodh Gaya and found Munindra, just as his son had described him.

Munindra strongly believed in the importance of Bodh Gaya and the stupa, says Denise Till: "He would always say that we could never really see what impact coming to Bodh Gaya would have on our lives, that every time you came it would completely change your karma, that you could not come here without some form of purification in your mind and developing merit."

Since Bodh Gaya is the place where the Buddha himself awakened, for all Buddhists it is the center of the universe and a sacred place. Munindra told Denise, "People struggled to get here hundreds and thousands of years ago and died on their way. Yet we've managed to get here just through a train journey and a bus. It's so remarkable for anyone to come here; it requires a great deal of good karma and good fortune." Perhaps that is why, in part, Munindra had such kindly relations with the many foreigners that showed up. He must have seen them through that lens, feeling a karmic connection to them, and taking on the responsibility of guiding them.

The more Munindra learned about Buddhist philosophy and cosmology, the more he embraced it. He would describe, at great length, different kinds of universes. Caught in the tension between spiritual faith and empirical science, Westerners imagined he was painting a religious fantasy, but he would confidently say, "You don't have to believe, but it's true."

Joseph "Joe" DiNardo says, "The biggest thing I take away from my experiences with him is that he was the rarest of individuals who was completely convinced of his vision of the universe—not intellectually convinced; he was convinced in his heart. In other words, all the things that the Buddha spoke about and taught were real for him, and he constructed his life, or his life unfolded, in a way that manifested all those principles of compassion and wisdom."

Abiding Confidence and Optimism

Munindra never abandoned—even for a nanosecond—his unequivocal conviction in Dharma's potency to transform. He projected it into the future for one and all, saying,

> It can be revived, it can be practiced again—this universal Dhamma. It's good for all beings. It can fill a wonderful role to have a better society, better world, better planet Earth. And not only this planet, but other planets also.... It can bring harmony, unity. Everybody can be happy, healthy, peaceful, and can live very long and supporting one another. [All countries] can help each other. One Dhamma, same Dhamma, for all people, all countries.

Despite his faith, or maybe because of it, Munindra was realistic, adding,

> But it will take time. Everybody has a role in it. Everybody has the responsibility. Even one person [who] becomes illuminated with the light... becomes an asset to himself, to society, to the whole world. So that is the essence of the whole teaching: It is universal love, goodness, beauty, abundance of health, happiness, prosperity. When the mind is pure, there is love; you see what is good, what is bad. You see for yourself.

Faith is the seed, practice the rain,
And wisdom is my yoke and plow....
Mindfulness my plowshare and goad.
—THE BUDDHA, SN 1.4 AND SN 7.11

saddhā: from *sam* (well) + *dah* (to establish, place, put). In effect, *saddhā* is well-established confidence or conviction in the Three Jewels (Buddha, Dharma, and *Sangha*). Although frequently translated as "faith," *saddhā* is not "faith" as understood in the theological and philosophical traditions of Western thought. It is not unexamined, unconditional trust, but an internal certainty, born of investigation and intuitive understanding, about the power of Dharma to purify and liberate. Such reasoned conviction grows through direct experiences that substantiate the Buddha's teaching. *Saddhā* becomes confirmed when a practitioner attains the first stage of insight—stream-entry (*sotāpatti*)—and the hindrance of skeptical doubt falls away. Faith and wisdom thus work together so that the former is not blind emotion and the latter is not merely intellectual or theoretical knowledge.

Saddhā is the catalyst that turns the experience of *dukkha* into the path toward liberation (*nibbāna*). It is one of the four streams of merit (*puññadhāra*), the five spiritual faculties (*indriya*) or powers (*bala*), the five elements of effort (*padhāniyanga*), and the seven treasures (*dhana*).

4

Give Everything with an Open Heart
Dāna (Generosity)

> *Thank you, now I can offer dāna to others.*
> —MUNINDRA

The Buddha made generosity a priority on the path to freedom when he said, "If beings knew, as I know, the result of giving and sharing, they would not eat without having given, nor would they allow the stain of meanness to obsess them and take root in their minds. Even if it were their last morsel, their last mouthful, they would not eat without having shared it, if there were someone to share it with" (It 26).

Whoever showed up at Munindra's door would encounter unmitigated generosity. He unfailingly shared whatever he had to give—food, time, knowledge, monetary and moral support, contacts, caring words, and spiritual friendship. Most of all, he loved to share Dharma, which he considered the greatest gift of all. And it was apparent that Munindra's outward deeds were an expression of an inward experience of wholesome motivation; feelings of loving-kindness and compassion impelled him to give.

In late 1996, Robert Pryor asked Paul Choi to bring some presents to Munindra at his family's home in Calcutta. (Munindra had been too ill that fall to teach in Bodh Gaya.) Being new to Dharma, Paul had neither a clear idea of who Munindra was nor a great interest in being with him; rather he was eager to play tourist in the city. But his unexpected experience of Munindra's bighearted nature left a lasting impression.

Paul recalls, "We chatted a little bit and Munindra said to me, 'Oh, you must stay the weekend with me and we will practice meditation together.' I kick myself now because if I had the opportunity again, I would take it in a heartbeat. But at that point I didn't even have reverence for the Dharma. So my thought was, 'Who is this guy anyway? Why would I want to spend a weekend meditating with him?' I said, 'No thank you.' Then he said, 'You must at least stay the night, and we'll meditate.' And I said, 'No, no, no.' He said, 'OK, at least you must stay the afternoon, and we could talk about the Dharma.' Again, I conveyed that I wasn't interested. He just smiled and said, 'OK, well, let me feed you.' I remember, quite distinctly, sitting down at his table and how carefully he attended to me, making sure I ate well. I begin to cry every time I recollect this. He kept standing up to serve food into my plate with such kindness, warmth, and generosity."

That was the extent of Paul's interaction with Munindra. "It's quite remarkable," says Paul. "As I've continued to explore the Dharma, my love for him has grown, even though I never saw him again. Especially when I'm on retreat, that memory will come back. Sometimes it will make me laugh and fill me with such joy because I felt—and I feel today—that that was such an example of his awakening, his selflessness and generosity."

Paul continues, "There was not a trace—at least not that I could feel—of him thinking, 'Doesn't he know who I am?' What I felt was him just doing whatever he could do to serve me. That has continued to reverberate through my life. I make a point of reflecting on that regularly, whether it's before teaching a meditation course or even going to see patients, because I'm training as a psychiatrist right now. I feel very grateful to him."

Alan Clements, who had much more interaction with Munindra, beginning in late 1976, echoes Paul's sentiments that Munindra had a remarkable sense of generosity. "You could not be in his presence without being served," says Alan. "You felt that you belonged in his space. He would see that you were fed, that you had drink, that you were comfortable, and he would answer the very reason why you were there. He gave himself beautifully, and he gave his few belongings beautifully."

Different Ways of Giving

There are various levels of and reasons for giving, such as prompted and unprompted generosity. We might reluctantly donate money in response to being asked because of feeling pressure to give or reciprocate, or because we would like to earn a fine reputation as a donor. We might respond spontaneously and compassionately to a need we notice and give because it feels good to do so. Finally, there is real generosity, not holding anything back and not confining our gifts to family members and people we like or to special occasions. As the Buddha said, such "kingly giving" ennobles and beautifies the mind, gladdens the heart, and causes happiness to arise.

Munindra was not someone who needed prompting to part with what he had; he never gave grudgingly. Without ever knowing the latest research findings from neuroscience—that voluntary giving makes the "feel-good" and "moral" areas of one's brain light up—Munindra was generous because he derived great joy from it and he understood its karmic implications. He gave unrestrainedly, for *mettā* (loving-kindness) and *karunā* (compassion) were inextricably linked with *dāna* in his character. He was as kind, loving, compassionate, and generous to strangers as he was to his family.

When Ven. Khippapañño came from Vietnam to India in 1967, Munindra not only taught him vipassanā, he also had the monk live with him at the Burmese Vihar in Bodh Gaya and offered him food daily. He guided him through the intense emotional experiences he suffered then and, upon learning about the monk's financial hardship, became his benefactor so he could keep practicing. Ven. Khippapañño says, "His heart is like my mother's—he is very soft and has so much compassion for me. I feel closer to Munindra than even to my father." Years later, when Munindra suffered various health setbacks, the monk raised funds to cover his medical expenses. *Dāna* generated by compassion led to more of the same.

Now I Can Give to Others

Munindra was a *dānapati*, a "kingly giver." Except for books and robes, he kept nothing for himself, including gifts. Dhammaruwan Chandrasiri says, "A lot of people came to our house in Sri Lanka to meet him. Once, a man offered him a bowl in the shape of a small Bodhi Tree, made out of brass. I was a little boy and said, 'Oh, this is very nice.' Munindra said then and there, 'I want you to have it.' So it was receive in one hand and give with the other. That showed me the character of Munindra, how much he didn't hold on to anything. Sometimes people would keep a gift like that for some time, to have it there on the table, and then give it away. But he was receiving and immediately giving."

Gopendra Prasad Barua (known as Govinda) says of Munindra, "Many things my brother got from people he distributed to those in need. Anybody who came to him, he used to give, always." Kamala Masters adds that whenever she offered him something, he made it clear that it was not just for him. He would say, "Thank you, now I can give to others."

S. N. Goenka, who was close friends with Munindra for more than forty years, found him "very humble, not greedy like some of the teachers in the East who want money, money, money." He adds, "As my teacher [Sayagi U Ba Khin] used to say, 'I am only at the giving end, not at the receiving end. Let people come and take Dhamma.' The same thing with Munindra, he was at the giving end. He was not greedy to collect money. For what would he collect money?"

Munindra once told Ram Sevak, "I don't take tobacco, I don't take wine, I don't take cigarettes—not even *chai,* only lemon water. I have no expenditures. Why spend money and buy these things? Instead, I can distribute this amount to other people. My daily habit is to give for Dhamma instead of for tobacco."

Gregg Galbraith says, "Munindra was very frugal and definite about not paying too much—he would not accept being ripped off—but he had a soft spot for the real needs of people. He spent a lot of time thinking about others. He was highly motivated to uplift people who had potential to better themselves and prosper but were held down because of poverty. If he knew that somebody was a good person, trying hard to get by, he would often be generous. His personal needs were small, and he was as content to be among villagers as he was with Buddhist students."

Munindra was especially keen to give for the sake of education. Though Bengali was his first language, while living in Sarnath, Munindra learned Hindi and thus was able to teach laborers and their children, who were too poor to attend school. Whenever he had some money, he gave it to them to buy books. When asked why he spent time teaching these people, Munindra said, "These people come from the village. They don't know Dhamma; they don't know neatness and cleanliness. They are good people. This learning will strengthen their character and good behavior. It is my duty to help them."

In Bodh Gaya, Munindra also donated food and clothing to elderly women and handed food or money to beggars. He made a special point of aiding girls to attend classes because the cost of dowries otherwise deprived them of schooling. Tapas Kumar Barua knows many students, including several research scholars from Gaya, Varanasi, Calcutta, Bangladesh, and other places, who benefited from his uncle's direct and indirect help. He says that

Munindra had a "profound interest in spreading common education to all," but he never cared to publicize what he did.

Understanding Greed

Munindra explained how greed blocks giving. There are three kinds of *vedāna* (feeling or sensation of mind, not body)—pleasant, unpleasant, and neutral. However, he noted, the root meaning of the word *vedāna* is "experience," moment after moment. In response to different forms of contact (visual, auditory, tactile, olfactory, gustatory, mental) with objects (sight, sound, touch, smell, taste, thought), a feeling arises. When it is pleasant, greed and attachment are likely to follow. When it is unpleasant, aversion is liable to arise, and thus condemnation. Lastly, a neutral sensation generally precipitates delusion because it often does not make enough of an impression on the mind and thus is not observed or understood clearly; that is, there is no mindful awareness.

"These are the three roots of all evils: Greed brings attachment; aversion brings hatred; delusion brings more ignorance," Munindra said. "Greed will not allow you to give, to share. The positive side, nongreed, becomes *dāna*—you can share, you can give." And *dāna*, he taught, whether small or large, as long as it is given with sincere intention, purifies the mind of greed.

Giving and Receiving with Wisdom

Although Munindra was spontaneously generous, he kept the Buddha's counsel in the *Kāladāna Sutta* that giving should be timely, with discernment, responsive to conditions, and devoid of stinginess (AN 5.36). Kamala Masters observed this at a train station in India. When a beggar began to pester her and pull on her clothes, Munindra told him to go away. After they left that spot, he took a banana from his bag and went up to a youngster—she is not sure whether it was the same beggar—and offered it to him. He did not give to everybody who came over, Kamala clarifies: "He gave when it was the right timing, when we weren't in a hurry, and it seemed like there was a connection."

Giving should be appropriate to the situation and carried out with discretion, Munindra advised. When visiting Kamala on Maui, he would inquire about her books on Dharma. One time she lamented, "Munindra-ji, I lend my books out and I don't get them back." He admonished her, "Don't do that. Your books are important to you. You must keep your books. It's better to tell the person what the book is and let them go get it, because then they have to spend their energy for it. They will have more interest in reading it."

To another student who had been generous to a visitor whose behavior seemed not to warrant it, he suggested not to give indiscriminately but to reflect on the usefulness of it: "To whom are you giving? For what are you giving? Why are you giving?" The Buddha said that one should give where the gift bears great fruit (AN 5.36).

Munindra also knew when to graciously accept *dāna* and when not to. Ray Lipovsky remembers being invited to join him for a Buddhist family funeral of a recently deceased man in Calcutta: "There we are, sitting in this place, and these extremely poor people are serving us with the finest that they had, honored to have us there and feed us all this amazing food. The widow is trying to press money onto Munindra, and he knows that she can't afford it. He refuses to take it and gives it back to her, 'No, no, you cannot give me this. We're just here to help.'"

Yet, on another occasion, Kamala Masters and two friends accompanied Munindra to the humble home of a *chai wallah* (tea vendor) in Sarnath and the lesson was different: "There I learned from Munindra-ji that if somebody wants to give, don't say no, because you are obstructing that person's *pāramī* (perfection of a virtue); so you receive. But somehow we knew that providing dinner for all of us was difficult for the family, so my friends and I right away agreed that we would give them *dāna*."

"They didn't have anything for us to sit on," Kamala recalls, "so they brought out their bed and we sat on it. We were outside under the stars—it was lovely. The whole family came, and, after we ate dinner, Munindra gave a dhamma talk in their language. There were about ten people sitting around formally, listening very respectfully, and very happily. This is how Munindra went around to teach, rather than making a poster or sign for people to come see him. That's the kind of person he was—not a lot of fanfare."

Tridib Barua adds that his uncle Munindra had a habit of visiting the marketplace or poor area of any region he was in so as to encounter the kind of people who would not necessarily approach him because of their low status. One monk in Bodh Gaya disapproved of Munindra's roaming from village to village "talking to useless people," but Munindra was happy to take the initiative to get to know them, never considering them worthless or a waste of his time. Kamala Masters saw this herself when she was with Munindra in

Sarnath: "We'd walk down the main street and it would take so long because, without fail, he stopped to talk to anyone who approached him, including the beggars who knew him from long ago. He was genuinely happy to meet up with them again."

Shopping

Munindra wanted so much to give to those who could not afford to get things for themselves that, when he was in the West, he sometimes overwhelmed his students with a penchant for shopping. In some of her dharma talks, Kamala Masters has recalled with gentle humor his great interest in shopping at Long's (a large drugstore) on Maui. While she was busy running errands, he would sit in her car resting quietly with his eyes closed. As soon as he learned that they were in the Long's parking lot, suddenly he was awake and alert, ready to go shopping.

"He told me at one point that he needed umbrellas," she says. "He saw umbrellas at Long's and picked up several of them. I asked him, 'Did you want one of these?' He said he wanted all of them, explaining, 'Look, where I live, there are many children that need things, many little children, so I want to bring them what I can.'" "It isn't as though he wanted all kinds of wonderful stuff for himself," Kamala remarks. "He didn't use very much. When we traveled in India, he had one cup, the same wide-mouth plastic cup that he had when he came to America. He kept it covered in some raggedy-looking but clean cloth. (No matter where we were, at four o'clock every day, he had to drink water.) When you see a person live like that, then you know all the stuff he wants to buy truly isn't for him."

Munindra always wanted the best quality for everybody, including himself. If there was fruit on the table, he would offer, "Why don't you take something?" And if the person took the smaller piece, he would say, "You don't see the bigger one? Why are you taking the smaller one?"

Bhante Vimalaraṃsi adds that Munindra was a living example of *dāna* and *mettā* simultaneously: "We would be eating a meal together, and he would find the choicest piece of fruit. He would always put it on somebody else's plate and say something about how important it is to share, especially when you're eating with other people."

Munindra believed not only in contributing whatever he had but also in not being deficient in anything. He thought it an unfortunate thing to not have enough, because one must be able to give and share with others.

Although the Buddha did not consider material wealth a lofty goal, Munindra pointed out, "Buddha never encouraged poverty, because good karma brings abundance," and abundance enables great generosity, creating even more good karma. This teaching is also found in the *Ādiya Sutta,* where the Buddha discusses five benefits that can be obtained from wealth that is righteously gained, including providing pleasure and satisfaction for oneself, one's parents, spouse and children, workers, friends, and associates, as well as offerings to followers of the holy life (AN 5.41).

So Much Stuff

Munindra especially delighted in going to flea markets to buy gifts. Ginny Morgan describes an experience she, Gregg Galbraith, and John Van Keppel had at a small flea market in Massachusetts. "We went up to one booth where Munindra saw a little piano keyboard for children. The gentleman behind the table looked like he had had a difficult night and wasn't with it that morning. He appeared tired and kept rubbing his eyes. Munindra held this toy up and said, 'How much for this?' The man looked at him and said, 'Ten dollars.' Munindra responded, 'Would you take five?' And the guy said, 'Are you crazy? Give it up. I'm not going to do it.' Munindra put it down and said, 'Please? I want to take [it] to the children in India.' This man said, 'Ah, jeez,' and hit himself in the forehead with his hand, walked back and forth behind his counter, and then finally got down on his hands and knees and dug around in a box.

"Munindra was very patient. The guy pulled out two batteries and plunked them down on top of the keyboard and handed it over to Munindra. He said, 'I don't know why I'm doing this. Five dollars, and I'll throw in the batteries.' Then he turned to me and said, 'Lady, I bet you bring him to do all your shopping.' Munindra folded his hands in the prayer position and looked at this man full on and said, 'May you be happy and peaceful. May you live with ease and well-being. And may you come to know full freedom from suffering.' I watched a red flush spread up this guy's neck and into his face—he seemed really shocked. He turned to me and said, 'Lady, we need this stuff.' And I said, 'Yes, we all need this stuff.' Then a woman in the next booth came running up and said, 'For crying out loud, it's Gandhi!'"

Munindra's accumulation of goods often presented a challenge. Vivian Darst recalls that he crammed suitcases full of used clothing they had found at a rummage sale in Seattle. "Throughout our trip to Europe," she says, "my friend and I were lugging around Munindra's luggage with all this stuff he was taking back to India. I used to give him a really bad time about it because I had to carry it into all these cars and planes. I used to say, 'You could buy it in India.' And he'd say, 'No, not the same quality.' I asked, 'What is it all for?' He wanted to give presents to family and friends, especially a lot of little children in Bodh Gaya."

Sometimes, Munindra could barely get on the plane with all he had acquired. David Berman describes what happened once at the airport in Boston. When Munindra checked in, his luggage was far too heavy. He had amassed so much at the flea markets, and he had a lot of books. The airline's overage charge for this extra weight was hundreds of dollars. David says, "He started to do the it's-for-the-starving-children routine, but that worked better at the flea market than at the airport, where they don't negotiate. I didn't have the cash or a credit card at hand. We were just stuck there. We weren't going to abandon the stuff, and it wasn't part of the agent's job to worry about the starving children of India. Just then Christine Yedica showed up to see Munindra off, and she whipped out a credit card. I think she was glad to rescue her teacher and solve the problem."

Though his intentions of generosity were heartfelt, Munindra was not always able to completely fulfill them. When he returned to India, the customs officials opened the boxes and suitcases and took what they wanted.

The Allure of a Generous Heart

Despite these challenges, Munindra's students fondly remember him for being an embodiment of *dāna*. A generous heart attracts the affection and friendship of others. Sunny Wootton says, "He was a wonderful man to be around—loving, generous of spirit, and kind. He saw the best in everybody, and gave me the best. He would have given me anything. It was, 'Do you want to have this? Do you want to have that? Just have it all.'"

Dhriti Barua says, "He liked one specific preparation of dried fish a lot. One day, he asked me, 'Do you like this?' I said yes. So after that, whenever he was here, he would instruct the cook, 'Take some off and keep it for *Goma* [daughter-in-law; Dhriti married his nephew Tridib]; keep some for Mumu [her nickname].' When I ate, he used to come afterward and ask, 'Did you eat it? I left some for you. Did you like it?'"

Offering food was something that Munindra did automatically wherever he was. When Akasa Levi sporadically paid him morning calls at the Gandhi ashram in Bodh Gaya in the early 1970s, he often found Munindra "squatting outside his room, making lemonade from a bowl of lemons, cutting and squeezing them mindfully." He says, "It almost looked like a Japanese tea ceremony. There were also raw garbanzo beans, soaking in a bowl, all fluffed out. He served these to me in a little tea saucer. He put down a little pile of these fresh-soaked beans and a little cup of lemon water."

People would constantly visit him on the Antioch Education Abroad Buddhist Studies Program in Bodh Gaya as well. Denise Till says, "He was very warm and inviting. We'd be giving him food, and he would keep it all piled up on the table to offer fruits and biscuits to whoever would come into the room." He did the same thing at Dhamma Giri. Barry Lapping says, "He would always give you something to eat. He was very health conscious. He would take a papaya, wash it, clean it, cut it up, and bring out a bowl of it to share."

The Greatest Gift of All—Dharma

The Buddha said there are two kinds of giving, sharing, and assistance: material things and Dharma. Of the two, Dharma is foremost and unsurpassed. From the time of his first realization until the day he died, Munindra spent his life sharing the supreme gift of Dharma and assisting as many people as he could to move toward realization too. His accessibility and availability for teaching Dharma are legendary. As Lama Surya Das comments, "He was generously and spontaneously giving in all ways. He didn't charge for his time or his knowledge. He wasn't enrolling, proselytizing, fund-raising, self-promoting, or empire-building. Munindra was so open that nothing could get built up because it was always flowing out."

Of his first trip to Calcutta in 1987, Danny Taylor recalls coming upon Munindra just sitting at the door: "I was struck by his willingness to talk to everybody, how easy and inviting it was to be in his presence, and an immediate sense of generosity. He'd never met me before. I was quite stunned at how easy it was to access a person of his reputation."

Munindra accommodated the individual and the situation. Without any sense of hierarchy or aloofness, despite his attainments, he would reach out to a reticent or shy yogi. Suil, who practiced with him in Bodh Gaya in late 1973, remembers, "If I didn't ask a question, he would ask me. He took that step forward in a certain way, starting the investigation or inquiry. It is a kind of generosity to like to share what you know and be willing to step out to do so. In my quietness, he would initiate some kind of dialogue that would end up being very useful as a reflection."

Daw Than Myint describes his guidance in Rangoon: "He allowed us to report to him any time, so we went to see him several times a day. Any new discovery we had during the sitting, we would go and tell him. It helped us to progress, because we could tell him at any moment about any difficulty. He showed how to overcome it or note it, so that we didn't stay at one stage very long." Becoming tearful, Daw Than Myint continues, "His door was always open. He was available all the time, helping and teaching, and always smiling. He wanted to pour his knowledge into us. He would be waiting, looking for the chance. So we learned a lot from him. That is very beneficial for us, and it's what I have seen with all the people he taught."

Peter Meehan says that even if Munindra was busy or walking down the street in the opposite direction, he would stop and make time for him. When Munindra was well into his eighties and in poor health, he still returned to Bodh Gaya to teach young Antioch students. Oren Sofer, a recipient of this generosity, was occasionally "frustrated that he didn't take care of himself more, that he would give so much." Oren often encouraged him to stop and rest for a while: "He'd be going on about the Dhamma in a very passionate way, but I could tell he was getting tired, so I'd say, 'OK, Munindra, it's time to go to bed. Everyone, let's leave.' Because otherwise he would just stay up, teaching."

Munindra shared more than direct teachings with his students. He would also take them to see places around Bodh Gaya that were important in the life of the Buddha. Fred von Allmen says, "At the end of the retreats in those winters, when it got really hot, Munindra would take us around Bodh Gaya, to the place where Sujata had offered milk rice to the Buddha at the river, and then talk about the life of the Buddha. And he would take us to the cave on the mountainside where the Buddha had practiced austerities. He'd take us to the Mahabodhi Stupa grounds and explain about the various places where the Buddha had stayed after his enlightenment."

Munindra shared Dharma in yet another way—through his observance of the five precepts. By abstaining from doing harm, he gave the gift of benevolence, fearlessness, and security. Kamala Masters remembers his saying that it is essential to strengthen all three pillars of Dharma—*sīla, dāna,* and *bhāvanā*—or the foundation of one's practice will not be stable, like a stool that cannot remain upright because it is missing a leg. She realized that when he was teaching her, *dāna* was not highlighted in the West; neither was *sīla*. At the time, the emphasis was on *bhāvanā,* mental development or meditation.

Munindra was also hugely supportive of other teachers. Rather than cling to students, he directed them to go practice with S. N. Goenka, Dipa Ma, the *sayādaws* in Burma, or even his Western students. Alan Clements says Munindra gave him a list of names of teachers to be sure he would seek teachings from them, including Mahāsi Sayādaw, Sayādaw U Sujata, Sayādaw U Jawana, and Sayādaw U Pandita. "Munindra-ji is responsible for the name Sayādaw U Pandita being introduced to the West," he notes. "He holds an extremely intimate and powerful place in this transmission legacy."

Itamar Sofer adds, "He was such a humble person. He recommended all of his students at that time to go and join the courses of S. N. Goenka. Many teachers would not do that; they would try to collect disciples. But he gave full praise to Goenka-ji. That's very inspiring."

Munindra provided opportunities that encouraged others to teach and develop confidence. He would facilitate an introduction, step aside, or actually leave so someone else would have to take over teaching while he was away or while he sat by quietly. Ruth Denison benefited from Munindra's support when she began teaching in the 1970s. By incorporating mindful walking as part of her practice, she did not adhere strictly to the method of her mentor U Ba Khin or his disciple S. N. Goenka, and she had to deal with some tension over it. Munindra answered her many questions and also understood why she included mindful movement, reassuring her that "Buddha said that teaching in a new culture had to be done very sensitively and had to connect to the culture at hand."

Unprompted Generosity—Teaching in the Moment

As a "gracious guest" in Kamala Master's home on Maui, Munindra shared Dharma with her daily, "because he felt that was the most valuable offering he could make." She says, "Every morning I went to his room to receive some guidance and instruction. His enthusiasm for sharing the Buddha's teaching was quite remarkable. Sometimes in the morning I would ask him a simple question, and he would take several situations that arose during the day to illustrate the Buddha's teaching in response."[1] Even when he was recovering from surgery, he continued to give her lessons while lying down.

One of Derek Ridler's strongest memories of his time with Munindra in Bodh Gaya was shopping in the market. "We must have been getting supplies for the retreat," he says. "I bought some food, including a bunch of those small Indian bananas. There was this young girl, about twelve or thirteen, who came over to me and wanted money. I gave her these bananas. Munindra-ji came right up to me and affirmed that it was a pure act of giving because it wasn't contrived. I can't remember exactly what he said, but something about the power of openheartedness or open generosity. That really stayed with me because he interacted with me in a very personal sense. It wasn't some abstract teaching but an immediate response to a circumstance that arose spontaneously."

In his early years with Munindra, Joseph Goldstein experienced a similar teaching on natural generosity. Ray Lipovsky remembers Joseph describing what happened: "Munindra was taking care of and feeding everybody, and Joseph all of a sudden realized, 'Hey, wait a minute. Here's this little East Indian guy giving us food, and we're these Western kids with all the money. How does he do this?' So he asked Munindra, 'Do you need some help with this? Should we be paying you?' Munindra said, 'If you like; it's up to you.' Joseph asked, 'Well, why didn't you ask?' And Munindra said, 'Because it will happen in its own time properly.' Which I took to mean that when there's unprompted generosity, it's a real teaching. You get to the place where you realize that generosity is appropriate, necessary, and obvious, so it happens. We all hear these *dāna* talks at the end of a retreat, but he wouldn't bring it up—he would live it. His attitude was: If it's true, it will happen; and if it doesn't happen, that's fine. He wasn't even thinking about it."

Years later, Munindra related this same incident to Robert Pryor and said that Joseph arranged to share his income with him. He explained that he did not ask for anything from his students because he felt he had no right to do so as a layman, only as a *bhikkhu* (monk). "If it comes, that's what I accept," Munindra said.

> I dedicated my life for Dhamma. Whatever I teach to people, I don't keep any proceeds; I don't keep something for me. I have given wholeheartedly everywhere. Wherever I've gone, whomever I've taught, I've given everything with an open heart. There is no closefistedness.

Munindra's dedication and generosity came from a keen awareness of Buddhist history:

Siddhattha Gotama became Buddha in India, but the tradition has been lost in India. I thought this was the best thing to share. "*Sabbadānam dhammadānam jināti:* The gift of Dhamma excels all gifts" [Dhp 354]. It makes a better citizen, better person, better individual.

Recalling his visit to Munindra at Dhamma Giri, Bryan Tucker was struck by his "amazing kindness and generosity." Bryan continues, "He couldn't help it; it was his nature to share the Dhamma. He would give you everything, absolutely. He also gave me food whenever he could and invited me into his room. Everything that he did, in the several days that I spent time with him, was showing me that though he was frail, he was still incapable of stopping his communication with people like me or anyone else around him, incapable of stopping his teaching, incapable of not giving. He made it possible for me to feel that being kind and generous does not have to be an exceptional mind state, but can be much more the norm."

When Munindra was dying, his mind was not troubled by fears about his future. Due to a generous nature throughout his life, he could recollect the many kindnesses he had shown others—teaching Dharma, providing material welfare for others, observing the precepts, and sharing the merit of his good deeds. Purifying his mind of greed, he could experience the peace of knowing that he had diligently followed the Buddha's counsel.

In this world, there are three things [of value] for one who gives. . . . Before giving, the mind of the giver is happy. While giving, the mind of the giver is peaceful. After giving, the mind of the giver is uplifted.

—THE BUDDHA, AN 6.37

dāna: from *dā* (to give, deal out, distribute). *Dāna* is the practical act of giving, in general, and, specifically, an offering to monks and nuns. As nongreed, *dāna* means relinquishing one's attachment to any number of things, ranging from worldly goods to family, to physical aspects of one's body and even life for the benefit of others. It is likened to "a drop of water that runs off a lotus leaf without adhering to it."

Dāna is the first of ten *pāramī* (perfections), for it is both common to everyone and easiest to practice. In Buddhist countries, children learn to give from an early age by putting a spoonful of rice into the bowl of a monk on an alms round. This establishes a pattern of giving that, through repetition, becomes ingrained as *cāga,* an attitude of liberality or generosity. This internal aspect is integral, since giving is not simply the external act of handing something over.

Dāna is an antidote to greed (*lobha*), one of the three unwholesome roots. It is also the first of three bases of meritorious action (the others are *sīla* and *bhāvanā*). As *cāga,* the inner virtue of generosity, it is one of the four foundations (*adhiṭṭhāna*) of an *arahant's* mentality, one of five blessings (*sampadā*), ten recollections (*anussati*), and seven treasures (*dhana*).

5

Take Care of Dharma and Dharma Takes Care of You

Sīla (Virtuous Conduct)

Be a blessing to the world by doing good karma and making the heart pure.
—MUNINDRA

In the West, people have generally entered the Buddha's Eightfold Path through meditation. But in Asian societies, *sīla* (along with *dāna*) is traditionally the first step that people are introduced to, beginning in childhood. This is certainly true in Munindra's case. His devout parents were both from Barua (literally, noble) families, considered remnants of the original Buddhists of India. His mother taught through her sweet, loving nature and her way of taking care of the family. His father instructed him and his brothers in the precepts for ethical living. As Munindra said, "I had very good parents. We were trained to observe *sīla,* to be a nice person—honest, not deceptive."

During the course of his life, Munindra witnessed and experienced personally how not being a nice person led to unhappiness of one kind or another. A seminal episode in his early years instilled in him the intention to not speak ill of anyone. When his father became a *sāmaṇera* (novice monk), rather than move to the temple, he continued his responsibility as paterfamilias by living at home. The Bengali villagers roundly condemned him for it. But all members of the family suffered from the hurtful words and ostracism. Until his death, Munindra made a conscious effort not to hurt others.

Nonharm

While the five basic precepts (*pañca-sīla*) refer specifically to refraining from killing, theft, sexual misconduct, lying, and intoxication, the principal motivation behind all of them is to do no harm. The extent to which Munindra kept *sīla* is evident in how he verbally and physically treated others, including the tiniest creatures.

"He would never harm a fly," says Uffe Damborg. "He certainly did not kill a mosquito." Munindra knew by heart the Buddha's message that any deed, word, or thought—no matter how inconsequential it appears—can have far-reaching implications. Actions that are skillful will generate uplifting results, while unskillful ones will produce unfortunate results. Practicing *sīla* helps avoid creating karma with unhappy outcomes in this life or in rebirth.

Even when insects spoiled what was dear to him, Munindra did not smash them. Michael Stein remembers a poignant incident in Bodh Gaya during monsoon season: "Munindra had all these dhamma books that he brought back from Burma—his only real possessions—and little, white, squirmy bugs started eating the paper of some of them. He had tears in his eyes. It was really touching. He just picked the bugs off, started cleaning up the books and putting them some other place that wasn't too damp."

Munindra tried to help others keep *sīla* too. Itamar Sofer recounts that Munindra used to rise early at Dhamma Giri and go out to sweep the walkway so that the yogis, who woke up at four o'clock, would not step on the leaves as they went to the pagoda to meditate and, thus, not crush the insects underneath.

Yet, if someone else was not as careful as he was, Munindra did not reproach the person. He was not self-righteously virtuous. He understood that the precepts are "steps of training" (*sikkhāpada*). (For example, when we chant the precepts, we say, "I undertake the training to abstain from killing any living being, from taking what is not given," and so forth.) So rather than judge and reprimand, Munindra was more likely to express compassion when a student reported a lapse.

Robin Sunbeam remembers his response when she broke *sīla* during a period in Bodh Gaya. "One morning, I woke up to find my forehead burning and covered with mosquito-bite lumps," she says. "There, lounging inside my mosquito net, was a lazy mosquito engorged with my blood. Fury rose in me, and I squashed the insect into a bloody pulp on the net. I had been practicing *mettā* very sincerely and strove to never harm any living thing. I went to Munindra-ji very upset because I had violated my practice and killed a living thing."

Munindra explained that it is bad to kill a mosquito, but not as bad as killing a dog—and killing a dog is bad but not as bad as killing a cow. Killing a cow is also bad, but not as bad as killing a man. And it is bad to kill a man, but not as bad as killing the king. And it is bad to kill the king, but not as bad as killing the Buddha. "If we had to swim across to the other shore with all our stones of karma, we would instantly sink to the bottom," he told her. "But our practice is like a boat to take us with our stones of karma to the other shore."

Munindra did not rebuke someone who killed many insects. One woman, overwhelmed by an infestation of termites in her kitchen cabinets, cried as she demolished all of them. When she reported what happened, he drew on his practical nature and said, "You have to think of your family's welfare, their health. You cannot let these insects eat your house."

Nonviolence Is Loving-Kindness

Munindra's observance of the first precept was born of several things. He had great appreciation for the preciousness of life and a natural empathy for all beings. He heeded the advice in the Dhammapada:

> All tremble at violence; all fear death . . . life is dear to all.
> Putting oneself in the place of another,
> One should not kill nor cause another to kill.
> (Dhp 129–30)

Instead of committing violence, however slight, Munindra extended love and kindness, for *sīla* is like a coin: While one side represents the cultivation of self-discipline and abandoning what is unwholesome, the other represents the cultivation of virtue and choosing to express what is wholesome. Munindra did not want his actions, though of good intention, to wound anyone.

Gita Kedia relates another instance of this at Dhamma Giri: "Munindra used to see a heap of dirt and rubbish from his room and think, 'There is nobody to clean, but if I clean in front of somebody, they may feel hurt that I'm cleaning the place.' So, one day, he woke up very early and cleared away the trash. Instead of causing someone shame, his act led to an interesting result—people started cleaning the area daily."

Oren Sofer recalls an incident involving rubbish in Bodh Gaya. He and Munindra were walking behind the back of the building where Munindra was staying. Looking out at the rice fields, Oren noticed a bunch of litter and commented on how upsetting it was to see the trash. Munindra said, "It is a reflection of our minds. By thought, by word, and by deed, we pollute the environment because our minds are polluted."

Sīla *as Gratitude*

Munindra's *sīla* was also a manifestation of deep gratitude. He believed that, in return for all that we receive, we should be an asset to society and a blessing to the world by doing good karma:

> I am grateful to Mother Earth. We have some debt to the planet because nature is wonderful, giving us so many beautiful things—food, fuel, everything. Do we deserve those things? Are we a good citizen of Mother Earth? By our thoughts, our deeds, our words, are we helpful to the world? If we are not doing that, we are unworthy children of Mother Earth and don't deserve to accept those things.

In addition to Mother Nature, Munindra was hugely thankful to his mother in particular and women in general. He noted, "In Buddha's teaching it is said that, on account of pregnancy and also taking care of the child after birth, mother is superior to father." He noted that one of the seven conditions of welfare, prosperity, or nondecline for a nation (*aparihāniya-dhamma*) is to treat women well. He said,

> I have greatly benefited by womenfolk from my childhood, from my mother and also [from] many women who accepted me as their son. I have [a] Bengali mother, Tibetan mother, Burmese mother, Ceylonese [Sri Lankan] mother, Japanese mother, Sikkimese mother, Bhutanese mother, American mother, Chinese mother—many different mothers. My heart is very soft toward women; I have great affection for them. If anywhere women are insulted and suffer, I feel sorry for them.

Empathy led Munindra to act on their behalf. He would offer assistance, through direct teaching or by other means, such as making it possible for girls in Bodh Gaya to get an education. He explained,

> In the state of Bihar, girls are neglected and badly treated. Boys and fathers take all the food. I have seen it with my own eyes. I was greatly shocked by all of this. People blame me for helping these girls in Bodh Gaya. I know what they say, but I don't care. If the heart is pure, there is nothing to blame. This is repayment of my loan from my mothers and sisters.

Munindra felt a sense of indebtedness and social responsibility not only to his parents, but also to his teachers and many other people for all the benefits in his life—body, food, clothing, housing, schooling, dharma training, and so on. He said,

> We should be grateful for this and also do good karma for them. That's why, whatever good karma I do anywhere, I share this with all the people to whom I am greatly indebted. Through our good karma—not being harmful in any way to society—we repay that debt; we gradually become debtless.

Harmony and Practicality

In making a voluntary commitment to *sīla,* Munindra recognized its intrinsic value in creating harmony. Honoring the precepts is considered a "great gift" (*mahādāna*) to others, for it creates an atmosphere of trust, respect, and security. It means we pose no threat to another person's life, property, family, rights, or welfare.

Peter Martin says, "What I observed in his relationships with the townspeople of Igatpuri is that everybody knew him and liked him. They all had respect for him, not only because he was in robes and was a teacher, but because of who he was as a person—honest, forthright. They knew that he wasn't going to try to get something in an underhanded way."

Munindra also did not allow dishonesty to go ignored. Practicing sīla is not just about creating harmony; it entails being practical as well. Many of his Western students remember watching him haggle in the marketplace to get a fair price for whatever he was purchasing—food, cloth, or other necessities. When there was a milk delivery, they noticed him step outside with a hydrometer to test the product and make sure he was not getting more water than milk. Walking the Buddha's path and following *sila* does not mean knowingly allowing yourself to be taken advantage of. Munindra often told students that being simple does not equate to being a simpleton.

If someone did not know enough to avoid being fleeced, Munindra would step in. Tapas Kumar Barua recalls that, on a walk around the Mahabodhi Temple with his uncle and some foreign students, one of the women became interested in gift items at a local shop. When Munindra overheard the exorbitant price the shopkeeper quoted her, he challenged him in Hindi: "Why are you asking such a high price? Because she is a foreigner and does not understand your language? The price which you are asking is absurd. Don't try to cheat people. Ask only what is reasonable."

Whenever the opportunity arose, Munindra tried to help others see that tolerating improper conduct did not serve Dharma. Shivaya Cain relates an anecdote that connects Munindra's practicality to the second precept (not stealing). There was a person who would come to Shivaya's house in Bodh Gaya and take things from him each time he visited. Sometimes he would leave things as well, for example, taking a Swiss army knife and leaving a ball of string. Shivaya told Munindra about this, and he remarked, "And you still let him come?" Shivaya said that he felt detached from money and possessions, that he found the situation interesting, and that maybe this person needed the things that he took. Munindra said to him, "Don't let him in your house! No one should ever take what's not given to them. You were not giving him those things. He had no right to remove them from your home. It doesn't matter that he left something in its place. He's still not following the path of Dharma."

My Path Is Not Yet Finished

The expectation of perfection of a realized dharma teacher led some Westerners to judge Munindra's behavior, because of any number of things: that he ate in the evening and thus did not keep the eight precepts; that he eagerly engaged in shopping; that he lodged in a student's home or that, due to his enormous curiosity and naïveté, he explored things that he might better have left unexamined. Some even accused him of denial and self-deception. Kamala Masters says, "Students still ask me, even today, 'How could Munindra stay with you?'"

Perhaps because of a different cultural understanding, his Asian students, as well as some Western ones, did not idealize Munindra or condemn any personal habit or isolated indiscretion. They knew the difference between a monk and an *anāgārika*. The latter is a Pāli term that means "one who does not inhabit a house" or "homeless one." During the time of the Buddha, it referred to those who had left home to follow a more ascetic life as his disciples. But in the early twentieth century, Anāgārika Dharmapāla of Sri Lanka, founder of the Mahabodhi Society in 1891, adopted the word to indicate an intermediate state between a layperson and a monastic, someone who has given up a home and family life, yet still lives in the world, not in a monastery. *Anāgārika* also refers to a monk's lay attendant, who is able to perform certain tasks that a monk is restricted from, such as handling money or driving a vehicle.

Daw Than Myint explains that a fluid boundary exists for an *anāgārika*, compared with the strict rules related to being a monastic. An *anāgārika* is a layperson who voluntarily makes the decision to be homeless and to take on or drop the precepts at any time. Such individuals might dress in white and engage in building or looking after pagodas, or simply being alone in the forest; at other times, they might become full-fledged laypeople anew. In contrast, a monk's responsibility is to uphold the entire Vinaya, the first of three main divisions of the Pāli Canon, or *Tipiṭaka*. It is the regulatory framework that includes rules governing the lives of monks and nuns along with procedures and points of etiquette designed to foster harmony within the monastic community and with lay supporters.

For twelve years, Munindra observed eight precepts (*aṭṭha-sīla*) as an *anāgārika* in India and then in Burma. In addition to the basic five, that meant abstaining from eating after midday; from dancing, singing, music and shows, and wearing garlands, scents, cosmetics, and adornments; and from using luxurious beds. During the year Munindra was a monk under Mahāsi Sayādaw, he fully observed the Theravāda code of monastic discipline (*pāṭimokkha*), which consists of 227 rules for fully ordained monks and 311 rules for fully ordained nuns. But when he returned to India from Burma, no longer a monk but an *anāgārika* again, and became ill, doctors and friends encouraged him to eat in the evening. From then on, he observed five precepts (*pañca-sīla*).

If Munindra ever slipped in his observance of *sīla*, it was not a cause for his most devoted students, who were aware of this fluid boundary, to censure the man they considered a huge benefactor in their lives. Rather, they acknowledged his humanity. They understood that he had not reached the final stage of insight and, therefore, was still subject to error. Dipa Barua clarifies, "*Anāgārika* is not *anāgāmī* or *arahant*. He's a good figure, educationally and religiously qualified, but he's like us, a human being. My mother, Dipa Ma, always advised me that in the world nobody is perfectly good and nobody is perfectly bad—there is a mixture."

Dipa adds, "Munindra's contribution to my mother and me was so great. My mother always said, 'Only through Munindra-ji's teaching and preaching, I came out from that shock [the death of her husband and two children], sorrow, pain, lamentation, grief, and also physical problems.'" If someone made a negative comment about Munindra, Dipa Ma would counter, "Maybe he has done wrong in his own way—maybe, I don't know, I didn't see [it] with my own eyes—but he's not doing harm to you. When he has done good karma and bad karma, then he will get a result for that. The Buddha said, 'First, look at yourself.' You have no right to judge him. You have many wrong things in yourself."

The very fact that Munindra was not perfect still inspires Kamala Masters. In particular, she recalls a few occasions when he mentioned that certain unwholesome states arose within him from time to time. Through mindfulness, he would see greed or anger coming and then going. By way of explanation, he readily admitted to her, "My path is not yet finished." Kamala understood this as an ongoing engagement in purifying his heart and mind of greed, hatred, and delusion; he was not yet fully realized. She says, "It gave me permission to be human and not to expect myself to be a perfect being."

No Nibbāna *without* Sīla

Munindra did not expect others to be perfect either. Because he could not control what others did, he sometimes had to endure their lack of *sīla*. According to Ram Sevak, there was a fifty-year-old Indian man at Samanvaya, the Gandhi ashram in Bodh Gaya, who persuaded Munindra to lend him money and promised to repay it in a couple of months. Time soon revealed his unethical intentions. One night, he left without a word. Munindra later learned that the man used the rupees to run off with a fifteen-year-old orphan girl from the ashram. Munindra wrote him two letters, but never heard back. He decided to confront him in person. He hired a car to go to the village and found the house where the man was living. But when the man heard Munindra's voice, he immediately closed the door. Munindra went in anyway, and there he saw the missing girl. He asked for the return of his loan, but the man said, "I have no money now." After Munindra left, he wrote to him again, but all to no avail.

"Why [do] people do these things—killing, robbing?" Munindra would ask. "Because of greed; greed makes the mind blind. Greed, hate, and delusion—these three are the root of all evils, leading us to darkness. By doing those things, we open up a darkening road, going backward, not forward." What we need to do instead, he pointed out, is cultivate "love, *mettā*, good discipline."

When it was obvious that repayment would not be forthcoming, Munindra decided to turn the man's theft into an act of generosity from himself. In his final letter, he wrote that the money was no longer a loan—he made it a donation instead—and strongly urged the man not to deceive anyone else. Munindra passed on the kindness that others had extended to him. He knew firsthand the great benefit of having a mind free from worry, fear, or regret.

During his first retreat in Burma, Munindra said he "felt the pinch" of incidents from earlier in his life. One day, as a young boy going to school, he bought some nuts, but forgot to pay for them. Before he left India, he neglected to return a dictionary borrowed from a monk. Recalling these ethical slips disturbed his mind during meditation. Conferring with Mahāsi Sayādaw, he made a donation in memory of the nut seller. He also wrote to the monk, inquiring how he could give back the book. The monk soon replied that Munindra should let go of his concern and now, with a clear conscience, concentrate on meditation instead, for he had donated the book to him. Having eliminated these obstacles, Munindra reapplied himself with vigor and had his first profound opening to freedom (the first of the four stages of awakening).

"If we do not observe the *sīla* of discipline—if we want to kill, want to rob, want to do all nonsense, and also practice," Munindra said, "*nibbāna* will not happen because these are two different things." Mahāsi Sayādaw had told him, "One who observes *sīla*, whose mind is pure, can complete any aspiration. This is a universal law: 'If you take care of Dhamma, Dhamma takes care of you.'"

Students remember this admonition expressed in various ways. For example, Grahame White says, "His main teaching was 'The Dharma protects' or 'If you look after the Dharma, the Dharma looks after you.'" Grahame adds, "He was talking about the precepts and practice. What I learned from him was that if you follow the precepts and if you practice generosity, it all comes back to you. Since I've been in business, I've tried to run on those principles. So I feed the monks or the nuns and so forth. The business just keeps getting better. It's so successful that sometimes I say, 'I've got to stop feeding the monks! It's getting too busy, too many orders!' On one level, that's what he was talking about. On the other level, he was saying that if you practice the Dharma, then your mind's protected."

Wise Speech

Although Munindra was known for speaking at length, he did so only when it came to Dharma. Itamar Sofer describes his first interaction with him at Dhamma Giri: "He didn't engage in just ordinary talk. He immediately goes to the teaching of the Buddha. He asked me a few questions about my life, where I came from, then back to the basics: How is your practice? How many years have you been practicing?"

"I don't think you could sit with him and just chitchat," Pat Masters comments. "It always had some dharma lesson or dharma connection. It was too important, in a sense, to waste that time."

Bhante Bodhipāla adds, "Whenever I met with him, I never heard any worldly talking, only Dhamma." So-called worldly talk is not what the Buddha had in mind when he described wise speech (*sammā-vācā*) to his disciples. He urged them to abstain from falsehood, talebearing, harsh language, and foolish babble. And if there was nothing worthwhile to be said, then they were to remain silent.

Interestingly, Munindra's name also reflects the Buddha's counsel. The term *muni* originally meant "to be silent" or "to take vows of silence," but later it was rendered as "a sage." Either way, silence or sagacity is applied to speech, body, and mind. Munindra said that his name means "Great Sage," and that it is also one of the Buddha's many appellations. "Shākyamuni" literally translates as "the silent one of the Shākya clan," but it can also be understood as "one who is gracefully or pleasingly silent."

Munindra was intentional in his silence. There were times when people spread rumors or spoke harshly about him. Knowing the truth of the situation, he did not let any gossip interfere with his practice of wise speech. He did not retaliate. Tara Doyle recalls hearing disparaging comments about Munindra and some other vipassanā teachers made by the students of another teacher. She says that the fact that Munindra never spoke badly of other teachers was "such a great gift he gave to us." She continues, "I was able to do vipassanā without having to see one thing as good and another as bad. He never said anything unkind about anyone."

Not only did he not strike back, Munindra never stopped encouraging students to go on retreats with the teacher who criticized him. Years later, he revealed to Robert Pryor that he had suggested to that teacher not to hurt others by wrongly criticizing them, especially without an understanding of what they are teaching. And when Kamala Masters once questioned him regarding a particular teacher in India, about whom there was much damning media, Munindra said nothing untoward about him. He simply commented, "A perfect rose can come from an imperfect giver."

Ram Dass says, "Munindra measured his words, considered his words, as if he wanted to not hurt anybody. He loved people very much." He managed this even when it came to difficult individuals. Gregg Galbraith recalls a temperamental man that Munindra had close dealings with as "kind of rough and irascible and sometimes a little deceitful." Yet Munindra refused to label anyone as evil or hopeless, and thereby solidify an identity. Instead of singling out the individual, he might acknowledge the misconduct itself. Gregg gives an example: "If a rickshaw driver knows that he's got you over a barrel and is trying to rip you off, Munindra would be matter of fact and say, 'That's not honest, that's not right. You shouldn't pay that.' He would focus on the behavior as being not valuable or not worthy, but he didn't condemn the person."

As Munindra told his students, "Nobody in the world wants to hear any unkind, rough, rude words. Nobody wants to hear scolding. Everybody wants to hear loving, sweet, soothing words."

Wise Action

On a visit to California around 1981, Munindra and coteacher Krishna Barua went with some dharma friends to see a documentary about Bhagwan Sri Rajneesh, filmed in Pune. Having known Rajneesh in India, Munindra was curious to learn more about his ashram. Sharda Rogell describes a specific scene in the film that captured his attention: "It showed a group therapeutic process where they were encouraged to act out whatever feeling or emotion or desire or aversion that arose—just to go with it. There were people fighting and lovemaking and just milling around. It was kind of like a circus, but it was real and authentic. Munindra was fascinated by this."

Sharda continues, "When we left, he was really upset. I think he was taken aback; he hadn't known that that was going on. He said, 'That is not Dhamma; it's not what we are teaching. That's misguided, a misunderstanding of freedom. What we're teaching is actually the opposite of that—that you don't follow your emotions, you don't follow your desires, you don't follow those thoughts.' He really gave us a wonderful dharma teaching: The whole point is wise restraint and not following the mind. He was not criticizing Rajneesh; he was criticizing what was happening there. He was pointing out that that's not Dharma. He could not understand in any way how that would help someone get closer to freedom." Munindra taught that real liberation comes from self-control rather than the total absence of restraint. Following thoughts and emotions blindly could lead one down "a darkening road."

Ajit Roy learned from Munindra that when upset, it is best to sit quietly, stay away, and talk later. "I learned from him that I don't have to express my anger; it's bad for me," Ajit says. "A lot of people—even nice people, good men—are in prison because one day they heated up and got sparked by the moment, did a bad thing, and now they're in a jail for the rest of their lives."

Dealing with anger presents difficulties, especially without an experiential understanding of *anattā* (not-self). "The anger is personified—'*My* anger! He made *me* angry!'—and then there is revenge and reacting," Munindra explained. "Feeding the anger, you also hurt yourself at that time, and those who are around you are fed by your anger. And also you pollute the environment, sending thoughts everywhere—thoughts vibrate. Your whole mouth becomes impure." That is why he cautioned everyone to attend carefully to the three doors of action—speech, body, and mind. Through any one of them can emerge harm or good. *Sīla* cuts off the external expression of the defilements and serves as a foundation upon which to build all kinds of virtuous qualities.

Although Munindra had cultivated *sīla* since he was a boy, his inclination toward *sīla* deepened after what he called "the spontaneous opening of the mind, the heart," during his training with Mahāsi Sayādaw. Munindra said, "When any wrong idea, wrong energy comes, negativity arises, it gives you a signal. When anger comes, you feel uncomfortable—'Oh, there is anger'—you see it. As soon as you see it, it dies out. All these negativities, pollution, come at the time of darkness; they cannot come in the light."

Right Livelihood

Munindra was a walking advertisement of "Do what you love." He derived great joy from helping others. "From my childhood, I was always a teacher, in the village and in the middle school, and when I came to Bodh Gaya and Sarnath—teaching all the time," he said. "How I learned, I don't know—by nature. Some psychic people told me I have been a teacher from many lifetimes."

Because of a shortage of instructors in his village during the 1930s, Munindra, having been the star pupil, was called upon to teach Bengali, English, geography, and other subjects. When he left his home for Calcutta, he taught Bengali and English to monks at the Nalanda Vidyabhavan, a Pāli study and research center established in 1935 by the Bauddha Dharmankur Sabha (the Bengal Buddhist Association), which was founded in 1892. In Sarnath, after learning yoga from others and practicing with the help of books, Munindra even taught yoga. He also instructed the unschooled sons and daughters of illiterate workers at the Mahabodhi Society, some of whom went on to be professors, doctors, generals, ministers, and scientists. It was another way of repaying his father's efforts to educate him and his brothers.

In Burma, on Mahāsi Sayādaw's request, Munindra became a teacher of Dharma, to which he dedicated every waking moment of the rest of his life. He lived solely on *dāna,* on whatever contributions came his way, whether as housing, money, personal goods, food, train and plane tickets, books, and so on.

Munindra not only loved to teach, he deeply loved his students, and they reciprocated. "Boys and girls used to love me very much, like a brother," he explained, referring to the early years. "They respected me. I never beat anybody, never scolded anybody. If I did not go to school, students came to my house asking why I didn't go, what happened. And they used to invite me to their house, with their family. I was a good teacher," he said, without bragging. "Whatever I teach, I teach wholeheartedly, not halfheartedly. If you are good to others, it is good for you. We are part and parcel of the whole universe. If even one person gets the light, Dhamma, he is an asset to the world."

Although Munindra encouraged some of his students to become dharma teachers themselves, it was not the right livelihood for everyone. He was open to many other possibilities. When people came to him and he asked about their livelihood, he was warm in his response, even when others were disapproving.

Arlene Bernstein remembers her initial meeting with Munindra in Bodh Gaya after someone suggested she pay him a visit. "I went and knocked on his door, and he invited me for tea. Just his presence was so lovely and embracing that I felt totally at ease with him." He asked what Arlene and her husband did for a living, and she told him that they grew grapes and made wine. Munindra said to her that that was a beautiful way to connect with the earth. "I had just left the retreat of another teacher," Arlene says, "where everybody was coming up to me and saying, 'You make wine? Well, that's alcohol. How could you do that? It's against the precepts.' To encounter such a different attitude was touching and affirming. I learned that it isn't about the thing itself, but it's one's attitude toward it. He saw it as connecting with the earth and participating in a process, and not that the end result is alcohol and alcohol is not good. There were no judgments attached whatsoever, and that just stuck with me. It was so gracious and spontaneous."

Clear Conscience

After facing many challenges in his own life, Munindra could freely offer advice to support others who were facing their own. Bhante Bodhipāla remembers his encouragement: "I know you are a very sincere practitioner, so you should keep *sīla* strong and you can progress quickly." When the monk was leaving India to reside at Taungpulu Sayādaw's monastery in northern California, Munindra saw him off at the airport and cautioned him, "America is a different country, a different culture. In America it is easy to get attached to worldly pleasures. You should not change your practice. Study deeply and practice deeply."

Despite some troublesome experiences, Munindra said,

> My motivation was good—to train people. When I went to the West, they asked me, "What do you want to see?" I said, "The best and the worst." I wanted to see both. I learned many things there. I am grateful to all these people; I learned from them. Even those who misbehaved, I learned from them also. So anybody who tried to harm me, put blame on me, I am grateful to them because I began to learn how it happened, to see past, present, and

future. This is called self-confrontation: Whatever you did that was wrong cannot be done any more. And good karma you have done, it can be increased again and again. So that's why no guilt feeling for anything.

> *Refraining from all that is detrimental,*
> *Cultivating what is wholesome,*
> *Purifying the mind—*
> *This is the teaching of all the Buddhas.*
> —THE DHAMMAPADA 183

sīla: from *sīlana* (composing), indicating "coordinating" or "right placing together" of bodily and vocal actions through volition; or signifying "upholding," serving as a foundation for profitable states. *Sīla* may also be derived from *śiras* (head) or from *sīta* (cool). *Sīla* means "nature," "character," "habit," or "behavior," but it is most often translated as "morality" or "moral discipline," "virtue" or "virtuous conduct," and "ethical behavior."

Sīla is about wise restraint (being cool-headed) versus heedlessness (acting hot-headed). According to whether one is a layperson or monastic, a varying number of precepts (five, eight, or ten) serve as guidelines in refraining from what is detrimental. A set of rules (*pāṭimokkha*) also governs the lives of monks and nuns. Precepts do not represent mechanical allegiance to commandments from a deity, but a voluntary training in self-discipline.

Because *sīla* is a cornerstone to practice, it constitutes the first of three aspects of training (*sikkhā*)—moral discipline, concentration, and wisdom—that comprise the Eightfold Path. Here, *sīla* represents right speech, right action, and right livelihood. As the preliminary groundwork, *sīla* is essential for progressing along the path. It is also the second of the ten perfections (*pārami*) and one of the seven treasures (*dhana*).

6

Say What You Mean and Mean What You Say

Sacca (Truthfulness, Integrity)

Truth never becomes old; it is always new, every moment.
—MUNINDRA

During the period Munindra worked at the Mahabodhi Temple in Sarnath (1938–48), he became friendly with some scholars who were dedicated members of the Ramakrishna Mission in nearby Varanasi. In particular, Professor Gupta, who taught science at a Bengal college, often invited him to discuss Dharma. But when asked to give talks, Munindra repeatedly declined: "No, I cannot because, [though] I studied Dhamma to some extent, certain things I do not understand." He acknowledged that he had some doubt: "I had trust in Dharma, in Buddha, but I was not clear that there was the *anattā* [not-self]." Professor Gupta also wanted Munindra to write books; again he replied in the negative—he felt the Buddha had already expressed everything. Decades later, he said, "Until I went to Burma and practiced and experienced, I did not give talks."

As Munindra demonstrated, truthfulness (*sacca*) represents a lot more than simply not telling lies. He wanted to learn the truth of the Buddha's teaching not merely through books but through his own experience. He was honest about what he did and did not know. Until he attained experiential wisdom from deep practice, he felt unable and unwilling to describe the true nature of reality.

It was this kind of integrity that exerted a pull on people to study with him, particularly counterculture Westerners who mistrusted so-called "authorities," given the lies they often fed the public (such as about the Vietnam

War). Yet here was Munindra, a man whose teaching was grounded not only in scholastic knowledge but also in authentic wisdom. For a generation that had read Robert Heinlein's 1961 novel *Stranger in a Strange Land,* Munindra was someone who could "grok"—that is, he so thoroughly understood Dharma that he merged with it. Ram Dass wrote in his introduction to Joseph Goldstein's first book, *The Experience of Insight,* that Munindra "so successfully absorbed the Pāli Canon of Buddhism... I found it difficult to differentiate him from the doctrine."[1] In Munindra, seekers found someone who taught from every level of his being.

From the Heart

Joe DiNardo recounts the first time he spoke with Munindra about Dharma, during a retreat with Mahāsi Sayādaw in Yucca Valley, California, in 1979: "It must have been ten o'clock at night when I went to see him. About three o'clock in the morning, my eyes were bugging out and it was hard to keep my head up. Finally I said, 'Munindra-ji, I simply have to go.' It wasn't that I was tired. It was just so overpowering—the inspiration that he evoked in me, the beauty of the way he saw life, and how genuinely he manifested all of the Buddha's teachings. It wasn't that he had read this someplace and was telling us about it, he *was* this thing."

Joe admits to some skepticism about spiritual teachers, no matter what tradition they come from, with respect to the depth of their experience. Despite this, he remarks, "I always felt that Munindra-ji was only talking about things that he had actually experienced." Joe was also struck by how human and normal Munindra seemed. "You would never expect to take Mahāsi Sayādaw to Niagara Falls, to a family reunion, or to sit down with him and have a conversation about whatever," Joe adds. "But with Munindra-ji, you could do that. He was accessible, yet he clearly had experiences in his life that had brought him to a place of oneness with what it was he was talking about. He wasn't teaching from having been taught, he was teaching from his heart. That's unusual; you don't get to meet people like that very often in life."

Gregg Galbraith also consistently observed Munindra's core integrity: "There are great teachers out there who teach really well, but then behind the scene, their behavior doesn't always match what they teach. They may be manipulative, possessive, angry, controlling, or lustful to the people around them. You can find that in many brilliant, gifted teachers; they have many good qualities, but they also have some Jekyll-and-Hyde kind of personalities. I can honestly say I never saw anything like that in Munindra."

Congruence

This congruence between knowledge and life experience as well as between the public and the private had a profound influence on Munindra's students. Jack Engler, for one, felt inspired to make several professional decisions. After spending a year with Munindra in Bodh Gaya, Jack proposed making vipassanā practice the subject of his doctoral research and asked Munindra to help him solicit subjects for the study. (He was interested in the unique changes vipassanā claims to bring about, and the mechanisms whereby these changes occur.)

Munindra was initially taken aback by Jack's request. Indian researchers had approached him a number of times, but they had no direct experience of practice. His response had been, "If they want to learn about the practice, let them do the practice." However, after much discussion about the value of scientific method, and because he understood Jack's personal commitment to the practice, Munindra eventually agreed to support the study and engaged the equally skeptical Dipa Ma and her Calcutta students in the project.

Jack says, "What I learned as a scholar was the importance of one's scholarship being anchored in real-life experience, that it not be just academic, coming from secondary resources or a library. I had planned on a career in teaching, but being with Munindra-ji convinced me that, when I came back from India, I had to get out of academic life and into some kind of clinical work in psychology. His example has always been an inspiration to me, a model in many ways."

Danny Taylor also saw Munindra as an inspiring role model in that what he said and what he did were one. Daniel says that he went to meet Munindra because he wondered, "How do you construct a life where consciousness is consistent with action?" Stories about Munindra became "a symbolic journey toward a human being who, in some ways, had cracked this." He adds, "Munindra was a person that I could be extremely inspired by, because it was obvious that this 'grokking' phenomenon had occurred, but he was different from some of the other meditation masters that I had come across in that he had a very expressive personality—he was happy to relate personally. Without even saying it, Munindra embodied in his being that it's OK for you to be whoever you are, yet your goal is to be one with the Dharma.

It gave me the confidence that I could be who I was and still progress in the Dharma—this was an incredible gift."

An Ordinary Person Who Was Not Ordinary

Students anticipating Munindra to be the guru of their fantasies found a man who did not feed their ideas of what a spiritual teacher is. Gregg Galbraith says that often people who came to meet Munindra would show up with all kinds of expectations: "somebody standing two feet above the ground, preaching some high teaching to you, and so on." Also, students often wanted Munindra to tell them what they should do. Gregg explains, "Munindra wasn't there to give out a specific regime. Some people couldn't get beyond their expectations. When you put all that aside, then you could fully see Munindra for everything he was."

Joseph Goldstein adds that, though it took time, one of the things he came to appreciate about Munindra a lot was that he was completely himself: "There was no pretense, no show of being a spiritual person. He was his own unique individual, and he was just out front with who he was. In a way, it was very liberating, even though there were, at different times, lots of judgments or raised eyebrows, but that didn't faze him at all. He wasn't out to please anybody."

Munindra was a teacher who saw himself as a spiritual friend (*kalyāṇa-mitta*), not a guru, and stayed true to that. James Baraz says, "Joseph [Goldstein] talked a lot about Munindra and described his personality, but it was so interesting to meet him. I had such awe and reverence for my teacher's teacher, and then, meeting him, he was just so naturally endearing, just so himself. It was disarming in a beautiful way. And I could just be myself. He had the courage to be unpretentious, to not be so concerned about the party line or looking good." As Larry Rosenberg puts it, "Although he was a holy man, he didn't have that kind of piety or self-righteous quality that is quite common among some spiritual people."

Grahame White adds, "Munindra didn't have a persona of sitting up there like a stuffed Buddha. He was an ordinary person who wasn't an ordinary person." This absence of hierarchical aloofness allowed anyone to approach him. Dhammaruwan Chandrasiri recalls playing around with Munindra during his boyhood and the good lesson it provided for him as a dharma teacher today: "He had that time to play with a child as well as to be a teacher. He was not a person who was very caught up in being a teacher."

Jack Kornfield says, "From the beginning I thought he was an amazing, wise, and brilliant teacher—and incredibly iconoclastic and willing to be himself. He made his own little costume and his own order. He taught in the way that he wanted to teach, which included this very deep scholastic learning, very deep meditation practice that came primarily through Mahāsi Sayādaw, and a deep dharma influence that came from what he had absorbed otherwise. Munindra had his own way and integrity. It was a very different flavor of the same deep teachings—open-mindedness, connectedness with people. He had some of the quality of the Dalai Lama. When you came in front of him, he was deeply interested; there was no sham or superficiality about him."

What's Powerful?

Jack Engler remembers occasionally hearing people say, "Munindra-ji is a nice man, but he doesn't have power," meaning he did not project the image of the typical guru or holy man. "He didn't look the part," Jack notes. "He was a small, energetic, sometimes excitable Bengali, with unending interest and curiosity about everything. He did not act the part of the restrained, composed, dignified teacher who projected mystique and seemed to know powerful and hidden things you didn't."

Jack continues, "He was alive, spontaneous, following what caught his attention, seeing the whole of life as part of the path. He was playful, impish, with a quick wit and sense of humor. He loved to laugh. He expressed himself in gesture as much as in words. He didn't teach as an expert or authority, but as a dhamma brother who had—by good fortune, good karma, and dedicated effort—walked down the road a bit ahead of you and so could tell you something about how to navigate it. That didn't mean he wasn't expert, only that he didn't interact with you or teach as an 'expert.'" Jack says that Munindra didn't speak dogmatically: "His style was more to invite you to experiment and experience."

Munindra also did not claim the psychic powers that so impressed Westerners at that time. According to Jack, "He simply was who he was, without pretense or guile or excuses. He knew suffering, but he loved life. He loved talking about the Dhamma. He loved to practice. And he loved getting to know those who came to him. In this, he worked in a much more personal and psychological way than most Buddhist teachers of any lineage I know."

Though Munindra was diminutive and soft-spoken, Eric Kupers respected him as "such a powerful man [because] there was so much integrity about his being. I just felt him to be very consistent. It was very much about the living truth of the teachings in the moment in a very down-to-earth way."

Maggie Ward McGervey adds, "You didn't feel just riveted by his spiritual or physical presence. It wasn't like some of the Tibetan teachers, where you feel their presence like a resounding drum. There was a real paradox, an irony there. The bigness was inside him." She also remarks, "I didn't feel like there was some kind of ego there that was seeking power or attention. Munindra's humility and his inwardness, his unimposing quality, was really a balm of healing, because many spiritual teachers are so into their whole role. There was never that with Munindra."

Without Pretense or Guile

Munindra's unabashed openness left some people perplexed: how to reconcile behavior that seemed idiosyncratic or contradictory with his level of realization in Dharma? Some simply projected negative traits on him. As Denise Till quips, "Munindra-ji didn't have issues with people; people had issues with him."

According to Robert Pryor, it was easy for people to be negative because "he didn't present a facade. You get thirty seconds with some teachers, but you could hang out with Munindra-ji. If you only saw the personality, he was kind of this odd little gentleman who had a lot of peculiarities. It confused people because they thought enlightened people didn't have a personality. He showed them probably more than they wanted to see. Maybe they wanted him to be on a pedestal."

A popular saying in Burma helps clear the confusion: "When the bottle's empty, there's still a smell." A person may be empty of greed, hatred, and delusion, but the personality remains. Realization does not mean perfection.

The majority found it liberating to interact with a teacher without pretense or pretensions. Tara Doyle says one of the things she learned from Munindra is that highly realized teachers (and she believed he was) "come in all sorts of packages." She remembers him as funny, loving, always kind, totally loyal, personable, even childlike. At the same time, the theoretical breadth he brought to speaking about the Theravāda tradition in a sophisticated fashion amazed her. Yet he also got grumpy about mundane things, such as the food he ate or when it arrived. Because Tara got to watch him "up close and personal," she found that "what you saw is what you got. And that's a relief—the good, the bad, and the ugly. It was all just there. I never felt he had any artifice."

Keeping Promises

A person without artifice is someone who engenders trust. Munindra's reputation for being genuinely dedicated in whatever work he did prompted people to recommend him as the first Buddhist superintendent of the Mahabodhi Temple in Bodh Gaya.

Robert Pryor and Tara Doyle knew firsthand that when Munindra made promises, he kept them. When he agreed to take on something, he did so enthusiastically. After they proposed the idea of a Buddhist studies program abroad to Antioch College, the administration encouraged them to explore it. In 1978, Robert returned to Bodh Gaya and asked Munindra to be the program's Theravāda teacher. He remembers Munindra's validation of the project: "I will lend you my wholehearted support. I will come and teach." And he did. Unless he was out of the country or sick, he participated from 1979 to 2002, a year before he passed away, even though he had to have a person on each side walk him to the meditation hall.

Munindra would honor his word despite unfavorable conditions. Gita Kedia remembers running into him at Dhamma Giri one time after she conducted a long course and telling him she would be leaving the next day. He said he would stop by to see her before she left. However, it rained so heavily the next day that she figured neither one of them could visit the other. Gita left for the train station in Igatpuri and sat down to wait. After a while, an old man emerged out of the downpour and made his way over to her. She was surprised to see Munindra. He waited with her till the train arrived, teaching her dharma stories all the while, and then gave her a blessing of *mettā*.

Munindra expected others to keep their word, too. One time, when a student failed to bring him something he had agreed to by a certain hour, Munindra rebuked him for being forgetful, unmindful, and unskillful. He felt it was essential to treat others with respect and responsibility. But once the lecture was over, Munindra dropped it, smiled again, and was warm and happy with the young man.

Being truthful and trustworthy, Munindra assumed the best in others too and believed what they told him. But they were not always worthy of it. It took strong evidence for him to change his opinion because he did not want to think ill of others nor condemn them. Several individuals betrayed his trust, such as the young man who insinuated himself as Munindra's traveling companion to the United States. When various people who generously hosted them reported his misbehavior—that he was not there out of a sincere desire to help his elder but to use his connections to obtain material goods—Munindra finally accepted what he had been blind to and, in turn, warned others not to have anything to do with him.

Another person who betrayed Munindra was the doctor in Calcutta who said he would perform hernia surgery but, instead, assigned it to some interns. Their carelessness resulted in Munindra's suffering an infection for two years, until he got medical help on Maui. On his return to Calcutta, Munindra saw the doctor and told him that an American physician found surgical strings in his abdominal cavity because "you didn't do what you promised, you didn't keep your word."

Munindra taught that "mind and body should work together—wholeheartedness. When you are honest and truthful, inner life and outer life should be in harmony. Then it is wonderful." He explained that people generally do not keep their word because they are halfhearted in what they do: "They work with a superficial mind. They talk—'I will do this'—but the inner mind does not accept it." He quoted a quality of the Buddha: "As the *Tathāgata* says, so he does; as the *Tathāgata* does, so he says" (It 112).

Straightforwardness

Although Munindra was known for his gentle and sweet nature, he did not sugarcoat his words or let emotions get in the way of teaching. Oren Sofer recalls, "Munindra encouraged me to get up very early in the morning, which I would. A couple of times, I overslept. He chided me at several points during my time with him, and it was always in a very gentle and loving way. One time, after I had fasted for a day (on Yom Kippur), a group of us went out for dinner. I ended up eating more than I was planning to, and the next day I got sick. Munindra said something like, 'This is because you have no self-control.' In his own humorous way, he pointed out to me the truth of what had happened."

On another occasion, during a retreat at Dhamma Giri, Oren was feeling emotionally overwhelmed and judged himself severely for it. Munindra's response surprised him: "He leaned forward and looked at me and said, 'You know, when I hear you saying this, when I see you crying, I feel so happy for you. You are doing so well.' This threw me for a loop, and I didn't know what to say. Then he said, 'You must enjoy the suffering.'"

Oren continues, "Munindra asked me, 'Why are you here? Why did you come here?' I said, 'I came here to see you.' He said, 'So, now you are seeing me. So what? What do you want? What is your aspiration?' I was so lost in what I was feeling that I didn't know. I said, 'I'm so confused.' But the question stayed with me. My heart was so open and vulnerable that it really went in very deeply and it was so powerful. Asking me that question gave me the opportunity to answer it for myself later in a really true and honest way."

One of the benefits of being straightforward is not wasting time and energy on conversations that bear no dharma fruit. Ginny Morgan remembers an incident at IMS during one of Munindra's visits. She and Joseph Goldstein were engaged in chitchat over dinner. Finally, Munindra tapped Joseph on the shoulder and said, "All this worldly talk—it's making me tired." They all looked at each other and laughed because it was true. Nobody really wanted to chatter, but only Munindra was willing to say so.

He was also straightforward in his actions, as Kamala Masters observed when he stayed with her on Maui. "Munindra-ji loved to watch the television program *Nature*. He even changed the day of our group sitting because of it. One day, an acquaintance came over while Munindra-ji was watching *Nature,* so one-pointed. I guess the guy had heard about this 'guru' at our house, so he just sat down and started asking him questions like, 'Can you levitate?' Munindra-ji gave him very short answers. I could tell he wasn't into talking with this man at all. So he got up, said, 'Excuse me,' and went to his room. *Nature* was still on. I followed him and said, 'Munindra-ji, are you OK?' He said, 'Yes, I'm OK.' I asked him, 'What's going on?' He said, 'Birds of a feather flock together.' It was his way of telling me that when they're not, then they go apart. He also said, 'Like attracts like.'"

At other times, Munindra would be direct with Kamala herself. When he was explaining how to meditate and she would be curious about why this, why that, or go off on a tangent and actually not do the practice, he would say, "Do you want to think or do you want to meditate?" If Kamala went on about certain difficulties she had endured earlier in life, he would say, "How long will you carry this?" Munindra was a great listener to people's stories, but out of compassion for her suffering, he also knew when to cut to the chase.

Munindra did not let his students deceive themselves. Whether it was thinking they had reached a certain stage in practice that they had not, or believing they were suitable and ready to become a dharma teacher when they were not, he stated what he thought. A particular interview still sticks in Joseph Goldstein's mind from his early years in India. When he reported having dropped into a state that felt totally free and open, Munindra simply said, "Don't recondition your mind," guiding him not to get attached to this state of mind or create concepts about it. And when Vivian Darst entertained thoughts of becoming a teacher, Munindra told her, "You have to have a lot of patience if you're going to be a teacher. And you are impatient with me, so how can you be a teacher?"

Munindra was also frank in expressing concern or amazement about things in the United States he could not fathom. He told Dale "Diinabandhu" Brozosky that he was shocked at the way American society abandoned the elderly. In Asia, children honored and took care of their parents until they passed away. Munindra noticed another peculiarity: "In India, if somebody doesn't have strong sexual desire, they thank God. But in your country, if people don't have desire, they think something's wrong with them, so they go to therapists to solve the problem, to be able to create great lust so that then they can enjoy their lives."

Dale says, "With Munindra, there was such openness and transparency it was disarming. It was like he was naked, not afraid to talk and express himself about anything."

Be Who You Are

Munindra's truthfulness and lack of pretense taught his students that it was OK for them to be who they were. Larry Rosenberg says, "In my years in Zen, I did hundreds of thousands of prostrations. I chanted in Korean, in Chinese, in Japanese. I wore special robes. I ate a certain way, in the Japanese style, in the Korean style. Finally a teacher is saying to me, 'It's OK, you can just be an American guy.' That was not small for me. Having tried all the traditional stuff, I had reached a point where I didn't want to do that anymore. I realized it's enough just to be Jewish-American. I don't need to pretend; it seemed superfluous and even a burden. So it was a big step just wearing ordinary clothes, honoring the Dharma in as ordinary and natural a way as I could. Munindra made it OK."

When Bryan Tucker visited Munindra at Dhamma Giri in 1994, he was struck by the absence of any self-importance. "His room was so small and unassuming, and it was packed with books and other memorabilia and things. He kept things neat, and it was clean." Bryan says that in his room Munindra took off his formal whites and his hat and sat in his *lungi* (a piece of cloth sewn into a tube and worn like a skirt). "He looked so small and old, weak and vulnerable, just like a human being, not in any way a powerhouse teacher or somebody that gets invested with all of the energies and projections that students might have about teachers. I felt a bit privileged that he didn't mind that I saw him that way, but he probably didn't care who saw him like this. He was that guileless as to allow people to see him behind the scenes, in ways that might not be flattering. I felt, if he's guileless, I can be guileless. Munindra really made me feel more comfortable in my own skin. Seeing him like this, I didn't feel less respect for him, I felt more respect for myself."

One time, several Westerners were crowded together on the floor of Dipa Ma's room on a steamy day in Calcutta. Jack Engler and Munindra were the only men present. While Munindra spoke about Dharma and practice, Dipa Ma sat resting on her bed with her eyes closed, for she had not been well. At one point, he mentioned (because he had read it in commentaries written after the Pāli Canon) that only men could become a Buddha. In an instant, Dipa Ma's eyes opened wide and she asserted, "I am a woman, but I can do anything a man can do." Everyone laughed, especially Munindra, who seemed so happy to hear her say this. He said to her, "You are my very much perfect student. There is no thing woman cannot do." Dipa Barua, her daughter, says, "He wanted always, whenever anybody came to him or during the course in retreat, to speak like this—to be honest."

Many did. Christine Yedica remembers how she felt sitting in a group of meditators in Bodh Gaya, when Munindra asked questions about their life and practice. At first, because she felt uncomfortable speaking about such things in public, she was relieved when he directed his queries at someone else. But when he turned and asked her to speak, she felt "it was imperative to answer truthfully."

Christine says, "For someone else to have asked those questions might have felt intrusive or invasive but with Munindra, after the initial couple of times, it just felt like it was an opening. That opening, in itself, was a teaching for me, and the feeling of being exposed was actually an offering on his part. The first time I experienced it, there was fear and wanting to close, but then I got it: 'Oh, this is real grace, to open in this way.' For the most part, people were truthful, and we inspired one another in working with the struggles that are sometimes part of the practice—you just keep at it."

Wanda Weinberger says that Munindra's honesty and authenticity affected how she dealt with the news of his death: "It really threw me, trying to figure out what to do with that information—what do I actually feel versus what am I supposed to feel? Society says you mourn death, you cry; it has a negative connotation. But then there's the other side; here's this beautiful person who touched my life, and to celebrate it. I cried a lot, but the celebratory side definitely came out. It was an interesting process to watch it. The teaching continues."

Staying True

For Erik Knud-Hansen, Munindra appeared to delight in truthfulness: "His attention was riveted to seeing what was true, and there was an inherent delight in staying true." Erik continues, "As dharma students, we might tend to see ourselves as being not the right kind of person, and so we learn to meditate, we learn Dharma, and then we try to act out a spiritual life. I didn't see him acting a part, and I think that was a very useful model for dharma students. He wasn't trying to act out what some people may have needed or wanted him to be. When you trust the Dharma that deeply, it's easier to assume that however you end up unfolding in front of other people is what they need, because you're not trying to micromanage your actions. You're not trying to be somebody for somebody else. You're just trying to be what genuinely comes out in that moment."

Erik adds, "I think that as students get older and understand the difference between the story-line world of our relative selves and the Dharma that the Buddha was pointing at, they'll understand why Munindra was an impeccable teacher and of extreme value. In my mind, one of the most limiting factors of the conditioned human mind is the need to conform and the fear of not conforming. Dharma is only understood by those willing to see outside the box, those willing to break the mold. Munindra tried to stay true to that and did so, for the most part, rather effortlessly. He had nothing else to express but freedom, and he tried to help people understand it and why they may want to go there themselves."

Munindra was a rara avis, or as Denise Till describes him, he was "quite eccentric, unconventional, and didn't follow the norm." Whether he was creating his own garb (white robes and a white hat), eating in the evening, traveling in the West, promoting the education of village girls, uplifting women as yogis and dharma teachers, or encouraging his students to practice with other teachers, Munindra remained independent in his thinking and in his actions. Criticism did not daunt him because he felt sincere in his heart. He stayed true to the truth he knew.

> *Like a beautiful flower,*
> *Brightly colored but lacking scent,*
> *So are well-spoken words*
> *Fruitless when not carried out.*
> *Like a beautiful flower,*
> *Brightly colored and with scent,*
> *So are well-spoken words*
> *Fruitful when carried out.*
>
> —THE DHAMMAPADA 51–52

sacca: from the Sanskrit root *as-* (to be, live, exist). *Sacca* means that which is "real," "true," or "truth"; "corresponding to reality," "accurate." As an aspect of character, *sacca* conveys a sense of truthfulness, honesty, integrity, transparency, and straightforwardness; the opposite of hypocrisy, treachery, doublespeak, and false testimony.

The Buddha synthesized all of his teachings in the Four Noble Truths (*ariya-sacca*): the truth of *dukkha* (unsatisfactoriness); its cause; its cessation; and the path leading to its cessation.

The seventh of ten perfections (*pāramī*), *sacca* is the foundation for the other nine, since without it, they become hollow and insubstantial. The hallmark of the Buddha's practice is nondeception. In his many lifetimes as a bodhisattva, he violated other *pāramī,* but never *sacca* because, as he said, "When one is not ashamed of telling a deliberate lie, there is no evil that one would not do" (It 25).

7

I Made Up My Mind

Adhiṭṭhāna (Determination, Resolve)

When your heart is pure, all things are possible.
—MUNINDRA

In the late 1940s, after India gained independence from Britain, the relics of two important disciples of the Buddha (Sāriputta and Moggallāna) were returned to the subcontinent. (They had been excavated from a stupa at Sanchi in 1851 and stored at the Victoria and Albert Museum in London.) The Mahabodhi Society exhibited these relics in Calcutta and at Buddhist sites around the country before forming a delegation to display them outside of India. Because of his work for the society in Sarnath, the organization invited Munindra along as an assistant. After their public presentation in Burma, Assam, and Nepal in 1950, the sacred relics were to travel to Sikkim and Tibet.

Earlier in his life, Munindra had read books about Tibet and longed to visit the Himalayas to see what people called "a mysterious country." The devotional lamas he observed in India had impressed him as well. Always eager to meet new teachers and hear new teachings, Munindra greatly looked forward to the trip and was absolutely determined to undertake it.

The mission journeyed from Calcutta first by plane and then by car to Sikkim, where they were guests of the *chögyal's* (spiritual king of Sikkim) government for two weeks. They received offerings from many people, including representatives sent by the Dalai Lama. Munindra later posed for photos wearing some of these gifts—Tibetan trousers, a fur hat, and boots.

In Sikkim, the original handful of Mahabodhi Society delegates swelled into a party of nearly one hundred persons. Armed guards from Sikkim led the group up the mountains to the border with Tibet. Four people, wearing special uniforms, conveyed the relics in a decorated palanquin. Others went ahead to cut a path through the snow. When it was too difficult to walk, the delegates mounted hill ponies; otherwise, they continued on foot, proceeding at a pace of ten miles a day.

All went well until the general secretary of the Mahabodhi Society succumbed to altitude sickness the first night at Karponang, a *dak* bungalow (travelers' rest house) at nine thousand feet above sea level. Sri Devapriya Valisinha wanted Munindra to return with him to Calcutta, but nothing and no one could break the latter's resolve to reach Tibet.

"No, I made up my mind to go," Munindra said.

"But you will have difficulty, you will suffer," said Sri Valisinha.

"Never mind, I want to go, I want the experience," Munindra insisted. The general secretary left, and Munindra remained with the mission.

When the group reached Nathu La, a 14,140-foot pass, they were fortunate to have a clear day and thus a panoramic view for hundreds of miles of the majestic Himalayas. Here the chief Tibetan general and his soldiers took charge of the relics. The delegation descended and passed that night at Chumbithan, another *dak* bungalow. Several more members of the party showed signs of severe altitude sickness but soon recovered.

Two days later, a formal procession, led by the Tibetan foreign minister, the lord chamberlain to the Dalai Lama, the chief general, and other officials and lamas, welcomed the delegation. Tibetan monks blew traditional long horns and embraced the travelers from India, presenting each one with a *khata* (a white scarf, an auspicious symbol of greeting).

Finally, they arrived at Dungkar Gompa, a monastery near Yatung, where the Dalai Lama had found temporary refuge, since the capital of Lhasa was currently threatened by Chinese invasion and battles in eastern Tibet. The mission had taken four days on foot to reach him. It was now March 8, 1951. The Dalai Lama, along with his tutors, ministers, other high officials, and the general public were all waiting outside the monastery. He received the sacred relics, carried them to the shrine room, and blessed the audience by touching their heads with the container housing the relics.

The Tibetans were warm hosts. Munindra remembers the Dalai Lama giving him yak-butter tea with great kindness. He did not recall what they discussed, only that the Dalai Lama was a young man (fifteen years old at the time) and "so sweet, very sweet."

Born and raised in the sea-level heat and humidity of Dhemsha, a village in the district of Chittagong in East Bengal (now Bangladesh), Munindra found it difficult to maintain his meticulous personal hygiene and dress in Tibet's climate. Generally, in India, after defecating, people clean themselves with water. But, in Tibet, water quickly turned into ice, impossible to wash with. "For that, you have to use a stick to clean," he explained. He also could not bathe, ordinarily a daily habit, except by arranging for someone to bring hot water to his room. He took a bath only once or twice during more than two months away with the mission, which took him to Kalimpong and Darjeeling after Tibet. Undaunted by the conditions and thrilled to have his dream come true, he said, "Very cold, but it was enjoyable."

Despite all his travels to other parts of Asia and the West, Munindra's trip to Tibet always remained a highlight in his life. Denise Till says, "He absolutely loved the Dalai Lama and had the greatest respect for him." Whenever they met again—often on the Dalai Lama's pilgrimages to Bodh Gaya—they greeted each other and embraced like old friends.

All Roads Must Lead to Dharma

Munindra's passion and determination for Dharma began in his childhood with a love of books. As a boy of nine or ten, he read a children's history that included the Buddha's life story. He was so impressed and inspired that, even at such an early age, he decided to strive for the same experience. He said, "I must know what he discovered, how he became Buddha, how he solved the problems of old age, sickness, and death." This resolve always remained in the back of his mind. Many opportunities arose for a conventional life—multiple offers for arranged marriages, land, buildings—but Munindra declined them all. "Wherever I am able to learn Dhamma, to understand, then there I will go," he said. "So I did not accept anything."

Govinda Barua, his younger brother, remembers that Munindra was so single-minded in this pursuit that he deliberately did poorly on his matriculation exam in grade ten. Because of his reputation as an excellent student—first in his class—his teachers were shocked and confused. He told Govinda, "I realized that if I pass my test, I'm going to do it very well. But what will happen? This will lead to another degree and another degree. I'm going to get caught up in degrees and I'll never be able to achieve the life I want. I want the answer to certain questions, like Buddha. I don't want to get tempted by a totally different life, moving away from the path I chose." This scenario played out repeatedly in the years to come. Munindra would be asked to sit for exams and invariably he would refuse. He insisted that he wanted to know, to understand what the Buddha experienced, rather than accumulate degrees.

Munindra let nothing get in the way of his learning, even while working full-time for the Mahabodhi Society. In Sarnath (1938–48), he was in charge of the temple, publications, and library. He also served as a tour guide when dignitaries such as Jawaharlal Nehru and Mahatma Gandhi came to visit. But when he was told to learn how to ride a bicycle so he could go to Varanasi, six kilometers away, he said no. He was determined to keep his time available for studying, not for running errands. Afraid of missing any chance to keep up his reading, he also rejected learning how to type because, if he had, people would have constantly requested that he type letters for them. As the first Buddhist superintendent of the Mahabodhi Temple in Bodh Gaya (1953–57), he was supposed to have a telephone installed in his residence, but he refused to get one. He felt it would interfere with his intention and waste precious time.

Fearless for the Temple

Because of its significance as the place of the Buddha's awakening, Bodh Gaya held a special place in Munindra's heart and called forth his commitment to the temple. For centuries, the local Hindu *math* (monastery) managed the Mahabodhi Temple in Bodh Gaya. Since the late 1800s, the *mahānt*, abbot of the *math* and a person of great power and influence—local people still refer to him as "the raja of Bodh Gaya"—had resisted handing over the Mahabodhi Temple to Buddhists. Then, in 1949, on Prime Minister Nehru's request, control was finally transferred to a government-appointed committee. Four years later, after the resolution of a final legal challenge by the *mahānt*, Munindra stepped into this highly charged situation when the committee appointed him the first Buddhist superintendent of the Mahabodhi Temple since the late twelfth century.

Munindra's reputation as a sincere and honest worker who had made improvements at the temple in Sarnath qualified him to take up more formidable responsibilities in Bodh Gaya. He had to handle not only the day-to-day administration of the most sacred site in Buddhist history—the place where Prince Siddhārtha became the Buddha—but also the delicate task of transforming ritual practices there from Hindu to Buddhist so that Buddhists from all over Asia would feel welcomed. In addition, he was involved in government plans to develop Bodh Gaya as a place of Buddhist pilgrimage. There was much pressure on him because the temple had to be ready for a momentous event in 1956: the Buddha Jayanti to celebrate the 2,500-year anniversary of the Buddha's *parinibbāna* (his death, with no further rebirths).

The situation at the temple was deplorable. Broken images littered the grounds. Due to a lack of guards, statues disappeared from niches in the temple walls. There was little money and practically no staff to turn the place around. The unpaved road from the railway station in Gaya to Bodh Gaya was in such a poor state that the ride by horse cart was extremely uncomfortable for pilgrims. Munindra said, "I felt sorry when people came from different parts of the world, seeing this disgraceful, filthy, dilapidated condition of such a wonderful, famous place. I was feeling ashamed for the country, for the people." He put locals to work cleaning out the pond there, setting up an irrigation system, and converting the despoiled land around the temple into a garden area.

Munindra also set up visitor books for people to write their impressions and make suggestions to better the temple. Determined to improve things, he sent these recommendations, along with his own, to Bihar State government. One idea was to relocate the impoverished potters' village that had sprung up near the temple and also to move shops in that area to the road. As there was no wall around the temple compound, the villagers, for lack of facilities, were in the habit of using the grounds as a latrine.

Although the *mahānt* had to agree to the changes, it was essential that Munindra be both cautious and courageous in exercising his authority. The *mahānt*, his henchmen, or his allies in the community could make things quite unpleasant for Munindra. Munindra was friendly with everyone, yet he was also aware that some local people were boiling mad and now considered him the enemy. He had no personal bodyguard to protect him, and it was clear that the *mahānt*'s cronies were not happy with him. The head of police, a fellow Bengali, advised Munindra, "As a friend, I inform you that they may do harm to you. You have to be very careful because the *mahānt* is a very rich man, a very powerful man. Please don't go alone at night to Gaya town." Nevertheless, Munindra remained committed to his vow to take proper care of the temple. He recalled:

> Many, many times I used to sit under the Bodhi Tree. The whole area was an inspiration to me; I enjoyed this blessing. It was an

opportunity for me to serve this man, Buddha. I dedicated my life to Dhamma. If I am killed for this, I have no grudge for anybody, but I want to change all this for better conditions.

They are good people, nice people, but they do not know. That's why I am friendly to them. Because I am going against their will, sometimes all my work is not preferable to them. That's why outwardly they [threaten], but they cannot do any harm. I used to come sometimes late at night from Gaya, but I had no fear about this.

Munindra left his temple post in 1957 to go to Burma and never took it up again, yet he would regularly visit later superintendents and continue to make suggestions for the temple's upkeep. Nearly five decades after he was no longer responsible for the conditions there, he was still determined that it be cared for properly.

In 2001, Kamala Masters visited Munindra in India, and, together, they made a pilgrimage to important Buddhist sites. Their stop in Bodh Gaya was particularly memorable because of what they encountered at the temple, where they would go to meditate early in the morning. Kamala recalls, "Munindra and I would be sitting under the Bodhi Tree before dawn, and stray dogs would ferociously bark and bite each other, fighting over territory. They came very close to us. One time, he said that he had to do something about them: 'It's a very sacred area. Whoever is in charge of this area now should make sure there are no dogs here.'"

Munindra and Kamala went to the office of the Mahabodhi Temple Management Committee. "Munindra respectfully greeted the monk in charge, putting his cloth down on the office floor and making three bows to him. Then Munindra sat down, and in his very sweet manner said, 'Bhante, I want to talk to you about something very important, very serious.' (He's really good at setting the stage; it isn't a complaint.) 'Why do you have these dogs here? This is a very sacred place. This is where Gotama Buddha was enlightened; this is where all Buddhas were enlightened. It is not proper for these dogs to be in the compound. It should be a place where pilgrims can sit peacefully under the Bodhi Tree. But the dogs are very noisy. They fight each other. They may even bite people.' He absolutely insisted that those dogs be brought out of the compound. The monk said, 'Yes, yes.' Munindra said, 'When? When can you do it? Can you do it now? Can you do it next week?' He really pinned them down. This was the most insistent I've ever seen him.

Then he also expressed concern about how the dogs would be fed, and they discussed that."

The Point of No Return

It was Munindra's dedication to Bodh Gaya that eventually resulted in fulfilling his life's goal. During his tenure as temple superintendent, he befriended U Nu, the prime minister of Burma, on his repeated visits to India. In 1956, U Nu invited him to Burma. The following year, Munindra was finally able to get leave for three months. As there were no teachers of vipassanā meditation in India at that time (organized Buddhism had died out on the plains of northern India during the thirteenth century), this was his first opportunity to learn directly from a renowned meditation master, Mahāsi Sayādaw, at his Sasana Yeiktha meditation center in Rangoon.

Six weeks after arriving, the two men accompanying Munindra decided to return to India and wanted him to come too. But he demurred, "I had a long aspiration from my childhood to understand Buddha, to understand Dhamma. I have not understood anything yet. I was born alone in this house [body]; I have to go alone. So, please, you go. If I don't experience Dhamma, I will not go back. If I have to die, I will die here."

As long as his companions were with him, sometimes disturbing him with talk, Munindra could not exert himself fully. Once they left, he pulled out all the stops. When people meditated during the day, he locked himself in his room and did not emerge for anything. To avoid interactions with anyone, he used a container to urinate in and bathed before the other meditators got up. At night, he walked in the dark—there were no candles or electric bulbs anywhere—yet he felt that everything was illuminated.

Early in his stay, when Munindra could barely sit in meditation and suffered from rheumatism, Mahāsi Sayādaw told him of a Japanese meditator who sat for hours at a stretch. Exasperated with himself, Munindra reflected, "This person comes from Japan, sitting for nine hours, and I come from Bodh Gaya, where Buddha attained enlightenment, and I am the guest of the prime minister and can't sit even half an hour. For days I have tried. It's too hard, so much pain. Oh, I am a useless person!"

Then Munindra recalled a Tibetan monk who made a vow to sacrifice some part of his own body under the Bodhi Tree where the Buddha awakened. While his fellow monks lit oil lamps to practice there at night, this lama dipped a piece of cloth in ghee, wrapped it around one of his fingers, set fire to it, and let it burn. He read and chanted by the light of his burning finger.

"Lama, why did you burn this finger?" Munindra asked afterward. "Buddha never said [to do] this in the texts."

The lama replied, "I did it for the welfare of many in the world. I could not give my whole body, but I gave a little bit in the name of peace in the world."

"Do you need medicine?"

"No, I don't want it."

"No pain?"

"There's slight pain, never mind."

Munindra invited him to stay and eat with him during his time in Bodh Gaya. After seven days, the remaining portion of the lama's finger fell off.

Recollecting all of this while he was in Burma, Munindra aroused the determination to sit longer: "I am sitting here. I feel pain. Heat arises. That man put fire on his finger and did not complain. Why should I not bear this inner fire?" He woke up at two o'clock, washed his face, and sat down to meditate. Then he vowed, "I am not going to move anymore."

The first two hours were excruciating; then the pain slowly dropped away and eventually disappeared, never to return. The sitting became pleasant, his mind peaceful. He felt as though he were floating in the air; and a cool light came, small at first, then bigger. He did not get up for meals or even a drink of water. Since no one had seen him all day, someone knocked on his door. Barely able to move, eventually he opened the door. The next day, he reported to Mahāsi Sayādaw, who said, "Continue your practice."

This episode was not a macho display of what Munindra could withstand. As Jack Engler notes, "It wasn't about being competitive, but loving challenges and setting them for himself, and testing the limits of what's possible." Munindra used to say, "If it can be done by people, then why not [by] me?"

Despite advancing in his practice, Munindra still had not fulfilled his lifelong aspiration. With only fifteen days remaining as a guest of the government, he was on the verge of giving up. As the sun was setting one evening, he was lying down, relaxing, and reflecting: "It is not important to be superintendent. Taking care of the temple is secondary; anybody can do it. But what I want to know, that is most important for my life. I'm not going back. I have not [yet] understood Dhamma. But I have no hope."

Suddenly, he was filled with inspiration and said, "I can! Let me practice!" Just as he was feeling the desire to rise from his cot and sit in meditation, he sensed a huge fire explode in his feet. It burned for a few seconds and then was completely gone, replaced by illumination and rapture, which lasted for three sleepless but joy-saturated days.

All of the Buddha's Teaching, Thoroughly

Munindra's experience of understanding the Four Noble Truths and the cessation of suffering (something he had longed for since childhood), led to unshakable faith in this path of practice. It also strengthened his resolve to do what he had been unable to carry out in India—to study the entire Pāli Canon (Tipiṭaka, "Three Baskets"). A vast collection of primary Pāli-language texts that form the doctrinal foundation of Theravāda Buddhism, it was originally written on palm leaves, but now printed editions comprise dozens of volumes covering the three main divisions: Vinaya Piṭaka (monastic discipline), Sutta Piṭaka (discourses of the Buddha), and Abhidhamma Piṭaka (philosophy/psychology). Munindra wrote to the Mahabodhi Temple Management Committee and also asked his friend Brahmacharya Jīvānanda, whom he had placed in temporary charge of the Mahabodhi Temple, to continue there. He had made up his mind to stay in Burma.

At first, Prime Minister U Nu wanted him to become a monk, but Munindra protested that he wanted to study Dharma thoroughly. "Monks are not always free," he explained. "Even [in] fifty years I will not be able to complete the whole Tipiṭaka. Let me study in my own way, as a layman, from morning to evening under eight precepts." Also, Mahāsi Sayādaw informed him there was no one at the meditation center to teach him. U Maung Sein, a wealthy local man, overheard their conversation and offered his help. He found the teacher best suited for Munindra's needs, U Maung Maung, and provided all the material support—lodging on the top floor of his family's building, meals, books, and incidentals.

It was a fortuitous match. Both Munindra and U Maung Maung, a highly respected scholar, were examples of the resoluteness necessary for such an endeavor. U Maung Maung was willing to undertake the task of going through the Pāli scriptures for free, but with one requirement: His student must agree to follow through day after day, month after month, year after year, until it was all done. "So both of our aspirations met," Munindra said. Accepting the generous proposal, he studied daily from six o'clock in the morning until nine or ten at night, pausing only for a bit of breakfast, one main meal, and some rest. Within five years, he accomplished what generally took ten to twenty. He became so immersed in his studies that he said it was as though the Buddha were right there with him in the room.

In the decades after his intensive practice and study, Munindra made clear to his students that they, too, could accomplish whatever they wanted, but not without paying a price for it. It was not a question of money, but "honest and wholehearted effort." He said, "You should be serious and have a strong heart for it."

To Be or Not to Be a Monk

Only after fulfilling his lifelong aspiration to understand the Buddha's teaching, experientially and scholastically, did Munindra become a monk. But the following year, in 1966, he decided to leave Burma and could not be dissuaded, even by his meditation master. Although he was offered Burmese citizenship, Munindra felt it was time to bring Dharma back to where it had been born. As he told Jack Engler, "It is my habit. I have an original way of seeing things. I am always going against the stream. Everything my horoscope predicted for me, I deliberately did [the] opposite."

Nine years after arriving in Burma to learn meditation, Munindra requested permission of Mahāsi Sayādaw to disrobe because he wanted to be able to teach everyone, and monasticism would prevent him from doing that. His teacher understood and consented. Munindra was determined to live his life fully and to spread Dharma as far as he could. He was prescient in this, for he wound up befriending men and women from around the world, teaching wherever he was invited, moving about freely in a way he could not have done as a Theravādin monk.

Where There's a Will, There's a Way

In preparation for departure from Burma, Munindra gathered all his books on the Buddha's teaching to ship to India. To make this shipment, one of his local supporters had been trying for six months to secure authorization from the military government, which tightly restricted what could come into and go out of the country. When his efforts proved unsuccessful, he advised Munindra to leave without the books; he would send them later. But Munindra was extremely disappointed and decided to confront the matter himself.

"I made up my mind," he said. "I came here, studied all of these books thoroughly. These books are very helpful for me, and there are no such books in India, so I must take them. Without books I will not go."

Munindra's supporter pleaded with him not to approach the military office: The people were rough and rude, would not help, and could even do him harm. Fearful of what might happen, still other people warned him not to go there. But Munindra set aside their concerns for his safety and reflected, "All the military people are not bad. There are only [outer] signs —[their] dress is like military—but they are human beings; they have [a] mother, father, wife, brother, friends. In every man, some good qualities and bad qualities are there. I will find a way to take the books to India."

Undeterred, Munindra decided to speak to the military officers in charge. Dressed as a renunciate, he arrived early in the morning at the first gate of the compound with his long list of donated books, including their prices.

"Where are you going?" the guard asked him.

"Because I have studied Dhamma here, I have to get these books to India," Munindra replied.

"Oh, no, not allowed. Please don't try, because nobody, not even Burmese monks or Burmese people living in foreign countries, are allowed. You will not get permission. Please go away."

"I want to meet the superiors. I want to talk to them. Without books, it is no use going back to India. All Dhamma is forgotten there. You have preserved Dhamma, you have kept all the books. My going will be beneficial. It will bring good relationships, [a] good name for Burma. It is your duty to send these books."

Munindra's sincerity was so persuasive that the man turned sympathetic and told him to move on to the second gate and inquire there. At the second gate, he went through the same routine, repeating the same explanation, and managed to continue to the third and last gate. The person in charge reviewed all his information and reiterated what the others had said. Nevertheless, Munindra was unrelenting.

He insisted, "I have studied all these books. Any teacher in Burma can test me because, without books, it is no use to go to India—there is nothing there."

In the end, they did not turn Munindra away but listened as he gave a short talk about what he had learned. Then he said, "Burma is my second home. Though I was born in India, I experienced Dhamma in Burma. I am deeply indebted to the Burmese people. I love this country. I have done my duty here—I have studied—but India is lacking Dhamma, so it will be very helpful for everybody. I should be given permission."

Officials came and discussed the matter and finally acquiesced: "All right, we have not done anything like this, but we will help you." They even made arrangements with the steamship and assisted with packing the books so that nobody could put anything else in the crates. They allowed him to leave the country with only fifty rupees and about ten sets of robes, which Munindra donated to monks in India. His circle was astonished that he obtained consent and wondered how he had dared to challenge the military. He told them, "I believe in human beings. Human beings I trust because all people have their essential qualities. When you can touch their heart, they respond. I trusted in their goodness and they all became supportive."

With a grand send-off by a large crowd at the ship's dock, Munindra left after nearly nine years in Burma. Indefatigable resolve had brought him there some thirty years after he had first read about the Buddha's life. Finally, in his early forties, he directly realized and understood the Buddha's experience. Now, at fifty-two, he was unwavering about bringing Dharma back to its country of origin. He would share what he had learned. Though, for a period, he became an international teacher, he felt a great need to serve India. As Gregg Galbraith notes, "His mission, close to his heart, was his home, his own people."

And twenty-seven crates of books did arrive in India.

You Must, You Must

Munindra was resolute not only with respect to his own aspirations but also in helping others to fulfill theirs. When Jack Engler arrived in India in 1975, he made his way to Bodh Gaya. The first thing Munindra did was secure a place for him. Staying in the tourist bungalow was out of the question, as it offered only short-term accommodations on a cot in one large, overcrowded room. (Jack adds, "The only lavatory I had ever been in that had more human excrement on the walls and floor was outside Jericho on the West Bank.")

Munindra promised he would help find him a suitable room: "We will ask at the Japanese temple." This temple had the newest and best lodging in Bodh Gaya, but it was also the most difficult to get into. Munindra asserted, "You are here to study Dhamma. They cannot refuse!"

"Witnessing the meeting between Munindra-ji and the head Zen monk was like watching an irresistible force meeting an immovable object," recalls

Jack. "The monk said no. 'But you must,' said Munindra-ji. 'Impossible!' said the monk. 'He has come from the West to study Dhamma. You must extend him hospitality,' Munindra-ji said quietly and cordially, but underneath he was steel. Finally the head monk told us to wait. He called in his assistant monk, and there was a brief consultation in Japanese. 'OK,' said the monk." Jack says that in this exchange Munindra was "never loud, never aggressive, always respectful, but just never stopped talking until his opponent simply gave up. For Munindra-ji, it was simply the duty of the *sangha* to stand by and support one another."

As Grahame White says, "Nothing was going to stop him from his goal of either looking after the Mahabodhi Society or looking after his students. He was always there for you." Jack Engler remembers, "He was home every day, all day, to whoever wanted to come and talk about Dharma or practice—or just talk. He opened his door at sunrise and closed it at sunset. Anyone and everyone was welcome."

Munindra gave this counsel to his nephew Tapas Kumar Barua:

> If you are desirous and committed to a cause, then there cannot be any obstacle that will stand in your way of achievement. Even if you find an obstacle, it will cause a temporary hindrance only, and ultimately it will melt and evaporate with the passage of time.

Fearful and Stubborn

As fearless and determined as Munindra was regarding anything connected to the Buddha, Dharma, and *Sangha,* sometimes he could be fearful and stubborn about other things. Understanding Dharma does not necessarily erase personal preferences or quirks, as Steven J. Schwartz realized when he took Munindra to Washington, DC, in the late 1970s, on one of his student-sponsored visits to North America.

Given Munindra's immense curiosity, Steven expected that he would appreciate seeing the subway system in DC, which is known for its breakthrough design. He comments, "Munindra was not only amazingly courageous, but he was also an adventurous kind of person. He always pumped his students for information about the West and how things worked there. He was scientifically minded, so I thought he'd love the DC metro system."

The metro is built in layers, with the various subway lines running underneath one another, so that some of the train platforms are very low underground and must be accessed by riding long, steep escalators. This was the case at the station Steven and Munindra were using. "Munindra was already familiar with escalators, so I just jumped on," says Steven. "But he stood at the top and wouldn't get on. As I was going down, I kept saying, 'Munindra, get on the escalator,' and he kept adamantly refusing, 'No, no, no, no, no.' I went all the way down and took the escalator all the way up. I asked him, 'What's wrong?' 'This escalator is going into a dark place,' he said. I said, 'That's true, but that's what the subway is about, it's in the ground.'"

Steven continues, "I could see on his face that there was uncontrollable fear, and it was such a unique moment. I had never seen fear in Munindra before, especially fear about a new experience like this. He would always take the first step forward, leading the group by walking fast, pushing the group mentally and emotionally. I had never seen him hesitate, and here he was stuck at the top of the escalator. He said it was too dark, too fast, and it might break. So I said, 'How about if I stand behind you?' He said, 'No, don't do that.' All of a sudden, I decided to do what he would do. I lifted him gently and put him on the escalator. His eyes went wild and he screamed, '*Arrey baba*! *Arrey baba*!' [Oh, my goodness!] He was completely terrified the whole way. At the bottom, he declared, 'I will never do that again.'" "Once we got down, he loved it," Steven says. "He just couldn't stand the escalator."

For the rest of the trip Munindra refused to use taxis—he only wanted to travel by metro. But, Steven adds, "He never got over his fear. Whenever we got to the station, he would walk down the stairs. When we arrived at our stop, I would say, 'Let's go up this escalator.' 'Oh, no, no, I won't go,' he would say. I would say, 'Up is easy compared to down.' 'Oh, no, no, it's like going into the light. I can't do that.' While I took the escalator, he would run up the stairs, taking enormous delight in beating me to the top. It was stunning both to see how scared he was and to see how determined he was not to let that fear stand in the way, because he loved the subway and knew it was convenient."

Stubborn or Resolute?

Ram Dass, who describes Munindra as one of "the warmest teachers," says, "Once he made up his mind, that was it. I mean, he was stubborn." Was he stubborn or resolute? Munindra's behavior was variously interpreted as either because an observer cannot necessarily discern the motivation behind it—to be of service or to defend one's ego? Is one determined to get one's way simply for aggrandizement or worldly gain? Or is the intention for attaining something beyond that? Also, how much does one hold on, and when is it time to let go?

Robert Pryor says that Munindra had the capacity to let go of what he was set on and, appropriate to the circumstances, to stop insisting. During his many years with the Antioch Buddhist Studies Program in Bodh Gaya, he had a reputation for making many requests, because he had a predilection for orderliness and cleanliness. But whenever Robert or another staff person explained to Munindra why something was not possible in that moment, he immediately dropped it and said OK.

The issue at hand could be as simple as getting a railway ticket or an extra bucket for bathing, or as complex as overseeing the establishment of a meditation center. Christopher Titmuss recounts Munindra's resolve—what others might have considered stubbornness—regarding the center. "In the mid-1970s, Munindra had various invitations to go to other places, in the West and elsewhere in India, including Calcutta, where Dipa Ma was," says Christopher. "But he was declining everything because his intention was to stay absolutely put in Bodh Gaya until he'd got the OK from the authorities in Patna or Delhi to start this center. Neither hell nor high water would move him, which was rather a brave thing to do, given the uncertainties, corruptions, and indecisiveness that all the red tape of Bihar involved. But I do remember he was absolutely not going to leave until this was sorted out. If I recall correctly, having patiently waited a couple of years, he finally realized that what he wanted to happen—starting up a significant meditation center—wasn't going to happen."

Munindra let go of the project, uncharacteristically letting go of his dream. Instead, he lent support to his old friend S. N. Goenka, who established Dhamma Giri, a major vipasssanā meditation center in Igatpuri, near Bombay. He encouraged hundreds, if not thousands, of people to go on retreat there. Munindra knew when to sustain his resolve to the utmost, but he also recognized when to set it aside.

And as a mountain, a rock, stable and firmly based, does not tremble in rough winds but remains in precisely its own place, so you too

> *must be constantly stable in resolute determination; going on to the perfection of Resolute Determination, you will attain Self-Awakening.*
>
> —SUMEDHA (THE BUDDHA IN A PAST LIFE), BV 154–55

---

adhiṭṭhāna: from *adhi* (prefix or preposition indicating direction and place, as in a movement toward a definite goal) + *ṭhāna* (literally, a place, region, or locality, but metaphorically, a condition or state, attribute or quality). This is translated as "resolute determination," "decision," "unshakable resolve," "vow," and "will." It represents the steadfast strength of mind essential for applying oneself to a specific end and the refusal to vacillate in the face of obstacles. Such a fixedness of purpose enables one to progress gradually toward attaining a mundane or supramundane objective, be it a state of meditative absorption, highly developed generosity and compassion, insight into the nature of reality, or the ultimate goal of awakening.

The Buddha spoke of four *adhiṭṭhāna*: to not neglect wisdom, to preserve truth, to cultivate generosity, and to train for calm (MN 140.12). The eighth of ten perfections (*pāramī*), *adhiṭṭhāna* is fundamental to attaining the other nine because perfecting them would be impossible without it. This resolve is directly related to the aspiration for complete awakening, for it is sustained determination to fulfill all thirty-seven requisites of awakening and overcome their opposites.

8

Slow and Steady Wins the Race

Viriya (Energy, Vigor)

Continuity is the secret to success.
—MUNINDRA

Stories about Munindra's remarkable physical and spiritual stamina are legion—from the great efforts he made to practice and study the Buddha's teaching to his tirelessness in sharing it. He could outpace students who were decades younger. And if someone needed him in the middle of the night, he was instantly awake, alert, and available. When it came to Dharma, Munindra's *viriya* was inexhaustible.

A combination of factors fueled his energy. A naturally wiry figure, he was probably genetically disposed to embrace high levels of activity. Insatiably curious and fervent about learning, he possessed infinite enthusiasm to keep exploring. Adept at mindfulness and inclined toward the wholesome, he was skillful in preserving strength for what he considered important and not expending it on what was trivial to his pursuit.

By Your Own Bootstraps

Since childhood, Munindra was aware of the Buddha's story—how long and how hard he persevered until his awakening—and willing to exert himself to learn what the Buddha knew. Having experienced the fruition of his own efforts, Munindra assumed that others could do the same. He encouraged them to be wholehearted in their endeavors and to understand why liberation was a matter of self-reliance: "Buddha only pointed the way. He cannot show you *nibbāna*. Nobody can do that. We have to make our own effort."

Tapas Kumar Barua remarks, "Every discourse, my uncle used to say what he experienced, and he wanted us to experience the same thing. But he told us, 'Unless and until you follow the path that I have traveled myself, you cannot do it. Unless and until you move your hands, you won't be able to swim. So you have to learn how to swim. That's your effort—how to keep yourself afloat."

For many people who went to Asia in search of answers to life's big questions, meeting Munindra was an occasion for building self-confidence in spiritual practice. He directed them to look within their own minds and hearts rather than outside themselves. His way of teaching both challenged and inspired them.

When unhappiness and confusion brought Sharon Salzberg to India at the age of eighteen, Munindra was one of her first teachers. He said, "Buddha's enlightenment solved Buddha's problem, now you solve yours." That she could actually accomplish freedom from suffering on her own was a revelation. She discovered that "the discipline, the structure really had to come from within," not from the teacher. "You had to take responsibility for your own choices, which was very good," says Sharon. "I saw that there was some amount of energy and effort and actual practice that was being called for from me so that I could step up to this experience of verified faith."

Because Khanti Moraitis was not looking for a guru but for somebody who could clarify things for her, Munindra's emphasis on *viriya* suited her needs. "The essence of Dhamma is love, understanding, and self-sufficiency, in the sense that you have to make your own way," she says. "In the Theravāda tradition, you have a teacher, you have the Buddha, you have the *sangha*, but all the work depends on you. It's your responsibility. It's not about some wonderful guru who's going to take you there if you don't do it yourself. This was what Munindra-ji was all about—he gave you minimal instructions. But his teaching was very clear from the beginning. Later, when I understood the importance of discipline—to really focus on something and put all your energy in that, and that's why you have to eliminate all the other disturbances—then I was able to do it."

Joseph Goldstein also appreciated Munindra's teaching style. Rather than adhere to a formal structure, students had to exercise their own *viriya* to get results. "In those early years, he wasn't leading retreats," says Joseph. "He was living in the Gandhi ashram, and I and a few Westerners were staying at the Burmese Vihar. We would go see him once a day, for a couple of hours in the morning. The rest of the time, we were on our own, just doing our practice." He adds, "How intensively students practiced varied a lot. It was all self-regulated; some were very motivated and some were less so. There was no course structure, there was just seeing him. Munindra was very open-minded and spacious. He didn't enforce a disciplined practice. It was all up to us."

If anyone questioned this approach, Munindra explained,

> According to scriptures, the teacher is called *kalyāṇamitta,* "spiritual friend," "spiritual guide." There is no guru system. Those who have experienced, who have walked on the path, they can show how it happens. They just point out the way; they show the path. Every individual has to make his own effort to realize the truth. No one can help you to realize it.

Phenomenal Energy

Although most of Munindra's students were of younger generations, his physical and mental vitality never failed to astound them. He would get up at two or three o'clock in the morning and go to bed at nine or so, sleeping four or five hours. By the time others awoke at five to get ready to meditate, he had already bathed, read, and dealt with his correspondence. As Patrick Ophuls remarks, "My predominant impression of him was of tremendous energy."

Munindra always had energy for students, even in the wee hours. Steven V. Smith says, "I remember times at IMS having really exciting things happen in practice and seeing his light on in the middle of the night and knocking on the door. He'd be up and invite me in. I'd tell him what was going on, and he'd take it all in and advise me, have me continue or give me some other instruction. I don't know that things like that happen anymore. It seems such a long time ago and how things might have been in the time of the Buddha."

Pat Masters recalls, "Munindra had bundles of unbelievable energy. He could walk those [college] students into the ground. He used to like to take them [from Bodh Gaya] over to Sujata across the river and to all these archaeological and historical sites, which he knew so well. They would be panting, and he would say, 'Let's go.' Even toward the end, he was still strong. He kept threatening to retire, but he just kept coming back [to the Antioch Education Abroad Buddhist Studies Program]. That was also pretty daunting on his part, because I know that he wasn't well. But he still maintained the incredible memory and his ability to transmit the Dharma."

Munindra's level of energy was not necessarily easy for everyone who hosted him. Sharon Salzberg and Joseph Goldstein remember a trip to the National Air and Space Museum in Washington, DC. "He needed to see every single exhibit," says Joseph. "I and the others that went with him were exhausted. He was quite tireless. I don't know whether it was his natural energy or his practice, but he had endless energy to look and to go places." Sharon adds, "We were there for about six and a half hours. Finally, I fell asleep on one of the couches. When I woke up, Joseph was across from me on another couch, and Munindra was going and going and going. He just didn't stop."

Bob and Dixie Ray also found Munindra "very high energy, very curious [i.e., hugely interested]." Dixie recalls, "He wanted to see everything, do everything, in Chicago. He didn't want to go to the circus only once but again and again and again. So we just took him everywhere and ran along behind him. He had more energy than we had. In that sense, he was challenging. But whatever he did, wherever he went, he was totally there, and then he would be through with that and move on to the next thing."

Sources of Energy

Dixie is describing, in part, why Munindra had so much energy—mindfulness. He was always present with what was right in front of him—the person or exhibit or animal or performance—rather than flitting back and forth to the past or the future.

"Until the last two or three years of his life, he was hard to keep up with, and that was very inspiring," says Robert Pryor. "The way I interpreted it, because his mind was freer than other minds, he just had more energy. I suspect he didn't waste his energy worrying, the way the rest of us do."

Worrying is not the only energy drain. Munindra explained,

> When the mind is influenced by anger, if you are not aware, then it gets food, it gets nourishment. If there is no mindfulness, anger has the nature to pollute the mind. When it is not observed, then it influences the body. Then we see these changes: The body becomes tense; eyes become red; the body trembles; the circulation of blood changes. Any reaction, any word you use at that

time becomes poisonous, hurting, because when the mind is polluted, all actions, deeds, words are polluted. On account of that, we burn a lot of our energy, and that's why we need more sleep, more rest. But if the mind does not react, if mind is not wandering, not thinking, but experiencing moment to moment, then it is restful, conserving the energy, not wasting it. That's why, when mindfulness is highly developed, you do not feel sleepy, tired, exhausted.

One day, without any forethought, Munindra demonstrated how the power of *viriya* to be mindful and to nudge the mind and heart toward wholesome states actually functions. Robin Sunbeam relates the lesson she learned: "I was trying to practice loving-kindness. He explained to me how anger and rage are the flip side of the coin of loving-kindness and how you could transform the energy of that rage so it becomes a fountain of love. Then I can't remember what happened, but someone came in and told him something, and he became enraged. I was standing only six or seven feet away, and I could see his face become a scowl. His eyes were burning, and he turned red. Then I could see his mindfulness snap in, and in a moment he was smiling his usual smile and being very loving toward the same person."

Kamala Masters adds, "As sentient human beings, we have the intelligence to incline the mind toward the wholesome. If something from the past has borne fruit in the present moment and it's unwholesome, then our practice is to not do anything with it—in our language, in our actions—to let it go. In different ways, Munindra would express that. We can't control outer conditions, but there's a great possibility that a wholesome state of mind, if nurtured and given energy and used, could lead to another wholesome state of mind."

Gregg Galbraith confirms this tendency in Munindra. "He honestly always looked for the good in people. He would not allow his mind to dwell on negativity, particularly related to other people. He would speak about their good side."

Toward the End of Life

About nine months before Munindra passed away, Uno Svedin came from Sweden to visit his old teacher and help in any way he could. Munindra was, by then, quite ill and weak. Nevertheless, Uno notes, "He still accepted people coming to make visits in the afternoon. He welcomed these visitors sitting cross-legged in the middle of the bed in his white clothing and brown cap. During these meetings, the visitors could get substantial time for discussions. And when dhamma issues were raised, he would light up: The entire flood of teaching enthusiasm grasped him, and the flow of Dhamma came uninterrupted in any suitable language for the occasion—Bengali, Hindi, Burmese, or, in some instances, English. A minidiscourse would fly out of his mouth, like in the old days." No matter what the circumstances, no matter his debilitated physical condition, he always mustered vigor for Dharma. He even asked Uno, "Is there still something unclear in the instructions given?"

Toward the end of his life, it was obvious that Munindra felt time was running out for him to impart Dharma and help others realize what he had realized. Various people noticed that *saṁvega*—a sense of spiritual urgency—strongly infused his teaching.

"There was an energy about him," says Rebecca Kushins. "Now that I've heard more stories about when he was younger, I know that he always had energy in his teachings, but he was very old when I met him [in the Antioch Education Abroad program] and he still had this energy. We were often told that if we were going to go chat with him, we should cut him off after a certain point, so that he could go rest, and not just let him keep going, because he loved to talk with us until he really felt that we got it. I remember he would always say to us, 'I'm giving you the shortcut.' I still don't know what he meant, but he was so insistent about it."

Munindra continued in this vein during a personal interview Rebecca had with him. "I told him I was having difficulty because I could only be aware of something just after it happened, not when it was happening. I remember the insistency and urgency—he really wanted me to get it. He kept saying this over and over again until the bell rang and it was time to go to the meditation hall again: 'Right at the moment of happening! Right at the moment of happening!' He would smack his two hands together and say, 'Be that clear! Right at the moment of happening!' He had this *saṁvega*. He really was very insistent, 'I'm giving you the shortcut! Now! No time to lose!'"

In his final period of teaching, Munindra did not have the enormous energy he had manifested in the early years of the Antioch Education Abroad program. "But when he got started teaching, the energy just flowed through him, and he was clear and his talks were accurate," says Robert Pryor. "There was this energy that he wanted to convey that was very strong, even though his body was really weak. I could see how much he cared that we got it, that blessing of the Dharma. I noticed very much a sense of urgency. It was like he was saying to us, 'Would you please get this! You've got to get this!' He didn't use those words, but almost. He had this tremendous desire for us to really understand the way he did. The sense of immediacy that came across was quite intense; it was so obvious that I could feel it. It was very moving, very touching. When he was teaching the Dharma, he got very powerful."

Oren Sofer observed that later in life Munindra could not talk for as long as he used to, though he still had the desire. He recalls one time when Munindra and he were conversing, and he encouraged Munindra to take a break. "He had been going on for a while about the Dhamma in a very passionate way, but I could tell he was getting tired. I said, 'Munindra-ji, why don't you lie down for a while and I'll sit.' He smiled and said, 'OK, OK.' He lay down and rested, and I sat for forty-five minutes or an hour. There was some pain in my leg that was getting to be unbearable. I shifted my posture and stopped sitting. At that point, he immediately woke up and asked me, 'What happened? What did you notice?' I thought to myself, 'His every single breath is devoted to teaching, living, and understanding Dhamma.' There was no sense of his wanting to take a few minutes to wake up or have some time to himself. As soon as he opened his eyes, he was right there with me, passionately curious about what happened for me over the course of the sitting."

Bryan Tucker had a similar experience at Dhamma Giri in 1994. To Bryan, Munindra would appear "on the verge of collapse, but then soon rise again and be a bundle of energy, constantly talking and taking keen interest in everything and everyone around him." Munindra walked with Bryan into town every day, which Bryan considered an enormous privilege. "I had tremendous respect for him as one of the great teachers of this tradition who was such a strong link in the chain of transmission to the West. As we would walk, he would talk incessantly about the Dharma or point things out to me. He would go up and down long flights of stairs with some difficulty. He was quite old, obviously, but his mind was like that of a young person, just continually asking questions. As I was speaking, he was thinking about everything that I was saying. He would cut me off and say, 'No, no, no. It's not like that. It's like this.' He was so quick thinking, it was sometimes unnerving."

"He used any occasion to speak about the Dharma," Bryan adds. "As we walked, he would urge me to become aware. *Paramattha* is a term that means ultimate reality, direct experience, clear perception of reality, rather than a concept. Munindra would say, 'Do you feel the *paramattha?*' And I would say, 'What are you talking about?' He was referring to just walking. He'd point to the ground and say, 'Do you feel that? Do you feel the direct sensations?' He used something as mundane as walking as an example of a high Abhidhamma term. He literally brought things down to earth."

Munindra also used the example of the burning bodies at the nearby cremation grounds in Igatpuri to infuse yogis with *saṁvega*. Itamar Sofer says that sometimes on their evening walks from Dhamma Giri, they passed by "the burning place." Munindra would say, "This is also Buddha's teaching about death. We are next in line. We should not be afraid to think about it. It is a very natural thing. Always think that you are dying soon so you will make your life very meaningful. Don't waste time!"

Wholeheartedness

Munindra used the word *wholehearted* often. Coming from him, it seemed synonymous with *viriya*. In order to attain one's greatest desire, it is necessary to strive for it with all the energy and effort one can exert. He would say, "Mind and body should be working together. Any aspiration you have can be accomplished, but you must be wholehearted, and you must know the way."

Munindra knew the way and made great effort to point it out to others. To be successful in traversing that path, he counseled (quoting from Aesop), "Slow and steady wins the race." He also stated that it is important to use wisdom in applying energy. Roy Bonney says, "What he conveyed to me was, don't apply effort to the point of discomfort" and, consequently, ineffectiveness.

Though Munindra had an immense passion for books and could have reached a greater audience by writing them, he never exerted *viriya* to author a single volume. He used to say, "I have always shared everything I know with everyone. You can write if you like." Munindra put all his energy into directly sharing Dharma, even with his last ounce of strength as an old and sick man. But, as Oren Sofer says, "The depth of his commitment and realization really had a huge ripple effect." Many of his students have applied their own *viriya* for Dharma and gone on to establish centers, write books, and teach yet more generations. Munindra's steadfast efforts live on through all of them.

Inactive when one should be active,
Lazy [though] young and strong,
Disheartened in one's resolves,
Such an indolent, lethargic person
Doesn't find the path of insight.

—THE DHAMMAPADA 280

viriya: from *vīrya* (literally, the state of a strong man or hero); from *vīra* (one who proceeds uninterruptedly in one's work); firm and unshaken vigor, energy, persistence, or effort.

Without the strength of *viriya*, one cannot carry out the resolve to fulfill an aspiration. It overcomes laziness, lethargy, and collapse. However, wisdom (*paññā*) must accompany *viriya* to ensure that it does not become the fierce grind of excessive striving or overexertion that would lead to mental and physical exhaustion. Rather, steadfast and balanced application of energy to the task at hand is akin to tuning an instrument so that the strings are neither too tight nor too slack to achieve the right sound.

The Buddha instructed that all on the path must exert the necessary effort to work out their own liberation. By example, he remained undaunted when beset by obstacles in his quest to awaken and to advance the welfare of others. Although not always physically robust, he never flagged in mental alertness and vigor. *Viriya* is not simply bodily power but also strength of character, will, and persistence; ardent and indefatigable effort to reach the goal serves to fortify all other qualities. The cause for marshaling such energy is a sense of spiritual urgency (*saṁvega*) that comes from realizing how unwise, complacent, and negligent one has been in accepting the usual and pointless way of living.

Viriya is one of the five spiritual faculties (*indriya*) or powers (*bala*), seven factors of awakening (*bojjhaṅga*), and ten perfections (*pāramī*). It is identical with right effort (*sammā-vāyāma*), the sixth stage of the Eightfold Path. As *sammāppadhāna,* it is the four right endeavors to avoid and overcome unwholesome states as well as to develop and maintain wholesome ones.

Munindra in Sarnath, ca. 1938–48.

Munindra, a wandering ascetic (right), and a bookseller at the Mahabodhi Society (left) near the Mahabodhi Temple in Bodh Gaya, ca. 1953–56.

Munindra (bottom left) and others with H. H. the Dalai Lama in Tibet, 1951. Photo by Heinrich Harrer.

Munindra as a monk in Burma, 1965.

Munindra with meditation students that he trained in Burma (including Depa Ma), 1965.

Munindra at the Gandhi ashram in Bodh Gaya, 1967.

Munindra in Bodh Gaya, 1969.

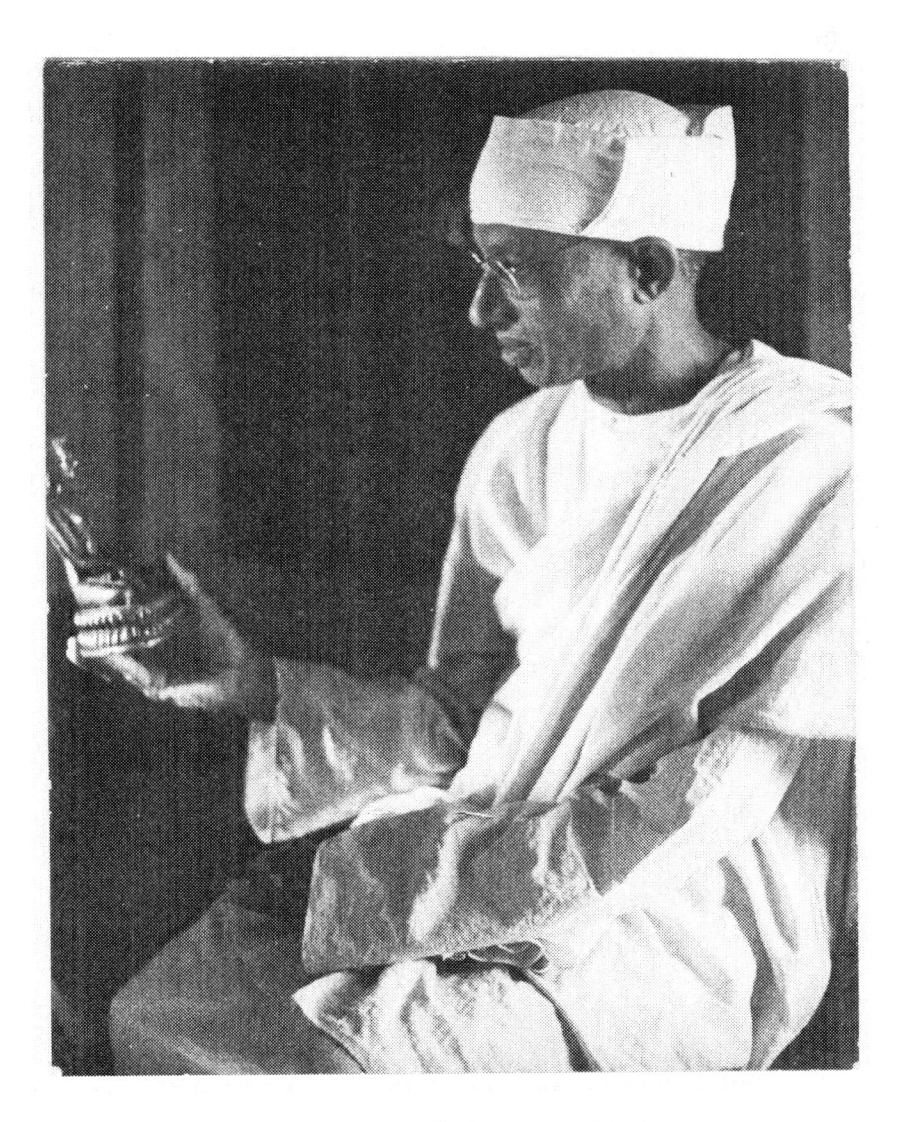

Munindra in Bodh Gaya, ca. 1966–69.

Munindra with his mother and others in Chittagong village, 1975.

Munindra with Joseph Goldstein
in Barre, Massachusetts, 1977.

Munindra at Disneyland, in Anaheim, California, 1977.

Munindra in Hawai'i, 1977.

Munindra with Joseph Goldstein and Mirko Frýba
(now Ven. Thera Āyukusala) in Barre, Massachusetts, 1977.

Munindra with Ven. Mahāsi Sayādaw and others, 1977.

Munindra, Dipa Ma, Dipa, Rishi, and Dixie Ray in Calcutta, 1980.

Munindra in Bodh Gaya, 1980.

Munindra with Joseph Goldstein, Ruth Denison,
and others at Dhamma Dena, ca. 1977–81.

Munindra at Barre, Massachusetts, ca. 1977–81.

Munindra with Joseph Goldstein
in Barre, Massachusetts, ca. 1981.

Munindra leading Antioch students in meditation
with Krishna Barua at the Mahbodhi Temple, 1986.

Munindra, S. N. Goenka, and Christopher Titmuss at the Burmese Vihar in Bodh Gaya, 1974. Photo taken by Roy Bonney.

Munindra with Antioch students in front of the Mahabodhi Temple in Bodh Gaya, 1994.

Munindra and Godwin Samararatne teaching the Antioch students in Bodh Gaya, 1996. Photo taken by Daniel Hirshberg.

Munindra at the Burmese Vihar in Bodh Gaya, 1999. Photo by Aron Weinberger.

Munindra at the Mahabodhi Temple in Bodh Gaya, 1999.
Photo by Aron Weinberger.

Munindra in meditation. Date unknown.

9

When the Fruit Is Ripe, It Will Fall from the Tree

Khanti (Patience, Forbearance)

> *Time is not a factor.*
> —MUNINDRA

When Robert Pryor first visited Bodh Gaya in the spring of 1972, the weather was hot and the park around the Bodhi Tree dry and deserted. Thinking that a leaf from the tree would serve as a good reminder of his time in this inspiring place where the Buddha awakened, he looked around. When he saw there were no leaves on the ground, he hesitated but then reached up to pick a leaf from a lower branch of the tree. Suddenly, a small man dressed all in white appeared and urgently requested, "Wait, wait until the leaves have fallen!"

"Of course, I immediately saw the value of his advice and realized that my desire for a *bodhi* leaf was leading me to an inappropriate action," says Robert. "This was my first meeting with Munindra, and it is a good example of his teaching. Not only was he protecting the Bodhi Tree, but at the same time he was giving me guidance about the necessity to let one's practice and one's life unfold in a natural way."

Munindra taught patience not only through the kind of personal advice he gave students but also through his general behavior and dharma talks. Jacqueline Schwartz Mandell says, "I can remember people talking to him about not knowing if they're progressing in their practice, and he would cite the benefits of training the mind rather than instant gratification. Of course, he spoke of liberation but also about the vastness of the Dharma. He had a long-range view of practice and life in general, and he certainly embodied that."

Joseph Goldstein adds, "Munindra used to say that in spiritual practice time is not a factor. Practice cannot be measured in time, so let go of the whole notion of when and how long. The practice is a process of unfolding, and it unfolds in its own time."

The Many Faces of Patience

Patience also unfolds in different ways. Munindra personified *khanti* in its various meanings: as endurance of suffering created by others; as forbearance of insults and other unwanted things; as forgiveness of those who wronged him in some way; as tolerance or nonopposition; as perseverance in his work for the welfare of others; as acceptance of what is; and as the absence of restlessness, neither craving rewards nor striving for fame or fortune.

On the mundane level, Munindra demonstrated the simple act of patience in something as basic as waiting for a train (in India, that could mean hours, even a whole day) or crossing the street. Bob Ray describes an experience in Calcutta: "We would come up to one of these impossible, very wide streets—total chaos, buses and animals, no traffic lights—and I would think, 'How are we going to get across? We might be here forever.' Munindra wasn't bothered by it particularly; he'd just stand there. Suddenly, there'd be an opening—it would somehow clear—and we'd walk out. But he was so calm, just very patient. He very quietly, and not even fast, walked across."

Dwarko Sundrani, head of the Gandhi ashram in Bodh Gaya, first met Munindra in 1954. He describes him as a "very gentle . . . very clean-hearted man," and remembers their talks over many years, especially their different beliefs as to who the Buddha was, what Dharma is, where vipassanā came from, and so on. "I think he was not convinced with this [Sundrani's Hindu claims]. He told his own things, we told ours. But Munindra-ji's nature was not to contradict, saying, 'Yes, yes, OK, OK.' His nature was not angry—no arguments."

Dwarko adds, "Because the name of this ashram is Samanvaya (harmony), here we also don't want to impose anything. We give an example of the rose flower. It is a good flower, but when we make a garland, we bring many kinds of flowers; but not because the rose has something less—every flower is perfect. In the same way, if we have different religion, different ideas, different philosophy, still we can live together. Munindra-ji was of that nature—harmony. Maybe he will not believe you, but he will not impose or contradict. There are many Buddhists here. They will not hear us; they say, 'We are right.' But Munindra-ji, maybe he will not agree with you, but he will never say he was right; he will keep quiet."

Zara Novikoff, who first encountered Munindra in Bodh Gaya in 1968, also noticed "he was never angry, never insisting on proving his point, but kind and humorous." According to Uffe Damborg, when meditators started arguing over something Munindra stated, he would say, "All right, yes, it's all right. You have your own way. You have to do it your way."

Jacqueline Schwartz Mandell found Munindra "was completely patient listening to how we learned, and he was also very open in terms of dialogue about different dharma points. He was modeling that I might have a different understanding of a dharma point and I can dialogue about my point of view without attachment."

No Grudges

Munindra went about his work quietly and patiently, even when others became angry with him. According to Dwarko Sundrani, during those early years in Bodh Gaya, various problems arose regarding the Mahabodhi Temple, and it was Munindra's responsibility as superintendent to deal with them. One conflict had to do with a ritual.

At the north end of the temple grounds, outside of the temple building, there is a long platform, about three feet high, known as the Jeweled Walkway. At the time, Tibetan pilgrims used to make offerings of small bowls filled with vegetable oil and a twisted cotton wick. These lamps were not only messy, because oil invariably spilled out and was impossible to clean up, but also destructive, filling the air with smoke and leaving carbon deposits. Visitors set oil lamps and ghee (butter) lamps right under the Bodhi Tree as well. The heat and the smoke were harming the tree. When Munindra told the pilgrims to engage in this practice at a distance, he suddenly found himself the object of antagonism. New to the area and unacquainted with local customs, some of them were rough with him, pushing and shoving as they protested, "This is interference in our *pūjā* [religious ceremony]. This is wrong."

Munindra simply endured the hostility: "What can I do? They don't understand." Years later, he said, "I had no grudge against them. It was a long habit. It is very difficult to change habits quickly. It took time." To resolve the issue, both Tibetans and the temple management committee built special structures so that the smoke of oil lamp offerings would not affect the temple or the tree.

That Munindra did not nurse a grudge was evident in his actions. According to Zara Novikoff, after class, he would pick up a papaya and walk over to the Tibetan temple: "I thought it was so nice because, on many occasions, even though it might be the same religion, people won't communicate, like Protestants and Catholics, almost as though they were considering themselves totally different. But Sri Munindra was not like that. He would go to the Tibetans, bring them something, and hold discussions."

Munindra extended patience to students, family, and friends alike. Zara adds, "He was a very loyal friend, and he was forgiving. I'm not perfect and might have said something that is not really polite, and maybe not even reverential, but he would smile and let it go." Clearly, Munindra took the Buddha's words to heart: "What is the way of impatience? If scolded, one scolds in return; if insulted, one insults in return; if abused, one abuses in return. What is the way of patience? If scolded, one does not scold in return; if insulted, one does not insult in return; if abused, one does not abuse in return" (AN 4.165).

Though people insulted him, spoke disrespectfully, objected to what he was doing, and even spread rumors about him, Munindra did not take offense or retaliate. His response was more likely to be one of compassion. People recall witnessing him concerned or frustrated from time to time, but not angry; they never heard him bad-mouth others. He might reprimand someone, but not with rage. Tridib Barua attests to this: "My uncle scolded me for something, saying, 'You should not do this. You should not be like this.' I was maybe ten years old. But the next day begins with a new Munindra-ji, fresh. Yesterday's uncle is totally absent. So maybe this is the reason he used to say, 'You live in present-to-present moment. What's yesterday has gone, so why worry about that? Today's today; today's not yesterday; today is not even tomorrow.' That was a teaching—not to carry over bad experiences or bad feelings."

More than likely, Munindra would encourage practice because of the fruits it would yield. Tridib's wife, Dhriti, says that before she had a baby, it was not a problem to sit, but afterward she found it very difficult to get up at four-thirty in the morning to meditate with the family. Munindra never reproached her. "I think he understood. He always told us, 'Whatever you've learned, if you like it, practice it; don't let it go. You will need it some time or the other. This is one thing that brings your mind under control. We are human beings who are likely to get angry very fast. We need patience. If you get angry too often, your relations with others will not be good. So don't go into that. If you practice, this will come.'"

Dhriti continues, "He used to clap his hands and say, 'What is happening now? Whatever feelings you have, that is happening now, but it will go after some time. So you must learn to be patient. There are so many things in life that you might not like, that you might need to handle, so this will help you.'"

No Anger

In the many years that Vivian Darst knew Munindra, she always experienced him as living without anger. She says that she kept a close eye on him during a five-month period that she traveled with him. "I never once saw him get angry in all of that time. I never even saw him get really irritated. I saw him be attached to books, attached to buying things in the market, but anger? I never saw it even arise, [at least] that was detectable. I saw him get a little bit restless with me sometimes, like if we were supposed to be some place and I was taking too much time. He would occasionally try to rush me along, but he wouldn't get angry with me. I thought that was really commendable because usually when you spend a lot of time with somebody, you see their angry nature pop up at some point. But I just don't think he had it; I think it was pretty much wiped out in him."

Rather than react with anger, Munindra might be baffled. Christina Feldman laughs about an incident in Bodh Gaya during the early 1970s. People were complaining about his absences on a course she did with him. She says, "He'd look so bewildered by these complaints—as if this were something out of the ordinary—and say things like, 'You have your practice. Why do you need me?' He wasn't at all offended or defensive about these complaints. I think he found them rather puzzling."

At other times, he might laugh at someone's outburst. Daw Than Myint tells the story of an old man in her neighborhood in Rangoon, a bachelor without any relatives who was often angry and had a drinking problem. She says, "He had no attachments to anyone and didn't go out with people, so he was very short-tempered. He used to go to the cinema and sit there for two, three pictures. So my mother and I asked him to try this meditation, and he went to Munindra-ji [at Sasana Yeiktha]. We supported him in whatever he needed, and he did meditation for some time."

Daw Than Myint continues, "Then, one day, his eyes all red, he came back with his things and, very angry, shouted from the road to my mother, 'Elder sister, I have returned and I'll never go there again. Oh, to such a place you have sent me!' But early the next morning, he came with his backpack and asked my mother, 'Elder sister, please come with me to the center.' He explained to us what had happened: 'This meditation made me very mad, so I went to drink and I was looking at the glass.' He could not drink it, so he left it and went to the cinema, and on the screen he said he saw only bones dancing. He could not watch the picture. Early in the morning he went to the center and shouted at Munindra-ji, 'Your meditation is useless. I am very wrong to come here.' And then he left, and Munindra-ji was laughing; he said nothing. When the man went back, Munindra-ji was smiling and received him quietly. This man continued and finished [realized Dhamma] and later became a *bhikkhu* [monk] for life."

Fully Listening

Munindra was not annoyed with students' ups and downs or their endless queries and issues. From Alan Clements's recollection, he seemed to have the patience of a saint. "The number one thing I remember him giving was his being, his presence. He had tremendous presence, and he did not indicate impatience. Someone would ask a question and he wouldn't see it as dumb. You know, a lot of people ask dumb questions, including me. [For] someone as seasoned in his understanding as he was and a scholar as he was, [he] was remarkably patient. He would answer the same question fresh."

During question-and-answer sessions, Munindra had a particular way of dealing with the impatience people experienced about what they were going through while practicing. Michael Liebenson Grady says that he had a "soft heart" toward all kinds of students: "He was not afraid to show sympathy to those who suffered around him, and he often attracted yogis who were quite troubled. He had so much patience with what many folks would describe as 'difficult yogis.' I always felt that Munindra had a healing effect on those yogis because he would listen and seem to have some concrete suggestion for them to bring away." Although Munindra did not necessarily recognize or understand certain imbalances or disturbed states identified by Western psychology, such as psychosis, he was willing to lend a patient ear to those who needed it.

Vivian Darst confirms that Munindra was "very, very patient with all of his students," for people would come to see him every day and ask the same questions over and over. She says she was able to talk to him about anything. He listened even to individuals who knew nothing about Dharma. She recalls his visit to her at Evergreen State College: "I had a roommate there who had not done any practice at all. She just opened right up to him and was crying, reaching some deep things that had been troubling her that I didn't know anything about. She just felt like he was a person that she could be open with, and he gave her some dhamma advice about how to work with negative states of mind or whatever she was holding on to, how to see it and let it go—be with the thing as it is, not judge, but just look carefully and fully."

"I never had any patience," Carla Mancari admits, "but I watched this little man so sweet with people, and some of them I think I would have hit over the head with a board. He taught me a lot about patience." As Lama Surya Das summarizes, "He was very broad and deep and accessible and wonderful and patient . . . very generous and patient with his time and his knowledge."

Impatience with the Teacher

Yet some of Munindra's students found themselves impatient with him at times. The flip side of his enormous capacity to listen to other people's stories was an ability to speak nonstop. Today, they laugh as they reflect on those trying sessions. Vivian Darst says, "Even though he was a great listener, he could talk for a long time and, from some people's perspective, sometimes get carried away. You ask one question and he's talking about Abhidhamma for three hours."

Steven J. Schwartz adds, "There was a complete absence of any sense of limit about how much one could either listen or endure, depending on the physical situation you were in. Maybe that's what he most wanted to press: challenging patience, which he did to the nth degree. He was unrelenting about going on. I thought of it as some combination of his deep interest in information and explication plus a total blind spot about how much other people could accept. But maybe he was very sensitive to what they thought they could take in, and he was determined to push their experience with patience, their capacity to absorb, or their willingness to sit still."

Because it seemed that Munindra could discourse indefinitely and because retreats in the West followed a specific schedule, Western teachers made an effort to limit his dharma talks. Erik Knud-Hansen offers another perspective: "Something that I saw pretty clearly then, and which is still misunderstood today, is the difference between drawing attention to something important and drawing it to oneself. I never saw him trying to be in the spotlight himself. Whenever he had your attention, he was talking Dharma. I've often used Munindra as a good example of the way some old Indian mystics would use *satsang* [devotional speech and chanting program]—they could talk for six, seven, eight hours nonstop."

Erik notes the irony that for most of us, it is quite easy to sit in front of a movie and pay close attention for two hours straight, or to read a book for a long period of time. He asks, "What makes it difficult to listen to Dharma for two hours? Who put this artificial forty-five-minute limit on a dharma talk? And what effect is that having on your mind? Do you start listening to a dharma talk saying, 'OK, I'll give you forty-five minutes?' At what point do you indulge your own boredom or your own distractedness and either see the nature of your own mind in that or not? Munindra, as well as others, tended to uphold the faith that it's OK to challenge people's attention spans and, hopefully, in some kind of inquiry or follow-up, see what exactly did occur in their mind that made it difficult." Erik adds, "The problem wasn't from the outside. It wasn't because somebody was talking too much. It was because someone wasn't listening openly enough that they had difficulties. I don't think anybody should have reined him in because people got uncomfortable."

Munindra could try people's patience in ways other than talking at great length. He had a different sense of time and schedule than most of his Western students. People who made arrangements for him to be in one place or another—Thailand or Massachusetts—would find themselves waiting and waiting for him to arrive, weeks into months. Or he would take hours to perform his daily ablutions. And if he were in conversation with someone, he would not allow himself to be pulled away in midstream. According to Gregg Galbraith, whenever people got anxious about the schedule, Munindra would say: "Time is for us; we are not for time." He patiently and mindfully remained focused on what he was doing and refused to be rushed.

Are We There Yet?

Impatient to experience insight, to be enlightened already, yogis would go to Munindra eager to be confirmed. "Is this it?" they would wonder. "Have I got it now?" Or they would have questions, the answers to which, he maintained, they needed to learn on their own. He would repeat certain phrases to them: "Just keep sitting and you'll see everything." "Be mindful and you'll understand." "Just continue your practice and you'll know." "Let it unfold naturally." In many dharma talks, Munindra expressed the essence of patience in practice:

> By practicing, it can happen anytime, at any door of perception, when one is ready, but not by expecting. Continue working. Every step is taking you near the goal. Continuity is the secret of success. Anyone who wants to know the art of living, who wants to experience this Dhamma, has to understand it clearly. But as long as you are expecting, then it will not happen.

When Robin Sunbeam felt stymied in her practice, Munindra taught her about patience. One time, she ran to him and exclaimed, "How come each time I get the realization, I still don't get it? How many times do I have to realize it until I *realize* it?" Munindra answered her by referring to the hordes of children and elderly with bandaged fingers who would break rocks with hammers at road-construction sites, making gravel for the roadbed. He said, "If the rock-breaker strikes the stone ninety-nine times and it doesn't break, yet it breaks on the hundredth strike, were the first ninety-nine wasted?" He continued, "Perhaps all ninety-nine strikes were needed before the stone would break, but at the ninety-ninth strike you may feel like you are making no progress at all."

Responding to others who felt frustrated or disheartened, Munindra might express it differently, as he did to Kamala Masters: "This is your karma. All these things come together for you to develop patience." Or, when she felt her practice was in a holding pattern, he would say: "When the fruit is ripe, it will fall from the tree."

Again and again, his students would learn the meaning of this aphorism. Khanti Moraitis notes, "Munindra-ji made me understand from the very beginning that meditation is a personal journey that we choose to embark on and that we will carry on our own terms, at our own timing."

Munindra's embodiment of *khanti* and his encouragement to cultivate it keeps rippling through his students. Eric Kupers says, "I learned a sense of steadiness in the practice and a sense of patience with the way that things unfold, just somehow a lack of melodrama around this spiritual journey. His example showed us that you don't have to worry about a lot of bells and whistles or [about] achieving something. You just keep plodding along on the path. That's inspiring to me, an acceptance for where I am."

> *Among ideals and highest goods,*
> *None better than patience is found....*
> *For the strong, guarding the Dhamma,*
> *Contentiousness is never found....*
> *Not giving anger for anger,*
> *One wins a double victory.*
>
> —SAKKA, *VEPACITTI SUTTA,* SN 11.4

---

khanti: from the Sanskrit *kṣam* (to bear, endure); literally, "patience." It is also understood as forbearance, endurance, forgiveness, tolerance, and nonopposition; a response of acceptance in the face of what is undesirable or even desirable in life. Rather than a reaction of anger or vengeance, there is gentleness and calmness. Patience manifests as endurance, fortitude, or perseverance on the path. The proximate cause is insight, seeing things as they really are.

Khanti is the sixth of ten perfections (*pārami*) and one of the highest protections or blessings, as the Buddha states in the *Mahā-mangala Sutta* (Sn 2.4 and Khp 5).

10

If You Love Your Enemies, Then You Will Have No Enemies

Mettā (Loving-Kindness)

You can bring a lot of happiness to people by being loving.
—MUNINDRA

Munindra's famously kindhearted and friendly nature first took root in the East Bengal home and village where he grew up, long before he ever learned to meditate. Without hesitation, he affectionately described his mother and father as "sweet and loving." He held nothing but profound gratitude and love for them, since he felt they had taken great care of him with tenderness. No wonder his Western students' complaints of lack of warmth and closeness in their own families—and subsequent negativity toward them—perplexed him. The result of his early upbringing and later dharma training was that Munindra loved and felt loved by everyone wherever he went.

"I was liberal in meeting people," he said, "because among Buddhists, there is no caste system. From my childhood, I find no difference among Hindus, Buddhists, and Muslims. Hindus and Muslims used to love me too, invite me to their house, bring books for me."

Only after Munindra left this peaceful rural community did he learn about intolerance. In 1938, when he arrived from Calcutta at the railway station in Varanasi to work for the Mahabodhi Society in Sarnath, he got his first glimpse of discrimination. Surprised to hear vendors calling out, "Hindu *pānī*, Muslim *pānī*," Munindra realized that they were selling water separately for Hindus and Muslims. In his entire life, he never allowed such divisions to penetrate his heart and mind.

Love without Discrimination

Anyone who spent time with Munindra witnessed a gentle and benevolent personality that did not discriminate as to who was worthy of his affection and who was not. "One striking thing that I find about my brother is the way he mingled with everybody, irrespective of age, sex, class, culture, or anything," Govinda Barua remarks. "He could get along with anybody. It didn't matter to him who the person was." Dhriti Barua, his nephew's wife, affirms that Munindra did not make distinctions between people. "If he gave my daughter an apple, he would give the maid's son an apple also. Whatever good he did for one person, he did it for another person."

Uffe Damborg noticed that when Munindra was busy with children in a Muslim village outside Bodh Gaya, even the appearance of an eminent Danish psychologist did not pull him away until he was ready, for "he was equal with everyone." This was true during a visit to Kalimpong as well, where a lot of different people—some of them very humble, others rich—came by to see Munindra and "he was the same talking to everyone." Gita Kedia comments that at Dhamma Giri "he was respected by all, from the sweeper to the highest manager and teacher, because of his love even to a poor person." Whoever they were, Munindra remembered their name and where they came from. Gita says the most important teaching from him was the *mettā* he was broadcasting to people all the time. She could feel it even after he passed away. For her, Munindra was simply "love, love, love."

Oren Sofer says, "I was always so surprised, humbled, and impressed by how he treated everyone the same. I say humbled because I thought that, since I was spending so much time with him, I was special. But he would give the same care and attention to anyone he saw or met." Rajia Devi, the local woman who cooked for the Antioch Education Abroad program in Bodh Gaya, remarks that Munindra always made a point of stopping by the kitchen to mix with the staff there and inquire, "How are you? How is your family?"

"He had a great heart," says Subhra Barua. "Uncle loved all the people; he did not differentiate between related or not related. He wanted them all to get free of suffering. That's why he wanted to give instruction. He wanted to inspire them to join in courses and to meditate." Munindra knew that the highest manifestation of love is showing others the path to liberation.

Tridib, Subhra's brother, adds, "Though Munindra-ji was uncle to me, I always had a feeling that he is a person who has a home, a family, in every part of the world. Even the way he speaks to a fruit seller or a rickshaw puller, as if they've known each other for a very long time, so close, so intimate—the whole world was his family. Such was his nature."

All in the Family

Robert "Buzz" Bussewitz was struck by how Munindra responded to his mother when she called up at IMS, though Munindra had not yet met anyone in his family: "He addressed her as 'Mama' and told her he loved her. He was saying that because he knew that she was a mother, my mother, and that was how he basically regarded mothers, as somebody he automatically could feel love, caring, and respect for. And he knew that, in this case, we had a troubled family. Nobody would have ever told my mother they loved her if they hadn't even met her, and he did. I was just touched by that."

When Max Schorr asked Munindra whether he had ever had any girlfriends, his playful reply surprised everyone: "I've had thousands of girlfriends, countless girlfriends who said, 'We were meant to be together.' I've had hundreds of love letters saying, 'We should settle down together.' But I love everybody." Munindra did not have "girlfriends" in the ordinary sense. He never felt a need for exclusive relationships with anyone, male or female. He explained that there are two kinds of love; one is positive and unrestricted. When we admire a beautiful flower or a big, empty sky, he said, "You can love it, but you don't want to possess it. Unbounded love is universal; it is pure. When all the dust [impurities] is cleaned away, only love is remaining. There is no hatred, only pure mind."

Part and Parcel of the Whole Universe

Munindra's kindly disposition toward others included all creatures in nature. Separately, Vivian Darst and Bob Ray took Munindra to the zoo in different cities. Both remarked about his keen interest in the animals. He insisted on stopping to look at each one.

In situations where people had to leave Munindra alone for a while, he would reassure them, "Don't worry about me. I have many companions: The ants are here, the mosquitoes are here, the birds are here, the *devas* are here. I am never lonesome." He consciously connected to and felt affection for even the tiniest insect. And he often repeated, "We are part and parcel of the whole universe. I feel affinity not only with human beings but also with the plants, with the trees. I feel very friendly with them."

Like a Mother

Perhaps because Munindra was as interested in someone else's well-being as in his own, his conduct often appeared motherly. Shyam Sunder Khaddaria remembers that when Munindra noticed a fellow leaving Dhamma Giri to travel, he said, "Wait, take some food." He went to the kitchen to get a few things for him and urged, "Carry some fruits with you." Jack Kornfield remarks, "I loved the fact of how well he cared for the people who were in front of him."

Ven. Khippapañño agrees, "His heart I feel is like my mother, even though he is a layman. His spiritual influence changed my life. His loving energy became a source of inspiration for my continued effort on the path." Barry Lapping also believes that Munindra was like a mother figure: "He was filled with love for his students because they were his children. He was always extremely available, always so happy to see you. He would sit down on the floor and hang out with you. I always appreciated that about him."

The Allure of Warmheartedness

Among the eleven traditional benefits of practicing *mettā* that the Buddha describes in the *Mettānisaṃsa Sutta* are happy sleeping and waking, a serene face, an ability to concentrate quickly, and love from other humans and non-humans (AN 11.16). Munindra certainly enjoyed these gains and more. In particular, his affectionate nature was like a magnet. His old students, family, and friends readily bring to mind this huge appeal. For James Baraz, it is "his warmth and welcoming heart as much as anything."

Shuma Talukbar says, "I never met anyone other than him who immediately would remind me of some affection; he was naturally affectionate." David Wong remarks, "I can recall his wonderful persona as vividly today as when I first met him. Every time I see him in my mind, I have this warm feeling of *mettā* and feel a smile on my face." Munindra's loving-kindness was so strong that Rev. James "Jim" Willems can still evoke the hug they exchanged after a long interview: "His heart was red-hot with warmth and love."

Jeffrey Tipp's first encounter with Munindra evoked trust because of such *mettā*. "Munindra had this sweetness that I thought, 'Oh, here's the result of practice.' It was very encouraging for me to see this. I immediately assigned who he was through having had a life of practice. That struck me, and right away I was prepared to trust what he told me. He'd respond to questions in a kindly, grandfatherly way. He was nondemanding and just supportive and lighthearted."

Gita Kedia says that Munindra's loving-kindness drew students toward him. "From the very first day I met him till today, without hesitation, there is that love. I appreciated the 'motherly' love he had for me. A kind of attraction just pulled me in. If you don't have that love, you cannot think to travel so far just to meet with him. You must feel that much attraction. This is the quality he had."

Manisha Talukbar elaborates on this aspect of Munindra's character, "He was affectionate to each and every one. Whoever came to him, he would just welcome him in such a soft and sweet manner, and instantly the person will say, 'I'm very close to him.' When he writes a letter, I have a feeling that he is conveying that feeling only to me, and yet he writes that personal way to everyone." He would give you the impression that 'you are the only person, you are my dearest one.'"

Manisha adds, "He talked to whoever sat in front of him in such a kind voice. I've met other teachers, even from different faiths, and many of them speak loudly, a little aggressively, or press to put their point forward. He spoke so softly. That's how I remember him, as the embodiment of gentleness—the way he walked, the way he talked, the way he was. He was an example of how one should live and what should be the most important thing in the relationship between one person and another—love, compassion."

Creating a Loving Atmosphere

When asked for the most important trait in a teacher, Munindra answered, "For a teacher to have love for the children because everybody wants to be happy." His love created an encouraging atmosphere. Ricardo Sasaki comments, "He had an openness that just accepted you as you were, no matter who you were, young or old, a scholar or just a beginner asking very basic questions. He was there for you completely, all ears. I don't think there is a better quality for a teacher."

For those who felt a certain coolness, dryness, or even severity in the Burmese Theravāda tradition, Munindra's gentleness provided a balance to their experience and brought them closer to Dharma. Ram Dass says that Munindra's *mettā* "made my heart go toward Buddhism. He was the person that pulled me toward it. He was so warm in his teaching method. He was inclusive: He didn't make me feel that I was cracking a secret society, but like it was family. He loved people very much. He was a sweet teacher that made me feel at home in Eastern thought."

Ruth Denison also reflects on Munindra's amiability: "I saw him like a softening atmosphere. Just to look at him and his smile and his friendliness and his delicacy. He acted not as a teaching assistant [to Mahāsi Sayādaw], but he was there as maybe the manifestation of loving-kindness and softness."

Jeffrey Tipp, who teaches in the Zen tradition, says that he learned a lot from Munindra's manner: "Zen has this really hard edge to it. People can get dry with the discipline and the uncompromising way the teaching is done. I've always known that a genuine teacher is especially lighthearted. There's a sweetness, a warmth—it's juicy—and that's really dharma teaching. It's inviting, it lets people in. Zen can be really daunting for folks. There's this mystique, and Zen has a certain aesthetic that everyone's entranced with, but it can be harsh. So I find myself just not going that way. I'm much more soft and kindly and very interested in meeting people where they are. I get that from Munindra because he was so much that way. His way of being was a teaching."

For Philip Novak, meeting with Munindra toward the end of 1976 in Bodh Gaya was his introduction to a life steeped in Dharma: "When I stepped in, Munindra was smiling and ready to see me. He was very friendly and kind, exuding *mettā*." Later, Philip saw him sitting in the sun on the porch of the Chinese temple, his "bald head above the white robes, children gathered around him," and it stopped him short in the road. As he approached the porch, he began "to see and to feel his beauty."

"Munindra could have been a great meditation master but a cold one, and I still might have learned something," says Philip. "But he was just wonderfully warm and welcoming. I felt real loving-kindness. I think that adds immeasurably to one's understanding of what one is doing while one is doing it."

Jack Kornfield concurs: "Munindra really fostered *mettā* and a kind of relaxation and graciousness that I now know are critical for the deepening of understanding and concentration." Holding positive thoughts and feelings of *mettā* counters the hindrances of ill will and restlessness and helps to lighten both the mind and the body. *Mettā* meditation also balances insight meditation (vipassanā), bringing the heart into wisdom.

We Are All Brothers and Sisters

In creating a loving atmosphere, Munindra incorporated a sense of belonging and togetherness. At the beginning of his first talk at his first retreat at the Stillpoint Institute in San Jose, California (June 7, 1977), he said,

> I am happy to meet you all, dhamma brothers and sisters. I'm new to you, but I've always been with you in spirit. *Spirit* means we are walking on the path of Dhamma, path of realization, of enlightenment. So we are all brothers and sisters. It is said that to be together in Dhamma, in practice, to meet noble beings and to live with them, is a blessing.

Ann Shawhan clearly remembers the message Munindra conveyed in his opening presentation: "We who are sitting here together are part of one family. When he said that, it was not just words. I really felt the kinship, like we've been here before and we are together like siblings."

Many years later, in the Antioch Education Abroad program, Rebecca Kushins experienced something similar through the way Munindra taught *mettā* practice. "I learned the geography of Bodh Gaya by listening to him send *mettā* out from the Burmese Vihar," she says. "It was our first month there, so we didn't know the place very well yet. At night we'd sit and do *mettā* practice. He knew Bodh Gaya like the back of his hand, and it seemed like he was sending *mettā* down every alleyway and into every shop, like he wanted it to find every place without obstruction. He would say, 'All the beings in the Burmese Vihar, and all the beings on the river road, from this temple to that temple across the river, to the Sujata village, and out to Bihar State.' We were part of a new neighborhood, a new universe, and the best way to learn it was to love it. When I would walk out into the town, it became a natural thing to say, 'May all beings on the river road be happy and well.' Then at the Mahabodhi Temple, 'May all the people here . . .' It's like that's how you travel, with love."

Winning Their Hearts with His

Munindra's behavior with everyone he met provided lasting lessons for his students. That he could speak so gladly with anyone was an eye-opener to many. One night he came for dinner at Vivian Darst's parents' home in

Seattle, after her return from Asia. She was duly impressed when Munindra managed to engage her own mother: "He actually got my mom to meditate, which was a feat beyond belief. My mom is a very outspoken, no-holds-barred kind of person. She was very vocal about what she thought of meditation. I remember watching him; he was great in how he handled her. He spent a lot of time just talking with her, and was really sweet and gracious, very kind and attentive. He was clearly attuning to her and her difficulty in sitting."

Giselle Wiederhielm, Vivian's mother, remarks of that and other visits: "You couldn't help but love him and smile and laugh when he was around. He had a way of making you feel good about everything. He was always such a sweet, pleasant person—I never saw him mad. He's the kind of person you could just open up to. I never felt restricted about what I had to say. We talked about everything. And you could depend on him being there for you."

Munindra taught all-inclusive *mettā* in everyday situations. Robert Beatty describes one such lesson in the late 1970s, during Munindra's first visit to California. "We used to go over to a lovely park just around the corner from the center [the Stillpoint Institute in San Jose] to exercise in the morning. There was a derelict sitting there, and my immediate experience was, 'Let's stay away from that guy.' Munindra, of course, went over, sat down, and started talking with him about the Dharma. He was really nice to the guy. I was very touched by that. There's no moral to the story other than that Munindra treated him like a person. The man experienced a little love in his life for a moment, and on we went."

Zara Novikoff appreciates that Munindra taught her about this kind of love. "It is hard for us to understand loving-kindness in a nonemotional sense, because we're emotional, and what we do always has an emotional lining," she says. "Loving-kindness doesn't mean that. It means wishing anyone who might not be attractive to you as a person [to have] the blessings of the dharma life and the blessings of the earthly life."

Bhante Vimalaraṃsi, who was part of the group at Stillpoint, as Marvel Logan, also shares recollections of Munindra's *mettā*. He says that his open heart had an unfailing power to transform others: "We would go out for walks in the area in the morning, and he had a kind of radar. He always seemed to be able to pick out the person who needed to have somebody that was very loving and kind talk to them. It didn't matter who it was, how they dressed, or any of that. Munindra dressed in white robes and that little Indian ice-cream hat, so a lot of people would stare at him. That didn't seem to slow him down the slightest bit. He would just walk up and get them started talking about some of the problems that they were facing, and because of his kindness, everybody liked him."

Bhante Vimalaraṃsi emphasizes that on these walks Munindra spoke to people about Dharma in everyday language. He adds, "It was very inspiring to be around somebody that had such an open heart. He always had everybody feeling good and laughing by the time they were done talking with him." Bhante Vimalaraṃsi says that there was one man in particular in the neighborhood who always seemed angry. Munindra stopped to talk to him and did loving-kindness for this fellow every day. In less than a week, this grumpy old man, who never had anything nice to say and was almost always cursing about something, any time he saw Munindra coming down the street, he would come out and talk with him, and he'd be smiling and happy and accepting."

Bhante Vimalaraṃsi notes that this man changed his behavior for Munindra only, not for anyone else. "So I started doing *mettā* for him, and he softened quite a bit, but he still had his up and down days. But the most important part of the *mettā* is not how it affects the other people around you, but how it affects you and the way you handle what arises. When there's no more reaction to a trying situation, and there's a response of openness and love, then your mind changes its perspective and you stop identifying with the negative thoughts and feelings and you start wishing that other person well and happy. It keeps your mind in balance, and that brings joy up. Munindra was really a living example of loving-kindness."

Oren Sofer also witnessed Munindra's *mettā* in a simple act. One time they were on their way to meditate at the Buddha hall of the Burmese Vihar when suddenly Munindra kicked a stone away from the path. Then he turned and said, "That is *mettā*, because someone might come and trip on the stone." Oren says, "I'll remember that sometimes when I'm just walking around and I see something really small that I can do that might help somebody else, something that has fallen and I pick it up."

Nonjudgmental Regard

Though others judged Munindra, he did not judge them. He once told Ajit Roy, "Nobody's perfect. I'm not perfect." So, despite what someone else might think of a person or of himself, Munindra would still extend *mettā*. Sometimes it was as basic as accepting how someone appeared. According to Khanti Moraitis, in those early heady days in India, when Western seekers showed up in droves, Munindra was nonjudgmental about their appearance or their habits. "People were outrageously dressed in those days. Everybody was smoking dope, and everything was going on," she recalls. "Yet I never heard him say, 'Don't do that!' He would say, 'Any substances that cloud your mind will not help you meditate.' But that's all. He never criticized anybody. Munindra had this way of getting to you, but without imposing himself on you. His was a very soft and sweet influence, which I think must have changed a lot of people's lives—it really did mine."

Munindra's easy acceptance of people also moved Stephen Strange, who says, "He had a great ability to inspire you to be better. Having seen him relate to other people, I would like to be like that—not to be judgmental, just to be open, just to have interest in others, in the way that a parent has love and affection for his children. I certainly thought of him as my sort of godfather."

John Travis found Munindra an inspiring figure as well and continues to feel his influence. "I wouldn't say I consciously invoke him, but there's almost a sense of affection that can help me act in certain ways in my dhamma teaching. It informs me," John explains. "Let's just say, in an interview, there's someone having a hard time and I recognize it. There's a part of me that goes, 'Oh, gosh, I've heard this story three times.' [*Laughs*] Then there's that other part—almost seeing the openness in Munindra's face, a kind of innocence. I will remember that quality and try to emulate it. Then I can bypass some of my own judgments or callousness to get back to that more open, truer sense."

Sometimes Munindra's nonjudgmental approach was hard for his students to understand. "I was so appreciative that he took time and cared about us," Peter Meehan says. "But he was like that with everybody, even people that I would have said, 'If you ask my opinion, Munindra, that guy's a loser.' He didn't care. He was nonjudgmental in a big way. Somehow he would lift up even the kind of people I thought were borderline nutty. I wonder whether, to a Westerner, he was too nonjudgmental. I don't know." Joe DiNardo agrees, "Munindra-ji was nonjudgmental almost to a fault" especially given that some individuals took advantage of his kindheartedness.

Seeing the Good in Others

Munindra had the uncanny ability to focus on the good in others rather than note their failings. In a situation where someone else might be smoldering in anger and resentment, he was forgiving and carried no grudge. *Mettā* had a calming effect when irritations might have otherwise riled him. "I believe in human beings," he said. "All people have their essential qualities, some good and some bad. I trust them in their goodness." Munindra knew that seeing the agreeable side of others is a proximate cause for *mettā* to arise.

Tapas Kumar Barua once asked his uncle if there were bad people in the world. Munindra replied, "There are indeed. It's not that the world is free of evil persons, but I never come across them because my vibration does not allow them to come." Munindra explained that even if someone was mischievous, by the time that person came into contact with him, he no longer was so because Munindra knew how to touch that person's heart.

Maria Monroe can vouch for the fact that Munindra found the good in others. She recollects being interested in looking through his small dharma library that was housed in several glass-fronted cabinets upstairs in the Burmese Vihar. Frustrated by their locked doors, the next time she saw him, she complained grumpily. Another yogi who was there seemed disturbed by her expression of negativity to their teacher and said, "Maria, you're so bad." But Munindra, ever kind and positive, countered, "No, no, she's good, but we must bring it out."

Unconditional Love

Munindra's unqualified regard left an enduring imprint and, for some, became a cherished healing experience. Reflecting on the years spent with Munindra in India and during visits to the United States, Jack Engler says, "I don't think first of his formal teaching, though that was immense. Nor of the many hours we spent talking. Nor even of living with him, or of his companionship, close and lasting as that was. No, what I realize I brought away from my time with him, the deepest and most important thing—and I am grateful for it to this day—was the conviction that he loved me and believed in me. That has been more sustaining than anything else. He saw my flaws and limitations, and he loved me anyway. And that, believe it or not, was a revelation to me."

Although the *Karaṇīya Mettā Sutta* likens *mettā* to the love and protection a mother expresses for her only child (Sn 1.8), for Rebecca Kushins, Munindra's loving-kindness evoked the memory of her grandfather. She describes the first time she and her group of Antioch students met him: "We were sitting in the dharma hall [at the Burmese Vihar in Bodh Gaya]. He came in, swathed in white. He just looked at all of us very lovingly with this beautiful, luminous smile, very quiet. He immediately reminded me of my grandfather, who I was really close with as a child and who had passed away some years before—I missed him terribly. If I had to think of somebody in my life who was my first dharma teacher, it would have been my grandfather because he was deaf and quiet, so I had a silent communication with him. With Munindra, I felt like I was learning from my grandfather. That was the kind of love I felt from him, the way that a grandfather would love a grandbaby."

Rebecca adds, "Mostly from Munindra I received what I felt was a totally unconditional love that beamed out from him. When I think of what Dharma is to me, that's the biggest thing. Even when he was talking about insight and these things that I tend to think of as maybe a little bit cooler (the wisdom side), there was always an easeful kind of love that wasn't so lofty. There was earth to it; I could relate to it."

Rebecca says that after the program was over and she returned to America, she wondered how to continue to practice without the guidance of this kind of teacher. "For at least a year, my whole practice was just to sit and remember Munindra's voice and, in particular, his way of saying the *mettā* phrases in his soft Indian accent: 'May you be happy and well. May you be loving and forgiving. May you be harmonious and peaceful.'" Remembering the way he was enabled her to sit with whatever came up inside. Rebecca continues, "You know how geese fly in a vee and use air from each other's wings? He was like a really big goose at the front, flapping his own kind of wings and I'm riding on that, just by remembering the way he would say things, like, 'No judging, no condemning,' or the way he would say the *mettā* phrases. If I could just remember the energy that he was passing along with the way he taught us, that love would carry me. He gave me a real sense of refuge."

For another student, Munindra's *mettā* was equally significant and transformative. "I came from a very abusive, dysfunctional family. I was surrounded by people full of anger and hate. The Dharma saved my life, because it focused on unconditional love, and I felt fortunate to be with people like that [Munindra and his coteacher Krishna Barua]. Munindra still influences how I deal with people. I always try to be open and not judge people. He would treat everybody the same way, with unconditional love and respect. It was just wonderful to watch and to be in the presence of it."

Love Yourself and You Won't Hurt Others

Munindra's *mettā* was like a stepping-stone for his students. He made it clear that it was not enough that *he* accepted and loved them. Invoking some of the Buddha's well-known phrasing, Munindra expressed the importance of self-acceptance and self-love:

> If I do not love myself, I cannot love others also. If we really love ourselves, we cannot think wrongly, cannot talk wrongly, cannot act wrongly. If you know how to love yourself, then you do not bring hatred anywhere. Mind is the forerunner of all good and evil. When mind becomes purified, it creates good karma. When mind is nonpolluted, then your action will be pure, the world will be pure. When you talk, it will be wise, nice, friendly. If you do not understand your anger and mind is influenced by anger, it becomes poisonous, and you suffer physically. When you act, it will create tension. It is the same for everybody.
>
> *Mettā* brings loving-kindness, makes you healthy. If you do anything good for others, it is good for you. Hatred never ceases through hatred in this world. Through love alone it ceases. This is an eternal law. There is no American love, Indian love—no difference. The mind is a wonderful force. Pervade your whole being with loving thoughts, from your pure heart. If you love your enemies, you will have no enemies. This is the only way, so you can be helpful to the universe.

Munindra also recommended forgiveness of oneself and others, for "it makes the mind flexible." As is traditional, before starting *mettā* meditation, he would say,

> If I have done any wrong toward my parents, my teacher, my elders, to anybody in the past, by thought, by deed, by word, consciously or unconsciously, may I be forgiven. If anybody has done wrong to me—if they have cultivated a grudge or complained or

accused or offended—by thought, by deed, by word, I forgive him completely.

More than any dharma talk, it was Munindra's *mettā*-filled presence that encouraged others to accept and love themselves. That is what John Burgess eventually grasped while driving Munindra around Hawai'i. At first, he thought, "My god, he's like Gandhi, he's like a holy man. How do I behave? What do you do if you're hanging out with the Buddha? He sees everything, he knows all about human nature!" Then being around Munindra, he realized, "I could just relax, be exactly the way I am, be friendly and kind, take care of him, and do the best I can."

Mettā, *Even When You Don't Want To*

Danny Taylor remembers an incident where Munindra patiently tried to teach the value of *mettā* to a yogi frustrated with the physical conditions at a retreat. "The German meditators couldn't stand the mosquitoes. Munindra-ji said to one who was complaining, 'You just have to love them.' He was so calm and encouraging. The German would come back and say he couldn't take it. In a very loving way, Munindra-ji would say, 'Well, you just have to love them more.' I've still got a picture in my mind of this handsome German guy saying, very agitated, 'I can't stand this! We've got to do something about it,' and Munindra-ji, very genuine, saying, 'Well, you just have to love them.' 'I don't think that will work.' 'Oh, I think it will work. You just need to be really mindful and really love them.' 'OK, I'll go and try.' Then he'd come back the next day and say, 'It's not working. I'm really having difficulty.' 'Ah, no, no, it will work. I love them all the time. They don't really bother me, because I love them.'

Danny says that everybody who heard these exchanges benefited from this teaching and could apply it to their own practice. He adds, "Munindra wasn't saying, 'I'm not going to listen to the practical needs that you've got.' He went off on the side and I think got extra netting for this character. So he was saying, 'Look, we'll be practical about it but, at the same time, you need to mend your mind here.'"

When Gregory Pai shared with Munindra that he was unsettled because of difficulty with his supervisor at work, he too initially balked at the advice he received: "Munindra said to me, 'I'll tell you what you should do. First thing tomorrow morning, you walk right into his office and apologize to him. Say, 'I am sincerely sorry for any misunderstanding or any kind of tension or problem we may have had or I may have caused in our relationship. I want to ask for your forgiveness and tell you it's my intention to be cooperative and work as much as I can in a way that you find acceptable and pleasing.' When he told me that, my first reaction was, 'No way. I'll never do that.' Munindra looked straight at my face and said, 'No, no, you really need to do this.' So I said, 'Well, I'll think about it.'"

Gregory says that he went home and thought about it, and he realized that Munindra was right. A few days later, he went in to see his boss and basically did as Munindra suggested. "I don't know how much it influenced my boss," he reflects, "but I think it softened him a little bit. But it was a kind of counterintuitive response. I mean, it's not the kind of thing you would normally do. But it is how you deal with difficult people in your life in a dharmic context to remove any cause for anger or ill will, as much as you can."

Gregory continues to recall Munindra's sense of *mettā* during moments of difficulty: "When I'm trying to figure things out or face emotional issues in my life, he comes to me—the thought of him. He was like a walking blessing, wherever he went, just by his personality and energy and wonderful, outgoing presence. I often think, 'What would Munindra-ji say or what would he do?' In a way, he's become a symbolic embodiment of the Dharma for me, a metaphor for all of that, a touchstone."

Do It, But with Loving-Kindness in Your Heart

For Munindra, living a life grounded in *mettā* did not mean allowing others to walk all over you. For instance, he clearly did not tolerate being cheated. Yet he was never nasty. "Even while haggling over every item he bought, he was always very kind," says Christina Feldman. And he advised his students to do likewise, for he was faithful to the Buddha's message in the *Kakacūpama Sutta* (MN 21): No matter how others treat you, you should train yourself to maintain equanimity, utter no evil words, and "remain sympathetic, with a mind of good will, and with no inner hate."

Sharon Salzberg recounts a memorable rickshaw ride through Calcutta with a friend that illustrates this counsel. In a back alley, she suddenly found herself in a terrifying encounter with a large man who stepped out of the darkness, blocked their way, and attempted to drag her out of the rickshaw. As images of rape and murder flashed through her mind, she felt helpless to do anything. Her companion managed to push away the drunken assailant and urge the rickshaw puller to keep running to the train station. Once Sharon was back in Bodh Gaya, she described to Munindra what had happened and wondered how she should have handled the situation. He asked her, "Did you have an umbrella?" "Yes," she replied. "Well, then, with all the loving-kindness in your heart, you should have taken your umbrella and hit that man over the head with it until he let go," he gently told her.

Where There Is Love, There Is No Separation

Saying farewell can be a cause for sorrow but, for Munindra, *mettā* flows beyond any impediment. Jack Engler recalls his final good-bye after an extended period of studying with him in India. "I was choked up," he says. "I remember standing on the path to his door in the Chinese temple in Bodh Gaya. I was not sure I would ever see him again. He came toward me, opened his arms, and gave me a warm embrace. His last words were, 'Where there is love, there is no separation.'"

Munindra constantly repeated this message in his correspondence, uplifting the recipients. Robert Pryor says Munindra's letters dependably gave him a boost. "I would be busy, working on arranging the Antioch Program, and then I'd see in the mailbox in the office this flimsy little aerogram from India. I knew what it was instantly. Just picking up the envelope and opening it, I would feel that same sense of warmth and support that I had from the first time I asked him to teach on the program. There would always be an opening like, 'I hope that you're well and that your practice is going well.' And there would always be a closing like, 'I promise to support you, and I appreciate what you're doing.' They were very warm and loving letters that always carried a blessing. It was really palpable."

Munindra consistently ended his letters with a long blessing that "went on and on—infinite *mettā*," says Ginny Morgan; and he signed them, "Yours in the Dhamma" or "Yours in the Service of Dhamma." He explained why:

> I have *mettā* always for them [the people he taught]. If they are honest and sincere, even if we are living not very close to each other, a long separation, still they are in my heart. If anybody is working for Dhamma in any part of the world, I appreciate them. I send them *mettā* for their growth, for their fulfillment. This way, though I am not physically supporting at long distance, mentally I am with them. That's why, whatever merits I have acquired, I

always share with all the people who are working for Dhamma, dedicated for the world. By virtue of these merits, may all of you live long, happily, healthily, peacefully, with prosperity, for the good, for the welfare of many.

Munindra did likewise when he said good-bye in person, began a practice session, closed a dharma talk, or expressed his gratitude. Sometimes the loving-kindness he intoned emanated in such a compelling way that, as Lynne Bousfield says, "you just got hit by the *mettā*." David Hopkins recalls such an experience at Dhamma Giri when he and a friend were ready to leave after a retreat: "Munindra stood there and said, 'Be happy, be peaceful, be liberated.' He had his hand up and I could see he was like telegraphing it with his palm. He gave us this blast of *mettā* that lasted the whole train ride to Bombay."

The send-off Bryan Tucker received at Dhamma Giri deeply moved him as well. Munindra put his hand on Bryan's head and said, "May you be happy. May you be peaceful." Bryan says that had someone else done this, he might have dismissed it as a prank or joke. But with Munindra, "it was genuine, completely unpretentious—a very, very powerful experience."

When it was time for Munindra to make his final good-byes, even as he lay dying he did not fail to radiate *mettā,* and he blessed everyone who came to see him.

> *For this is the escape from ill will, friends, that is to say,*
> *the freedom of mind wrought by universal love.*
> —THE BUDDHA, DN 3.234

mettā: from *mid* (to soften, to love) and *mitta* (true friend), as in *kalyāṇamitta*. *Mettā* is translated as "loving-kindness," "amity," "goodwill," "benevolence," or "fellowship." It is that which softens the mind and heart and results in a warm, friendly disposition that is not based on self-interest. As such, it is the strong wish for the welfare and happiness of all beings (including oneself) and generally leads to compassionate action (*karuṇā*) on their behalf.

Mettā's root meanings include "gentle," like a soft rain that saturates and cools all areas without exception, and "moist," thus overcoming brittleness and hard-heartedness.

The first of four *brahma-vihāra* (sublime abodes), *mettā* is "boundless" (*appamaññā*). As universal and impartial love, it embraces all living beings, regardless of class, wealth, ethnicity, religion, politics, or species. Unlike romantic affection or erotic lust, it is nonpossessive and without expectation of reciprocity, for it is informed by wisdom rather than delusion. It is love that leads to spiritual freedom, not to attachment.

Mettā is the ninth of ten perfections (*pāramī*) and a powerful healing formula (*paritta*). Because it purifies the mind of ill will, it safeguards one's well-being. The Buddha said that developing a mind of goodwill, even for a second, is a greater deed than providing hundreds of platters of food in *dāna*. He advised his disciples to constantly abide in loving-kindness, whether standing, walking, sitting, or lying down.

Mettā is a mental attitude as well as verbal and physical conduct toward self and others; cultivation of an innate capacity; and a meditation method leading to absorption.

11
Can I Help You?
Karuṇā (Compassion)

As we purify our mind more and more, automatically compassion comes.
—MUNINDRA

Munindra took seriously the directive that the Buddha gave his disciples to go forth and share Dharma for the good, welfare, and happiness of many, out of compassion for the world and the *dukkha* that everyone experiences. He never faltered in assisting those in need, whether spiritually or materially. He physically tended to others by making sure they had food and drink, clothing, a place to sleep, even medicine, and he cared for them when they took ill. Above all, he taught Dharma to help them come out of their suffering.

Alleviating Physical Distress

If Munindra could relieve another's physical discomfort, he stepped forward to do so. When someone showed up at his doorstep, he asked at once, "Are you hungry? Have you eaten?" And he always inquired first about a person's health.

Jack Engler arrived in Bodh Gaya early one morning in the winter of 1975 after spending several days traveling by plane, train, bus, and finally by rickshaw. Although he was cold, tired, hungry, and disoriented, this was his first visit and he was eager to get started with Munindra. Jack announced, "I'm here. I'm ready to go." Instead, Munindra queried, "How are your bowel movements?" Jack says, "His question completely threw me. As a matter of fact my bowel movements weren't too good! Anyone who has been to India knows the intestines are a first order of concern. He had the priorities right:

bowels first, then everything else. We spent the first two weeks attending to my bowel movements. Dharma teaching consisted of instructions on the use of flaxseed husks and garlic pills . . . his father had been an ayurvedic physician."

When a situation called for his urgent attention, Munindra responded without hesitation. In Bodh Gaya in 1980, Derek Ridler woke up one morning feeling very sick. "I had an Asian flu and amoebic dysentery—a double whammy. Munindra-ji pretty much dropped everything that he was involved in, which was a lot, and we got into a carriage and he took me into town to different ayurvedic and homeopathic doctors. I can remember being almost unconscious, sort of semiaware of what was going on. To me, that act was a living embodiment of the teachings. It wasn't an abstract Buddhist philosophy; it was a very human, very touching quality that really endeared me to him."

Barry Lapping also recalls Munindra's immediate compassionate action when he became ill: "I had just taken a train from Hyderabad to Calcutta and was going to fly to Burma. I was fainting and felt absolutely horrible. I was dehydrated. Somebody told me I had cholera, but I don't know. Munindra was there at the same time and he started taking care of me, and I started getting better. I still went to Burma. He was like that—he would take care of you with his own hands. In that sense, he was being the mother—and this was well after I became a Goenka student—he never stopped."

In Sarnath, Munindra became friends with a Punjabi man, Harilal, a Theosophy scholar. What happened is reminiscent of the story about the Buddha personally looking after a sick monk that his fellow monks had abandoned lying in his own filth. Munindra related the incident with Harilal:

> Harilal used to teach me Theosophy, making charts, diagrams, and all these things. He was very loving and sweet. After some time, he became very sick—boils all over the body. There was nobody to take care of him because he was always criticizing the monks; he did not like their behavior. The monks became angry with him and they stopped giving food also. So I served him, took care of him, sharing my food with him, cleaning his boils. Then one monk complained about me to the general secretary [of the Mahabodhi Society]. Mr. Devapriya Valisinha asked me, "What are you doing here? Why?" I said, "He is a guest here, living in the society. He is sick, has no support, so I am taking care of him. If

he suffers, if he dies here in that way, Mahabodhi Society will be blamed. Sir, I am fulfilling my duty toward the society because I have been grateful for living here." He appreciated my idea and agreed with me.

Even when Munindra could not offer physical ministrations to ease someone's pain, he tried to help in other ways. Saibal Talukbar was ailing from an eye disease when he went to meet Munindra in Calcutta in 1991. His condition was so bad that he could barely see. After Saibal recounted the story about his eyes, Munindra asked, "How is your fear? First, you will take a vipassanā course and come out of fear." After his first retreat, Saibal's fear was gone and his faith surfaced. He was no longer disturbed by not seeing well and became eager for further retreat. In time, his vision improved.

There's Always Room for One More

By the time Kamala Masters arrived late for her first retreat, in 1977 in San Jose, California, she was exhausted. She had had to make arrangements to leave work and have her three children cared for, and now all the regular beds were already taken. Assigned a sleeping space on the floor in the upstairs hallway next to the large bathroom for the teachers' use, she saw Munindra walking toward her. "As he approached, I remember feeling totally at ease with his presence, which was unpretentious and light," she says. "His grounded composure helped me to relax. I somehow thought he would say something mystically profound. But he just stood there for a moment and looked curiously at the mat I was putting down on the floor, then at my haggard-looking face, then at the mat again. He surprised me when he asked in a matter-of-fact way, 'Is that where you will sleep?' After a short conversation, during which he found out I was so tired mainly because I was a mom, he paused, figuring out what to do next. What I remember most about our encounter was the look of concern and compassion in his eyes, when he said (as I recall his words), 'You cannot sleep here. You must take good rest in order to practice. I will take your mat, and you take my bed.'"[1]

Kamala was not the first person Munindra made room for. While living at the Mahabodhi Society in Calcutta, he kept assorted sleeping paraphernalia on hand and shared his modest room so any visitor had a place to spend the night. At the Chinese temple in Bodh Gaya, he invited Jack Engler, studying at the Nalanda Pāli Institute of Post-Graduate Buddhist Studies, about thirty miles away, to stay with him on weekends.

Bhante Bodhipāla describes the second time he met Munindra, at a vipassanā retreat at S. N. Goenka's center in Igatpuri. Upon arriving without a reservation, he found that there was no room for him and that he would have to leave and return in the future. Upset over the state of affairs, he suddenly remembered Munindra was there and went directly to him: "The first thing he did was give me my lunch because time was running out [monks must eat before noon]. The second thing, he said, 'OK, sit, and I am coming back soon.' After ten minutes, he had arranged everything for my stay and the course."

Easing Mental Distress

There was no boundary on Munindra's compassion. As he once told his nephew Tapas Kumar Barua,

> People are very much suffering, so whatever knowledge I have learned in Burma and other places, I'll try to share so they'll also see the suffering and come out of it. Most of our problems are because of our ignorance; we are not aware. Dhamma means to become aware.

Uno Svedin still has a vivid and intense memory of Munindra's unfettered compassion during his first meditation training with him in Bodh Gaya at the end of 1966, shortly after Munindra returned to India from Burma. One night Uno was gripped by intense desperation and fear. "It was four o'clock in the morning, and normally Munindra-ji withdrew around ten o'clock at night, after having tea or a little chat with me. The next time for contact was around six in the morning when he opened the mosquito net door, which was locked during the night. Yet here I was, really going to pieces. In the end, after lots of consideration, I knocked softly at the door, fully knowing this was very unorthodox and outside the rules."

Uno continues, "At first, there was no response. Then I heard Munindra saying, 'Who is there?' 'It is Uno, and something terrible is happening to me.' A warm voice then came, 'I am coming, I am coming.' He opened the door and there he was in his nightclothes. I burst out crying bitterly, shaking, wobbly from the terror I felt. He put his arm over my shoulder and let me in.

'What is happening?' he asked. 'I will put on some tea and we can talk.' What a wonderful bridge to sanity and order! Just listening to his voice provided lifesaving medicine. Later that morning, when my tears had dried up, he gently put me back to practice in a reencouraged way."

Almost forty years later, as he recounts this episode, Uno's eyes fill with tears and the warmth of gratitude wells up in his throat. He says it was one of the most powerful moments of his life, "to have gone over the cliff and to be saved by Munindra's sheer presence and kindness at the right moment."

Munindra's compassion was clearly gentle. In 1989, when his elder brother Sasanka Mohan Barua passed away, his daughter Subhra was overcome with grief and sadness. After a few months, she went on retreat with Munindra, but she was in turmoil there. "When meditation was going on, I felt it increased my sorrow because it came out from a deeper area of the mind," she says. "One day, it came out so big that I could not control myself and I cried when I was sitting in meditation. My uncle told me not to meditate: 'You just rest in your residence and watch it. Don't hold on to it. Just release it automatically. Just be mindful.'"

The story of how Dipa Ma emerged from all her suffering is perhaps the most dramatic of Munindra's compassionate interventions. According to her daughter Dipa, a series of tragic events caused her mother so much *dukkha* that she fell into a highly disturbed state. "My mother was married at twelve years old, but not until age thirty-three did she have her first child, a girl. But after four months, her baby died. I was born two or three years later. Then, two years after my birth, a brother was born, but he lived only a few days and died. My mother became like a mad person, very crazy—sorrow, lamentation, everything. From this shock, she got high blood pressure and heart disease. About five or six years later, in 1956, my father died. This was another great shock and she became more crazy. She could not speak, she could not do anything, not even walk properly. Our neighbors looked after me. (I was six or so years old when my father died.) People tried to console her, saying, 'Don't be like that. Everybody will die. Please pay attention to the dhamma life and to Lord Buddha. Please do *pūjā* [religious ceremony].' But at that time, it was no use."

Dipa continues, "About one or two years after my father's death, Munindra-ji heard about my mother from some people at the Mahāsi Sayādaw center and came to see her. Because she was in such shock and couldn't speak properly, Munindra-ji was talking, talking, talking—preaching the Buddha's words: 'Everything is impermanent. Everything is suffering, sorrow, and lamentation. We have to remove all of these. As long as we live in the world, we have to do good karma, good deeds.' She became a little bit calm and quiet. After his talking for about one hour, she said, 'My life is no use. I do not want to stay any longer in this world. I don't know what to do.' He kept trying to calm my mother. He spent at least two hours talking with her that day, and he came regularly, every day, for at least two weeks. After three or four days, she was improving a little bit. Then, after two weeks, she was twenty or thirty percent better."

At that point, Dipa says that Munindra visited her mother once a week or so. "After two or three months, when she became calmer and quieter, he advised her to come to the Mahāsi center and meditate there. My mother said, 'I have Dipa here. She's going to school. Who will look after her?' Munindra-ji told a neighbor who had three or four children herself, 'Please look after her like your own child.' She said, 'Yes, OK.' Then my mother went for two months. Munindra-ji showed her the technique, the process, and Mahāsi Sayādaw preached, but my mother doesn't understand the Burmese language. When Munindra-ji told Mahāsi Sayādaw what was happening with her and some other Bengali people, he said, 'Whenever I preach in the hall, they can come and meditate and, after that, any report or anything they want to ask about meditation, please talk to them.' After the retreat, she was fully recovered from mental misery, and also physically, by the practice of meditation. Through Munindra-ji's advice and guidance in vipassanā, she advanced very much and very quickly. Everything happened through the guidance of Munindra-ji. His contribution to my family was so great, so great."

Once Dipa Ma released her extreme suffering and was healthy again in mind and body, Munindra encouraged her to teach others because of the depth of her realization experience. She became an accomplished meditation master in her own right.

The Thief Who Refused Munindra's Help

Not everyone was keen on accepting Munindra's help. While he was staying with Kamala Masters on Maui, a curious incident occurred. Because Kamala was working, she had to leave Munindra alone at home for hours at a time, but she would come back in the middle of the day to check on him and bring him lunch. On one such day, Munindra told her he had heard someone walk in, so he emerged, in his white robes and shiny, bald pate, from the back room into the hallway to see who was there. His unexpected and unusual appearance not only surprised the intruder—whom Munindra described as looking disquieted—it also terrified him. The man screeched and ran out of the house into the backyard, where he had left his bicycle. Munindra followed him, calling out, "Wait, wait. Can I help you?" He had no clue as to why the man had illegally entered the house, but his first inclination was to offer assistance to someone in obvious distress.

Only when the police arrived to ask questions did Munindra learn the facts. For one thing, the man was actually trying to rob the house. People in the area knew that he broke into homes to find drugs in the bathroom. The neighborhood also believed that Kamala's house was haunted. It had stood empty for a long time before she and her then husband bought and remodeled it. The intruder thus assumed that Munindra was a ghost. But all he was trying to do was extend his compassion to a person who seemed disturbed.

Do What You Can

Although Munindra had no training as a psychotherapist, social worker, or counselor, he still tried to be of service when he heard of difficulty in a family. During one of his visits to IMS in the early 1980s, he learned that Buzz Bussewitz was dealing with a challenging conflict between his mother and sister. "He ended up coming back to my house with me. It wasn't solely to be an intermediary, but he kind of presented as somebody who offered help as a Buddhist emissary. I think the fact that he was from another culture made him, if not more objective, at least an outside person," says Buzz. "It's not like we sat down and had great talks with my folks, but it helped us bring about some change regarding my sister. All in all, it was some years before that intolerable situation got resolved. Anyway, Munindra was brave enough to step into a hornet's nest. Almost nobody did that. I felt a lot of appreciation for him to do this. That actually was more meaningful to me than most anything else that he did."

Even when he could do nothing directly, Munindra's compassion shone through. According to Jeffrey Tipp, during a retreat at Cultus Lake, Oregon, in the late 1970s, one of the yogis had a psychotic break. "Munindra-ji was really concerned for him and he said, 'You have to be sure to stay with him; don't let him be alone.' We were to walk around with him and be with him," says Jeffrey. "I think he talked with him too, a bit, but it didn't matter what you said. I mean, he needed medication really. So we just kind of shepherded him through the retreat and, when we got home, stayed in touch with him."

Munindra knew that, sometimes, the most compassionate action is simply to be with someone, without doing anything special. Oren Sofer describes their last meeting: "My heart was really in anguish at leaving him and knowing that I might not see him again. We were on the stoop of his little cottage [at Dhamma Giri] and I was just crying and crying. He started walking with me as I left because I was still crying. I think his arm was on my arm. There was this sense of he didn't know what to do because I was so upset, but he was staying with me. We walked a couple of yards, then turned the corner onto the next path and took a few more steps. I stopped and turned to him, took his hand, and said, 'It's OK, Munindra. I'll be OK.' And he sort of nodded and said, 'Oh, OK,' and turned around and walked back to his cottage."

Compassion without Burnout

Munindra's bountiful compassion never led to the burnout so prevalent in the helping professions, because he balanced it with wisdom and equanimity. He knew that each person is heir to his or her own karma, something about which he could do nothing. He was able to volunteer succor without overly identifying with or taking on another individual's problems. Yet his sensitivity was "just remarkable," says Gregg Galbraith. "I saw him doing interviews. Someone would come in and was troubled, struggling to understand the teachings. He understood that they were troubled, maybe emotionally or with some personal trauma, and he would address that. Rather than try to throw the Dharma at them or take them somewhere where they weren't ready to go, he spoke to people on their level. He was very gifted at that. People knew that he heard them, connected with them."

Gregg continues, "He saw a person as a whole and would communicate with all their interests. Sometimes people would come to talk to Munindra as a teacher and his whole conversation with them might be very mundane, about their family or situation. But behind it, he was really fulfilling something in them, helping them connect to the Dharma and also going to the heart of the matter. You can preach to somebody, but it may not be what they need to quench their thirst. He was a brother to anyone on the path. He wasn't there to take you; he pointed the way. He was truly a *kalyāṇamitta,* a spiritual friend."

Compassion for the Dead

Munindra's caring extended even to the dead, specifically to the suffering of a female ghost in Bodh Gaya. Brahmacharya Jīvānanda, the superintendent in charge of the Mahabodhi Temple after Munindra left for Burma, told him several times that a spirit was living in the large shady tree in front of the temple committee office. He had seen it himself on various occasions, because he used to walk around the temple reciting *suttas* (discourses by the Buddha) at four o'clock in the morning. The sound of crying, along with big birds flapping their wings, started in a tamarind tree in the Muslim burial ground and then moved to the big tree. He saw a white shadow coming down from the tree and going toward the corner, by the side of the temple, toward the village.

Munindra discussed the matter with some monks. One of them, a psychic, said that a spirit was suffering and if anybody were to do some good karma and share the merit of it, she would be released from her sorrowful state. When Munindra inquired in the Muslim community, a mullah (a local Islamic cleric) passed on a comment he had heard that a long time ago a pregnant Muslim lady had been killed and buried near the tamarind tree. Munindra asked whether anyone would like to do a good deed for her, but nobody did. So he took it upon himself to carry out the Buddhist custom of *sanghadāna* (donating food and clothing to monks), with the intention that the merit he earned would be transferred to this suffering spirit and free her from her turmoil. He invited ten monks to the temple committee office and gave them their daily meal and new robes. After this, no one heard the sound of crying or saw the white shadow again.

Inspiring Compassionate Action in Others

Munindra's selfless compassionate behavior inspired others to follow his lead. Some of his students went on to become dharma teachers themselves; others are engaged in various fields for the greater good. Gregory Pai reflects on how Munindra profoundly affected him, especially since his retirement from government work in early 2002. "Basically, I started to do the kind of things that I wanted to do while he was still alive: to spend more time taking longer retreats, deepening my practice, and getting more involved with teaching, but not the traditional sort of dharma teaching. It's been more in the area of working with hospital patients, prison inmates, and veterans. I'm currently running several programs that bring the Dharma to people who ordinarily wouldn't have access to it. It's not been an easy path; there have been some successes and some not so successful attempts. I don't know what it is that drives me to do this work, but somehow I see Munindra-ji behind all of this. The poor, uneducated, and disadvantaged don't even know that the practice exists, and these are the ones who probably need it most. Munindra was a big influence in my moving more and more in that direction."

Understanding the Nature of Compassion

Pat Masters recalls Munindra's help in better understanding what *karuṇā* is. "He said the actual term denotes an active element; it's almost a verb. In order for it to really be compassion, it necessitates intention and action. There's no distinction between self and other, of course, and then [there's] the idea that you're [not only] feeling with but you're also acting with."

When someone asked where compassion comes from, Munindra explained its development:

> Automatically this comes because meditation is actually cultivation of nongreed, nonhate, nondelusion. Greed, hatred, and delusion are the factors of darkness—they darken the mind. Where there is hatred, there is no *karuṇā*; where there is love, *karuṇā* automatically follows. As we eliminate more and more the impurities, the defilements, the mind becomes purer and purer. Then compassion comes. When we cultivate meditation, at that time the mind is pure, so inherently you are developing *karuṇā*. But there is also a special way to develop it by meditations of loving thoughts.

Munindra was referring to the instructions that the Buddha gave over and over to pervade each of the four directions with a mind imbued with compassion: also above, below, around, and everywhere, to oneself and all beings, "abundant, exalted, immeasurable, without hostility and without ill will."

Unlike human beings, animals cannot meditate, but they can perform acts of compassion, good karma. Barry Lapping remembers an occasion when Munindra and S. N. Goenka were walking along the main road in Bodh Gaya and they saw a male dog taking care of abandoned puppies. He heard

Munindra say, "That is the kind of act that would help bring this animal out of the lower realms."

Munindra was clear that compassion is essential for peace and happiness not only in this life but also in future rebirths. His own behavior reflected not a trace of enmity toward anyone. Even when others criticized Munindra or abandoned his friendship, he was likely to express compassion for them—out of an understanding of karma and ignorance—rather than anger and resentment. Nor did he hold grudges about whatever had occurred. Even as he lay dying, he was more concerned for the visitors who came to pay their last respects than for himself. As long as he could speak, he shared Dharma with them, hoping that it would lead to the relief of suffering.

Develop meditation on compassion; for when you develop meditation on compassion, any cruelty will be abandoned.
—THE BUDDHA, MN 62.19

---

karuṇā: from *kar* (to do or make). Translations include "compassion," "compassionate action," and "active sympathy." *Karuṇā* is the desire to see the end of one's own or another's suffering and distress.

The second of four *brahma-vihāra* (sublime abodes), compassion is *mettā* directed toward suffering. It is not only empathically wishing for all beings to be free from *dukkha* but also trying to do something about it. *Karuṇā* is an antidote to its direct enemy—coldness, insensitivity, callousness, and heartlessness—for it purifies the mind by eradicating the unwholesome root of ill will.

Compassion is not a headlong rush to do something—anything—but is most effective when tempered by wisdom (*paññā*). There is awareness and understanding that all beings and phenomena are interdependent. *Karuṇā* is not grief or pity, its indirect enemy, because it is not overcome with sorrow.

As with the other three noble states—universal loving-kindness, sympathetic joy, and equanimity—there is no limit to *karuṇā* and no distinction as to whom one extends it. Thus, it is also called "boundless" or "immeasurable" (*appamaññā*). The Buddha advised pervading all directions with a mind imbued with these qualities. *Karuṇā* is therefore three things: the wholesome motivation behind efforts to end suffering; actual behavior to do so; and an object of meditation leading to absorption.

12

There's No Pizza in Nirvāna— Are You Still Interested in It?

Nekkhamma (Relinquishment, Renunciation)

> *On account of greed, great suffering.*
> —MUNINDRA

Too often, freedom is defined as unlimited choice—to do and get and say whatever we want. But what if that definition is actually misleading? What if, instead of contributing to happiness, it leads to confusion, tension, indecision, and dissatisfaction? Fewer options may be more conducive to a sense of well-being. Through his simple lifestyle, Munindra demonstrated that a certain degree of renunciation—not being entranced by overwhelming possibilities—ultimately leads to greater freedom, to liberation from the *dukkha* of craving.

The concept of "renunciation" (*nekkhamma*) is unpopular in a society that wants instant gratification. It smacks of deprivation and denial, of hair shirts and flagellation. Munindra did not engage in such austerities—he was no ascetic. Although he had no house of his own, no secure position, no guaranteed institutional support, and no steady income, he glowed with happiness. He knew what he liked, yet he was not fiercely attached to obtaining it, unless it was Dharma. For Munindra, renunciation became the positive assertion of dropping what might stand in the way of his deepest aspiration. Nothing—no particular food, no dwelling, no modern convenience, no special status through degrees, titles, or wealth—was as desirable as the freedom of *nibbāna* that the Buddha's narrative indicates is possible. That is why he used to ask his students, "There's no pizza in *nibbāna;* are you still interested in it?"

Munindra revealed another way to be contented: It is not about how much we can acquire but how much we can release. Knowing what is most important gave him a clear direction; in turn, this freed him to make clear decisions. He took to heart the Buddha's advice:

> If, by giving up a lesser happiness,
>   One could experience greater happiness,
> A wise person would renounce the lesser
>   To behold the greater.
> (Dhp 290)

Munindra simplified his life by eschewing whatever he felt would keep him from pursuing Dharma—anything from a telephone, bicycle, or typewriter, to marriage and property.

The Emptiness of Sweetness

In his talks, Munindra stressed that "the highest goal is freedom from greed, hatred, and delusion." Kamala Masters recalls that his emphasis on what one relinquishes at each stage of the path gave her the understanding that the purpose of practice was not to reach something or get anything. Rather, "there was always this connection with what was let go of and the purification of heart and mind."

Munindra's story of his addiction to Indian sweets illustrates how abandoning a sense desire can reduce the suffering that comes from lusting after certain pleasures:

> In Sarnath, I was very fond of sweets. I used to go to Varanasi [on foot], six miles away, to get some. It was disturbing for me, but there was a hankering to eat them. One day, I thought, "I have to finish with this somehow." So I went to a big Bengali sweet shop, the best one, and I bought several kilos of all kinds of sweets. I wanted to eat as much as I could. I went to a tree outside town and sat down under it. I thought, "I'm not going to give any portion of this to anybody. I will try to eat the whole thing." But when I opened the bag, the various smells of the sweets all together made

me sick. I tried to force myself to eat. I told my mind, "You, mind, you are always troubling me to eat sweets. Why not eat this now?" I felt a vomiting sensation from nausea and I could not eat anything. I said, "From now onward, I give up this habit." I read in a yoga book that whatever you hanker after, go into it fully, and then you become fed up. It worked.

That is not to say Munindra never ate such foods again. When he traveled in the West, people encouraged him to try the sweets they loved. To be gracious, he would taste a little bit, but he found that he was no longer used to such sweet foods and truly had no desire for them.

Munindra explained that the sense pleasures we crave, whether of sight, sound, smell, taste, or touch, are like a mirage:

> On a sunny day, at noontime, if you look in the distance, it appears there is water. But as you go nearer and nearer, you know there is nothing—it is empty. So everything is like that. From childhood, we go after this color, after this sound—oh, this looks good! All these years, we have been looking outside only, going after these sense pleasures. We misunderstand, because we think something is better there. If daily we are mindful, fully hearing the sound [or tasting the sweet], we see that it is empty, like a bubble, arising and vanishing.
>
> Once you understand, you get tired of running after this. Greed keeps the mind unbalanced; on account of greed, there is great suffering. And when something unpleasant comes, then hatred comes. When we understand this, there is the end of suffering. Unless one is fed up, disgusted, detachment never comes. And detachment brings liberation, detachment brings deliverance.

Munindra clarified that the "disgustedness" that leads to no longer hankering after something is not the same as aversion or hatred. Rather, it results from seeing the illusory nature of sense objects.

Never a Householder

From a tender age, Munindra expressed the intention not to become a householder. "I don't want to get married and have a family life," he told his brother Govinda. "I don't want to get involved. It has too many complications. If Buddha renounced everything and many years later found the answers to so many questions, why can't I follow the same path and get the answers to the questions that I want?"

Munindra said people would comment on what a handsome boy he was: "Ladies used to kiss me and pet me, and tell me about marriage. I used to cry at this." Nevertheless, according to custom, his parents made marital arrangements for him. But he did not want to get married simply because it was customary. "From the beginning, I wanted to go against the stream," he asserted.

Munindra's father made the first arrangement quite early, with the understanding that the children would marry when they grew up. Munindra "saw her and liked her." Then, as the story goes, one day she glimpsed a vision while passing a haunted house on her way home from school. Suddenly, she came down with fever and began vomiting. In less than two days, she was dead. "Her face became so ugly and fearful," said Munindra. He added that he felt neither sad nor relieved, but disgusted and detached with respect to life. "Such a beautiful girl can die in this way," he said. "I saw life is like that."

The family received two more marriage proposals. Because these girls died as well, a wedding never took place. Eventually, Munindra asked for permission to leave home and his parents granted it.

Munindra did not renounce marriage because he discounted or reviled women. On the contrary, the high regard he held for his mother is the attitude he maintained toward women his whole life. Vivian Darst remembers that "on more than one occasion, he talked about how women are really important—all that they have to go through in the raising of children." He said, "The father gives only one drop; the mother gives all the flesh and blood. This body is from a woman. We are indebted to mother. So always we should pay respect to women." When he was finally able to, he went to Bangladesh (East Bengal before Partition), where his mother still lived in the rural area of his childhood, so he could teach her Dharma.

Given Munindra's rejection of marriage, it would be easy to think he would dissuade others from it as well. By example, he did influence his brother Govinda and their niece Subhra not to marry, but he did not automatically counsel anyone against the householder life. He made it clear that "as a householder also, one can get full enlightenment. There are many beings living the family life who have attained enlightenment during Buddha's time and now also there are beings who attain this path."

From Monk's Robes to Anāgārika's Robes

Munindra did not suggest that monastic life was the only option for those who wanted to pursue Dharma. When it was necessary to do so, he gave that up too after obtaining consent from Mahāsi Sayādaw, his preceptor. He took off his monk's robes, relinquished his affiliation with the meditation center, and went back to wearing white robes and leading the homeless life of an *anāgārika,* but now with his head shaved.

Munindra left monasticism behind in Burma for at least two pragmatic reasons: survival and hierarchy. Having experienced the challenge of monkhood firsthand, Andrew Getz attests, "India is not a Buddhist country. It's not a place where the Buddhist Vinaya is understood or appreciated. You run into all kinds of practical problems. I think it was wise of him to recognize that and not put himself in that position." Secondly, there is always a certain distance between a monk and a layperson. "What I've learned cannot be shared with a layman if I become a monk," Munindra explained. "There were many people who wanted to know about Dhamma, so I wanted to reach out to them, to share my experiences with them."

Female students benefited from this decision. Tara Doyle says that "the kind of invisible barrier that one feels with Theravādin monks when you're a woman—you can't get too close or be in a car or room with them alone—simply wasn't there with Munindra. He was really like a great uncle." She continues, "I felt absolutely no sexuality coming from him. That, of course, is important and felt clean with me and our students. He was almost neuter—kind of female, kind of male, kind of neither, really, in a way that I know monks and nuns are supposed to be, but there's so much restriction around them when you're a woman. With Munindra there was just sweetness and accessibility."

As Bill "Chaitanya" Samways comments, "He wasn't exactly a monk, but he was a monk. He wasn't exactly a teacher, but he was available for teaching." This in-between status inspired many students. Christina Feldman says that Munindra was unique because "as a nonordained figure, he embodied an important bridge in lay life and yet, within that, [he was] so committed and undissuaded in his path."

Shaun Hogan says that the false dichotomy we set up between a monk and a "regular" person reminds him of feeling, "Oh, if I really had my act together, I'd be meditating somewhere as a monk." Munindra, Ed Hauben comments, was "a powerful force in understanding that one's spiritual development is not dependent only on sitting on a cushion in a monastic setting, but it's in every moment in our lives."

Being such an example was really important for the Western *sangha,* according to Jack Kornfield, because Munindra "supported many of the best things that were part of what we were creating with a dharma community—open-mindedness, curiosity, graciousness, deep devotion to Dharma—and that you don't have to be a monk to do it. By his presence, by his words, by the way he was, he supported us all in doing it."

In remembering Munindra as a renunciate, Lama Surya Das remarks, "He didn't have much stuff with him, but his stature, the breadth of his heart and mind, were huge. But no big deal, no big show. He was really a model of how to be in the world but not of it. And he didn't have a monastery. He carried his own *sīla, samādhi,* and *prajñā* with him—his own floating buddha field."

The Challenges of Renunciation

The *anāgārika* lifestyle suited Munindra's objective to share Dharma as widely as possible—from Bengali housewives to young Westerners. Still, living as a renunciate also tested his mettle. Luke Matthews remarks, "He chose a pretty tough path: being homeless and sort of prey to the winds of fortune—not an easy life. You obviously have to trust in your karma and the Dhamma to take care of you."

Not having a permanent home meant moving from place to place. In Calcutta, he lived in a room at the Mahabodhi Society or at his family's residence; in Bodh Gaya he stayed at the Gandhi ashram, the Chinese temple, or the Burmese Vihar; in Igatpuri he resided at Dhamma Giri; and during his travels he was a guest at any number of homes and centers. Ann Shawhan calls his *anāgārika* lifestyle "a very portable way of living the holy life."

Gregg Galbraith explains that while studying in Burma, Munindra had his needs met without having to ask. But once he was back in India, his situation was awkward. "He lived extremely simply and had few possessions, similar to a monk. He didn't have a job; he didn't have a means of support. He was a teacher. Generally speaking, if you're a Buddhist monk in Asia, you're taken care of because you're associated with a monastery. Munindra was not. He gave up all forms of institutional support. The only way he got to America or got around—even to go from Calcutta to Bodh Gaya—was based upon the generosity of people. He lived by the graces of his relatives or the Mahabodhi Society or Burmese Vihar and what little gifts people would give him."

Gregg explains that, for the most part, the monks Munindra knew in India had not studied vipassanā meditation themselves. (Buddhism in India had languished to the point that it consisted mainly of certain rituals and text study.) Therefore, if Munindra had lived as a monk, he would not necessarily have been respected, because he would have been outside the norm. "The people he taught meditation to were primarily laypeople who became interested in the Dhamma and Buddhism but not in a ritualistic way," says Gregg. "He taught people to go beyond the structure, the ritual, and to actually take up practice. There were many people in Calcutta who learned meditation from him, and the monks didn't like that a whole lot either. They accepted Munindra and they liked him, but it was sort of undermining their authority for a layperson to be teaching meditation. In many parts of Asia, sometimes laypeople think meditation is a job of the monks and only the monks can achieve anything. I think, politically, Munindra knew he was walking on thin ice."

Yet some monks did appreciate Munindra's precarious position. Ven. U Nyaneinda, the abbot of the Burmese Vihar in Bodh Gaya, had known him since 1976. At a commemoration of Munindra's death at the Temple Management Committee office in 2003, Robert Pryor heard him publicly acknowledge his insight into Munindra's character as a renunciate: "We monks talk about not being attached to worldly life, but most of us have temples that we manage or other responsibilities. Munindra was truly homeless. Even though he was not a monk, he lived like a monk. And he was a better monk than some of us."

Not Letting Things Control You

Although Munindra lived simply, he did not renounce quality. According to Govinda Barua, he had high standards. "If somebody brought him a rickshaw or taxi that was shabby or unclean, he would say, 'What are you bringing me? Why couldn't you get a nice clean one?' He always believed in having the best and also taking others in comfort."

Munindra admitted to indulging in and enjoying the fine accoutrements that his hosts presented to him around the world. But he was never sad to be in India without those luxuries. This provided important modeling for Dhammaruwan Chandrasiri "to just be simple, relax, not to hold on to things." He notes, "When you say *anāgārika* in the Eastern countries, it's a person who won't be traveling in jet planes and going to countries. Munindra-ji was playing around with the modern gadgets, but he didn't let them control him."

That Munindra felt free to take things or leave them was clear during one of his early visits to the United States, when Steven J. Schwartz brought him to Washington, DC. "I had spent a fair amount of time trying to organize this trip and also find a place that would be comfortable, respectful, and private, all those things that you would like to do for a teacher without spending an extraordinary amount of money. I arranged to have a friend's two-bedroom apartment to ourselves. I was going to give him the main bedroom and I was going to be in the little guest room. When we came to the apartment, he looked around. He thought it was totally delightful and immediately went into the smaller room, put his stuff down, rolled out a bed mat, and ended up staying there. It was quite a touching moment to see how, as much as he enjoyed comfort, he always leaned toward simplicity."

And when S. N. Goenka offered to have a *kuṭī* built for Munindra at Dhamma Giri, which would be attached to Goenka's own residence, Munindra declined. He preferred his small space (*kuṭī* K-9), far from the center of visitor activity.

No Attachment to Status

Just as Munindra did not let certain luxuries or foods dominate him, he did not let status go to his head. He was willing to resign from his work as the first Buddhist superintendent of the Mahabodhi Temple in Bodh Gaya, the epicenter of the Buddhist world, and leave the familiarity of India. Derek Ridler says, "What I appreciate and find inspiring was that I felt he put his life on the line. He left his homeland and went to Burma to practice hard. He took a leap into the unknown."

In the same way, he did not take on the persona and perks of being a "guru." Robin Sunbeam relates a story about how Munindra clarified his role. One day he told her that S. N. Goenka would be giving a retreat at the Burmese Vihar and suggested that she attend. "I was initially confused because I thought Munindra-ji was my guru," she says. "He told me that he isn't anyone's guru. He said he has no disciples and explained that he is like a signpost on the road: If I go too far to the left, then he points me to the right, and if I go too far to the right, then he points me to the left. He didn't want to be a guru because he didn't want attachments. He just wanted to be unencumbered and give freely."

Fred von Allmen notes, "He seemed always very unwilling to be caught by possessions, by formal courses or retreats, by somebody or something. He was somehow free-floating." Each time Munindra received offers of buildings and money, the guarantee of a place to sleep and a full stomach, and the run of a monastery in India, he declined. "I avoid all these temptations," he said.

Nonattachment and Humility

Part of not being attached to having followers was also not being attached to their adulation and obsequiousness. Christina Feldman says, with a laugh, that Munindra was definitely "not into occupying a throne. He was actually so humble in the teacher role, so unassuming and unpretentious. This was ultimately very inspiring and helpful to me."

It was as well for Ricardo Sasaki, who went to the Mahabodhi Society in Calcutta upon first arriving from Brazil in 1987. When the monk in charge informed him that he would have the room next to Munindra, Ricardo wasted no time in knocking on his door. "My first and lasting impression of him was one of deep simplicity, one not affected by fame or accomplishments," Ricardo recalls. "After our first talk, immediately he invited me to join him for breakfast in the following days, in his own nearly bare room. I guess it is the hallmark of spiritual men—as I would notice in subsequent years of my spiritual journey through Buddhist places—expressing *viveka* [detachment] and contentment in a shining way. He used to cook himself. I well remember his chapatis!"

Maggie Ward McGervey reflects on Munindra's nonattachment and simplicity: "There's so much distraction and materialism, outward-seeking, and attention-seeking in the world. It seems a very rare person who has that level of humility, sweetness, and nonattachment. He was a demanding person in some ways, kind of persnickety about certain things, like the temperature of his tea. But to have the experience of knowing somebody who was so pure in his understanding of nonattachment, so blissful and humble, is really important."

Renunciation with Preferences

For all his renunciation and nonattachment, Munindra did have preferences. In Rangoon, Daw Than Myint noticed that he was quite fastidious in everything, even in keeping a bunch of small towels. "He had one towel for wiping his head, one for his face, one for this, one for that. He liked everything very neat and tidy and clean."

Daw Than Myint also remembers preparing lime juice with sugar for Munindra, but she did not taste the juice before offering it to him. He would shut his eyes and drink, no matter how sour it was, and he would never ask her to put more sugar in. He may have been picky, but he did not complain.

Some old friends and students still joke about Munindra's style and the seeming contradiction between renunciation and having strong preferences. Tara Doyle says, "At the big level, he seemed to have been pretty free, and in the little things, he was particular." But he was also able to not get upset about the little things, according to Robert Pryor: "He would say, 'I really need a certain kind of chili, Denise [Till].' And she might say, 'Munindra-ji, we can't get that today.' He'd say, 'Oh, OK.'"

Attachment to Dharma Books

While Munindra was willing to give up what most others would not care to, he did not let go of his dharma books until the end of his life. He loved books even as a boy. Because he was such a good student, his village teacher permitted him to take whatever he wanted from the school library and to select a prize for being first in his class—any book on a list from Calcutta. Between books at school, his father's books, and what people gave him—all translated into Bengali—Munindra read widely as a youth, including such Hindu classics as the *Ramayana, Mahabharata, Bhagavad Gita*, the *Upanishads*, and the *Puranas*.

Munindra's love of books also translated into collecting them, especially because he welcomed literature on the spiritual life from any tradition. As a result, he received thousands of publications from people wherever he resided or traveled. By his own account, when he returned to India after nine years in Burma, he brought twenty-seven crates of books and booklets on Dharma in Pāli, Sanskrit, English, and Burmese. Unfortunately, due to improper storage, rats ruined many of them.

Munindra created libraries wherever he was. The first one was in his parents' home, where he built a bookcase himself. Later, he was responsible for the Mahabodhi Temple libraries in both Sarnath and Bodh Gaya. He kept a personal library in his own room. He also donated many books to existing libraries. When he passed away, he was in a bedroom across from the library he had established in his family's meditation room.

Lama Surya Das remembers Munindra's library in Bodh Gaya. "He was staying at the Gandhi ashram, but many of his books were in a locked bookcase upstairs in the meditation hall at the Burmese Vihar. People were always trying to pry it open (the lock would hold, but the doors would bend a little), and Munindra didn't like that. The books he had, nobody else had or could get in Bodh Gaya. And he really didn't want them all to disappear and end up in one person's hands instead of being available to groups. One could say, in a loving and laughing way, he was very attached to his books. That's probably the only thing I remember his owning or being attached to."

Happy Everywhere

As a renunciate, Munindra did not let go of everything, only that which was superfluous and unwholesome to his life in Dharma. Relinquishment was not a rejection of the cornucopia the world offers but a means that moved him toward contentment. Instead of the restlessness of wanting this or that and the anxiety of keeping and protecting it, he felt the ease of not grasping. He gave freely of whatever he had and thereby gained peace of mind. The absence of a house, money, or other possessions held no negative connotation; rather, he enjoyed the richness of its benefits. During a stay at the Barua family house in Calcutta, Oren Sofer once asked him, "Munindra-ji, does it feel good to be home?" He replied with a smile, "Wherever I am, I am home, so I am always happy."

If, having seen the drawback of sensual pleasures, I were to pursue that theme; and if, having understood the reward of renunciation, I were to familiarize myself with it, there's the possibility that my heart would leap up at renunciation, grow confident, steadfast, and firm, seeing it as peace.

—THE BUDDHA, AN 9.41

***

nekkhamma: from *naiṣkramya* (to go forth or out, as into the homeless state of a monk); or from *naiṣkāmya* (turning away or departing, specifically from *kāma,* sense desire). It is understood as the absence of desire, the presence of nongreed, freedom from sensual lust, or renunciation of worldliness. It is also the relinquishment or restraint of unwholesome mental states, such as anger, and unskillful actions of body and speech.

Rather than deprivation, *nekkhamma* points to the choice of abandoning that which leads to more *dukkha* so as to cultivate that which brings lasting happiness and peace instead of momentary pleasure. The third of ten perfections (*pāramī*), it serves to reinforce virtue (*sīla*). As *nekkhamma-sankappa* (thought free from lust), one of the three kinds of right thought (*sammā-sankappa*), it is the second link of the Eightfold Path. A sense of spiritual urgency (*saṁvega*) is the proximate cause of *nekkhamma.*

13

Joy Is a Factor of Awakening

Pīti (Delight)

> *Dhamma doesn't mean you have to look for suffering.*
> —MUNINDRA

Although the Buddha articulated the first noble truth as the reality of *dukkha* (unsatisfactoriness), sculptures and paintings depict him with a smile on his face, not a frown. Munindra acknowledged this teaching: He was never in denial about the pain of loss, sickness, aging, and death during his long life. But he was not grim or dour. His default setting was joy, not despondency or querulousness. Photographs and videos show him smiling, even beaming.

Munindra knew that zestful interest and enthusiasm are highly important to awakening. Otherwise, one would become sullen and indifferent to Dharma, averse to meditation, and even morbid about practice. His cheerful demeanor and exuberance for life were exactly what spiritual seekers needed to lighten their solemn attitude.

Natural Joy

Students and family alike recall that Munindra went about with an overall lightness and ebullience. His brother Govinda Barua says, "Wherever he went, he enjoyed everything." Whether engrossed in study, taking care of a temple, teaching, or sightseeing, Munindra definitely enjoyed himself. And others enjoyed him. According to his nephew Tridib Barua, "Because of his childlike nature, he used to attract children."

Munindra's delight arose spontaneously whether alone or among people. When someone asked him, "Do you ever get bored?" he replied,

> Why should I be bored? I enjoy my life. I enjoy nature—trees, plants, sky, insects—observing the smallest thing since my childhood. When I first came [to Bodh Gaya], at that time, there were no monasteries here. I was alone, but I didn't feel lonely in my life. I used to visit the river [the Niranjana, a dry riverbed in Bodh Gaya]. It was like a desert. On the sand, I used to see different kinds of ants collecting food and some little plants with flowers of beautiful colors. I felt friendly with them. It gave me great joy seeing this nature. Alone in the dead of night, sometimes I used to walk—cricket noise was there, sometimes moonlight. I enjoyed my aloneness. I learned many things being alone.

Years later, when students expressed concern about leaving him by himself in the house or having him wait in a grove of trees while they hiked higher up a mountain, he reassured them, "Don't worry about me. I have many companions here. I am never lonesome."

A Sense of Humor

Although serious about practice, Munindra had a sense of humor. "He was always cracking jokes," David Gelles comments. "Maybe they weren't one-liners, but I certainly remember his laughter. He was amused, but not in a trite way; he was able to laugh at circumstances." Jeanne Smithfield adds, "Everything was funny with Munindra-ji. He was a sweet, sparkling little man trying to learn to be in a totally new Western world sharing Dharma. He approached almost everything with humor. He was a lot of fun."

Munindra used laughter as an aid to teaching. Carla Mancari observed how he handled groups of people who came to visit him during a stay in Lake Worth, Florida, while recuperating from an unexpected recurrence of malaria in 1983. "I remember him teaching with stories. He'd always tell some funny stories and make people laugh. He made everything very light when he was teaching. He seemed like a little boy to me because he laughed so much."

Munindra's good humor and lightheartedness—what Peter Martin calls his "impish, elfin quality"—extended to a willingness to play along with his students, even to letting them dress him in Western garb. John Orr recalls an episode at IMS that many found hilarious. "The staff and some of the teachers put on a skit for the yogis on Halloween night. Munindra-ji came out with a black wig on, combed out very nicely, and people just howled, it was so funny."

Larry Rosenberg concurs, saying, "He knew how to have fun." He relates an incident that occurred in the staff dining room at IMS after a meal. "The custom then was that everyone washed their own dishes. Munindra-ji left his dishes, so one of the staff, a cook, very shyly said, 'Excuse me, Munindra-ji, but here we have a division of labor.' He was trying to say, 'Please wash your own dishes.' It was the second or third time Munindra-ji had left his dishes there. Munindra said, 'Yes, yes, yes, I believe in division of labor as well: You cook and I eat!' He wasn't being a wise guy, and everyone broke up. I don't remember how it got resolved, whether he washed his dishes or someone swooped in and did it for him."

"He enjoyed living, and that is infectious," Larry adds. "It was also not in opposition to what he was teaching. It was the same thing."

Contagious Joy

"Unforgettable was Munindra's capacity for joy," says Matthias Barth. "He could shake with laughter; but, even deeper, was his silent joy." Matthias remembers making parcels of secondhand clothes with him, to be sent from America to India. Suddenly, Munindra stopped and started to celebrate a formal sharing of merit. Matthias continues, "He shared the merits of our good deed with all the beings in the house, in the surroundings, in the country, in the world. And, in doing so, he created a joy of such intensity that it overwhelmed my emotions. He really was a master in this field."

Andrew Getz recalls the effect of Munindra's friendly and warm presence in Bodh Gaya: "Every time he came around, he'd exude a kind of joy and lightness that was very inspiring. One day, it was Christmas Eve and I was going into the Mahabodhi Temple and he was coming out. He just had this big smile on his face and was saying, 'It's the birth of Christ. It's the birth of Christ.' He seemed so happy about it, and it was infectious. It made me think what a joyous moment it really was."

Sara Schedler recalls, "His presence was so sparkly. He just got a kick out of everything. He had this ability to make himself laugh. Folks who are pretty developed spiritually really get a kick out of life and themselves. They can make fun of themselves so easily, but not as any kind of weird ego trip. It's just totally natural."

Grahame White noticed that Munindra would joke and tease even with his Asian women disciples, who would afford him absolute respect in the traditional way.

A Lighter Side to Dharma Life

Munindra offered many people a taste of the joy that comes with following the Buddha's path. Peter Skilling feels that he taught not only through his exemplary behavior but also because he was "always very full of good spirits." Peter continues, "Within the Pāli tradition, he was one of the most learned people and also one of the most pleasant and human. The learned Burmese monks who teach meditation that I've known are usually rather somber. Munindra-ji was never somber. He wasn't frivolous, but he always had a certain kind of infectious joy. He's one of those people who live the Dhamma in their way and show people that it's a good way to live, precisely because of their compassion and happiness. Especially for people who happen to be in a miserable or embittered state, such a person is very important because they see that there are other ways to live."

Although we tend to think of suffering as the catalyst for evoking compassion, Sharon Salzberg suggests that rejoicing can also generate a feeling of deep connection with others. When someone once asked Munindra why he practiced meditation, his students expected an exalted response. Instead, he replied, "I practice meditation to notice the small purple flowers growing by the roadside, which I otherwise might miss." Sharon says, "When we start to notice the small purple flowers, we come to want others to also see them, for their solace and enjoyment. This is the compassionate wish to share delight."[1]

Munindra talked a lot about being happy, says Giselle Wiederhielm. "That was his big message—happiness. He tried to live his life that way. In the true sense, he was following his heart and his gut feelings. He really loved life, and he showed it. I'm sure he had some unpleasant moments and disappointments—I even witnessed that—but he dealt with that too and really practiced what he was preaching."

Arousing Joy in Others

The combination of Munindra's lightness of being and emphasis on joy affected many students, including Steven V. Smith: "He really incited that joy factor right to begin with because he'd been practicing for so many decades, and yet he still had this novicelike, childlike interest in everything. It was his enthusiasm, his zest, and his deep love of the Dhamma that ignited my interest. Whenever I would hear him talk, I would experience a lot of *pīti* in my mind. I felt happy around him. I'd go off feeling a lot of inspiration and excitement." Even now, Steven hears Munindra's voice suddenly pop up in his mind and say, "Keep it simple. Be light."

Memories of Munindra still touch a place in James Baraz's heart: "If I'm talking about something and remember him or hear his name, his unique energy tickles me, in the best sense of the word, just with delight and joy. I have an image of his face, his eyes twinkling and a big smile. And I can hear his chuckle. It's like he was always seeing life as a delightful surprise and blessing and gift and could full on open to life as it is, with a deep sense of appreciation."

If You're Too Serious, Your Practice Lags

While inspiring students with his zestfulness, Munindra also dispelled a misinterpretation too many made about practice. He kept things more lighthearted so that people could practice without feeling so grim. Bhante Vimalaramsi says that one of the things that drew him to Munindra was "a spontaneous kind of laugh that would just open your heart—that was really magic." He explains, "Vipassanā had a tendency to make you overly serious, and he wouldn't allow that to happen. Many a time, I remember him saying something that would make somebody smile and giggle to themselves, maybe not laugh out loud. One time, I did ask him about that, and he said, 'Joy is an enlightenment factor.' If you have joy in your mind, your mind is very alert and your mindfulness is very quick. When you don't have joy, you might lose that enthusiasm for the practice."

This was a valuable lesson for Wanda Weinberger as well because her first exposure to the Theravāda tradition left her feeling it was a heavy, impersonal, and solitary practice. "Munindra-ji showed me what was missing, which was lightness and simplicity. He opened the door for me to see the Dhamma as light and beautiful and to find the joy in it all." Wanda says that Munindra taught her that this is "a practice with a smile," and she recalls a particular incident involving Munindra's smile. One morning, just before meditation practice was about to begin, Munindra was standing by the Buddha hall waiting for people to enter. "All of a sudden," says Wanda, "he put his hands to his mouth and turned around to walk back to his room. He realized he'd forgotten his teeth! He came back with a big smile. This was my first introduction, and this sparkling, beautiful man was just breathing and living it."

Munindra's scholastic and experiential knowledge of joyful types of consciousness not only inspired students, it also enabled him to guide them. Matthias Barth says, "In the middle of days of intensive practice, he wanted me to offer a small gift to the most disturbing meditator in the room, who was a source of anger to many of us. When I did so, the bliss of heaven descended upon me! Munindra's understanding of the mind states of his students was very precise. He knew just when it was time for a hint or a teaching. 'There are sixty-two kinds of happiness,' was his simple commentary when I reported my experience."

The Joy of Dharma

As much as nature evoked great delight in Munindra, nothing gave him as much joy as Dharma. Howard Cohn remembers asking him numerous questions about it and thus provoking a reply that seemed to include the entire Tipiṭaka—the Four Noble Truths, the Eightfold Path, the seven factors of awakening, and so on. "It would all come as a response to the simplest question," he says, laughing. "He was like a flood of Dharma. It was joyous to be in his presence and to listen to that, even though I would shake my head because I would get this massive teaching, which was very useful and wonderful, but more than I asked for. What most comes through is his brightness and effortless capacity to share the whole Dharma—the full monty—and the joyousness with which he held it."

Philip Novak says, "There was a palpable delight in him over being able to expound the Dharma to another human being." Sara Schedler adds, "I felt like he was really joyful working with us young folks, who had our whole lives ahead of us. He seemed really excited to introduce us to the Dhamma."

Maggie Ward McGervey describes the way Munindra did that: "He never used a big, strong voice; it was always very soft. Now, with my older, more mature perception, I see that there was a sense of rapture, an ecstasy in the way that he expressed his love of the Dharma, yet it was so unimposing. When we think of rapture and ecstasy, we often think of a passionate kind of outward energy. He wasn't that way at all. He was just steady, calm, and unimposing. He was so blissful, but in such a quiet and self-contained way. His voice and physical stature were quiet, yet when he spoke, it was coming from a place of absolute certainty and bliss when it came to the wisdom of the Dharma and the wisdom of impermanence."

Sympathetic Joy

Munindra both personified and taught the quality of sympathetic joy (*muditā*). He was inspirational in terms of living simply, but he also told Jacqueline Schwartz Mandell, "You just don't need a lot of things. Whenever anyone gets something, you can have sympathetic joy for them. You can be very happy for them, but you don't have to have that thing." Jacqueline observed that when somebody did get something, whether a material item or an insight, he was visibly pleased.

Munindra never fulfilled his dream of creating a dharma center, but he was supportive of the efforts of others to create retreat centers and shared in the happiness of their success. As he once told his nephew Tapas Kumar Barua, "I have not been able to make it, but somebody has, so why don't you make use of it? Take benefit of it."

"Here was somebody who had been an inspiration and a guide and a teacher to so many people," Peter Martin adds. "He'd come to the West many times. He was Goenka-ji's dhamma brother—they had come up together in India as teachers. And with all of this, he was living in a tiny *kuṭī*, in K-9 [at Dhamma Giri in Igatpuri], with nothing but this little space, and he was happy with what he had. That in itself spoke so much: no pretensions, not needing anything more than that."

Munindra confirmed, "I am most at home in Igatpuri. That is where I most enjoy. From my own room, I hear [chanting from the meditation halls]. It brings innermost joy in my mind when I hear Dhamma there. It brings feelings of joy, joy, joy."

Absolute Joy

Although Munindra experienced all kinds of joy—from books and nature and people and traveling—it was his realization of Dhamma at Mahāsi

Sayādaw's center in Rangoon that delivered a rare kind of *pīti*—the ecstasy of illumination, of the unconditioned—which lasted for three days. During that time, he said,

> I could not practice meditation anymore because body was in rapture: Body was dancing, body was jumping, body was floating in the air. [A] very strong force. No sleep. Just joy, joy. After three days, it became quieter. Then a state of equanimity. Faith, confidence became very powerful.

He knew that the delight of *pīti*, though pleasurable in itself, is merely a stage progressing toward other refined states and eventually to the ultimate joy of *nibbāna*.

> *For a bhikkhu with a peaceful mind,*
> *Who enters an empty dwelling*
> *And clearly sees the true Dharma,*
> *There is superhuman joy.*
> —THE DHAMMAPADA 373

pīti: from *prī* or *pī* (to refresh, gladden, satisfy, please, invigorate). It is translated as "zest," "accompanied by joyful feeling and pleasurable interest," but also as "rapture," "refreshment," "elation," "delight," "ecstasy," "exuberance," and "blissfulness." *Pīti* is not momentary pleasure derived through the senses, but the result of not clinging to ephemeral mental or physical satisfaction. In addition, *pīti* inhibits the hindrance of ill will or aversion.

Aside from delight experienced in everyday life, various degrees of *pīti* occur at certain stages in insight practice (vipassanā) and meditative concentration (*samādhi*). As inner chatter ceases and the hindrances drop away, rapture can arise as strong and joyful interest in the object of attention. Energy moves freely and refreshes both body and mind. Five kinds of *pīti* range from subtle to intense: Thrilling joy raises the hairs of the body; instantaneous joy streaks through the body like a flash of lightning; a flood of joy washes over it like ocean waves; transporting joy lifts it; and suffusing joy totally pervades it.

Pīti is the fourth factor of awakening (*bojjhaṅga*). Eleven things support its arising: recollection of the Buddha, Dharma, and *Sangha;* recollection of virtue, generosity, *devas,* and peace; avoidance of immoral individuals and association with good people; reflection on discourses inspiring confidence; and the inclination toward joy.

14

Come and See for Yourself

Dhamma-vicaya (INVESTIGATION, CURIOSITY)

> *Self-discovery is the most adventurous path.*
> —MUNINDRA

Munindra's curiosity is legendary. Like his dharma colleague the Dalai Lama, he had a fascination with how things work and liked to examine them up close—from subtle points in Abhidhamma to the details of a Danish castle, a lawn mower, or vegetables and fruits in a market. He often asked "ten thousand" questions, for nothing and no one was exempt from his orbit of interest. They started with his boyhood yearning to know what the Buddha discovered under the Bodhi Tree: "Why did he leave the common world when he had all kinds of riches? What had he attained? How did he get relieved from old age, sickness, and death? What is enlightenment? What is Buddha?" Munindra said, "He solved the problem of life, but what he found was not mentioned in the history book. That curiosity remained in my mind. It compelled me to learn the scriptures and study many philosophies under many teachers in India, but they could not give me satisfaction."

A Lifelong Student

Munindra felt there was something to learn from everyone, including his little great-niece, Pallavi "Piyu" Barua:

> I'm always learning, everywhere I go, from every person I meet. I am interested in exploring new things, new ideas, new paths. There

is unlimited knowledge in the universe! No end of knowledge! So from every side—from all plants and trees, insects and animals—I've been learning.

Not even old age, and the physical debilitation it brought, stifled his lifelong affinity to be a student at home or abroad. As Matthias Barth notes, "He wanted to see and know everything. Already on first arriving in Switzerland, on the train from the airport to the city, he stood at the window and asked specific questions about local agriculture and the operation of city buses."

Most of all, Munindra loved to examine the Buddha's teaching through any possible venue. Ron Browning says, "What struck me was his mind's constant investigation of dhammas and his intense curiosity and interest to not just see things superficially but to really penetrate them deeply: What's the Dhamma in this?"

In the spirit of scientific inquiry, Munindra could turn any event—even watching TV and movies—into a dharma lesson. Bryan Tucker remembers that in the early 1980s, Munindra asked someone at IMS to bring him the most horrifying movie, and he wound up with *The Texas Chain Saw Massacre*. He told Bryan why he watched:

> I am interested because I test my equanimity about fear. I watch my emotions rise and fall as I look at the TV. I just want to see. I know that they're not real images, but it's amazing how the mind thinks of them as real. So I'm curious about that.

One time, in India, he joined his nephew Tridib Barua and his friends to see a typical Hindi movie, *Rājā Rani*. The discussion afterward surprised his nephew: "We generally see this movie as nothing special—popular, not artistic, not very rich. Even in this very common cinema, Uncle pointed out certain qualities of people. That impressed us very much. He's a meditation teacher—he doesn't see movies a lot—but he found something special in this kind of movie. So he showed us that if you are aware, you can have some lesson from anything in the world."

Even when he did not personally view a film, he wanted to hear about it. Michael Zucker relates one such episode during Mahāsi Sayādaw's visit to the United States in 1979, which he helped organize and manage: "Munindra-ji was there for all or part of the trip. While we were in DC, I went out one evening to the movies. When I returned to the place where we were staying—a Zen center, I think—all of the doors were locked. I walked around the house. There was light on in Munindra-ji's window, so I knocked. He bid me to climb through the window, as if this were the most ordinary thing, and then insisted that I tell him the entire plot of the movie I had just seen (*Picnic at Hanging Rock*), coaxing me along and asking questions."

A movie Munindra liked to watch repeatedly was *The Princess Bride*, says Xuan Huynh: "He really enjoyed the part about the smart guy asking so many questions." Perhaps it resonated with his own questioning nature, as Robert Pryor indicates in a story about a trip to Sri Lanka in 1980, where Munindra was teaching for three months. Unexpectedly, Robert had a chance to go with Munindra to meet a renowned monk, Ven. Balangoda Ānanda Maitreya, who was then eighty years old.

"We went to a hermitage in the countryside outside Colombo. It was quite remote and lovely," he recalls. "They spoke to each other in English because they didn't share a native language. It was amazing to watch Munindra-ji in action and to benefit from his curiosity. Ānanda Maitreya was a great scholar—his room was mostly full of books—and Munindra-ji loved books, a great passion of his life, so he asked, 'Bhante, you have all these wonderful books. What kinds of books are they?' They talked about books, and then Munindra-ji started a line of questioning about what Bhante did all day long: 'When do you get up? What do you do when you get up? What do you have for breakfast? Oh, you study in the morning. What do you study and how long do you study?' Munindra-ji was very detail oriented." Robert continues, "Halfway through this discussion, a bird came to the door and Ānanda Maitreya excused himself and went to feed it. When Munindra-ji was done [asking questions], I had an incredible sense of how this amazing scholar/meditator/monk lived as a hermit. It was quite a blessing to get a glimpse into somebody's life like that. It inspired me: Now I will sometimes ask those kinds of questions of people because it's so illuminating."

Munindra requested details even when the subject was not as lofty as the life of a revered monk. While staying with Kamala Masters, he would stand, robed in white, and look on as her then husband David, covered in grease, fixed a car in the carport. She says, "David would get under the car and Munindra-ji would ask, 'What are you doing now?' And David would explain, 'You see, a car is like a human being. This is what the parts of the car are like. It has a heart and a liver—a pump and a cleaner. The tires are like the legs.' And Munindra-ji was so curious and interested."

When he had a chance to learn about another kind of machine, Munindra literally jumped for it. Kamala and Gregg Galbraith were walking with him in up-country Maui when a big old tractor came lumbering down the road after work at the reservoir. Kamala recalls, "We were sitting, taking rest, and Munindra says to the driver, 'What is this?' So the guy asked him if he wanted to come on the tractor. And Munindra says, 'Oh, yes, why not?' We lifted him up on the tractor, and he was looking at everything."

"Munindra's love of new experience and new information was startling," notes Steven J. Schwartz. "It played as much in experiencing a new environment as it did in understanding the truth about practice."

Ehipassiko

Munindra encouraged others to examine and probe too. When Westerners expressed a desire to know themselves, he extended the Buddha's invitation of *ehipassiko*—come and see for yourself. "If you want to understand your mind," he told them, "sit down and observe it." Inquiry leads to insight into the true nature of everything.

During a three-month course at IMS, Munindra urged James Baraz to engage in such an inquiry. "I was reporting an experience to him, and he asked about some subtle aspects of it. I tried to describe them. Then he started chanting and, when he got to '*ehipassiko, ehipassiko, ehipassiko,*' he had such an excited look on his face. He touched his index finger of one hand to the palm of the other, and said, 'Look! Look carefully! It's so magical—life and this moment of experience and the nature of reality. It's so compelling and fascinating—if you let it be. Take a look for yourself. *Ehipassiko.*'" James adds, "It was an instruction, but the gentlest kind of instruction. It wasn't, 'You should really look more.' It was, 'Let yourself be fascinated by it.'"

Sometimes, Oren Sofer says, Munindra would touch his shoulder or chest and say, "The whole world is right here. Once you understand this mind and body, then you will understand everything." Oren adds, "This is what I love about Munindra. There's that clear possibility of direct understanding of the absolute nature of existence in our bodies, in this world." On another occasion, after Oren had posed a slew of questions, Munindra asked, "Do you have any more questions?" He replied, "I have so many questions, but I feel like I could spend all day sitting here asking you and hearing you answer and I would still be missing the point." And Munindra said, "Yes, you are right. You have understood. Some things you can ask me, but other things you will have to see for yourself in your own experience."

Penetrating the Mind-Body Process

What Munindra wanted his students to see for themselves were the Four Noble Truths, the three characteristics of existence, the elemental nature of experience, and other features of the Buddha's teaching. He said,

> *Dukkha*—this is the noble truth of suffering. This is to be investigated. This is to be explored. This must be examined and discovered. Then comes the cause of suffering. What is the cause of suffering? One must understand, explore, investigate this.

Munindra would ask, "What is mind? What is mindfulness?" and explain:

> To understand this, the whole process of mind and body, the psychophysical process, must be investigated: What am I? Who am I? To know these things, we have to understand the composition of the whole being. According to Buddhist psychology, the whole being we call "me" or "I" is composed of two things: mind and matter, *nāma-rūpa*. What is matter here? It is body. This physical body is composed of four primary elements: earth, water, fire, air. These four elements are individual; their characteristics are different.
>
> When we say "earth element," what is earth element? There are certain layers of it. It is also known as the element of extension, the occupation of space. On the gross level, it means the hair, nails, bones, skin, flesh—there are twenty solid aspects of the body. Still, when the mind becomes silent and not talking, if you go deeper, what will you find? Their nature gets unfolded.
>
> When you sit for meditation and sometimes you feel heavy or stiff, this heaviness or stiffness is a characteristic of the earth element. Sometimes you feel hardness—it is the nature of the earth element. So, on account of hardness, we sometimes feel uncomfortable. This is called physical pain. So that is the earth element, we understand at that moment. It shows its nature, and mind knows it; mind is the cognizing faculty. So things are working in harmony: mind and matter. Earth element means matter. It does not know; it has no cognizing faculty.

When we say, "I feel heavy," "I feel stiff," "I feel hard," this hardness is not "I," not "me." It is just characteristic of earth element. When you say, "I am heavy," that is called "ego," "self-illusion," and it is wrong view about what is going on. This ego becomes a hindrance. As soon as we identify the earth element as "I" or "me," we get involved: "Oh, I don't want this!" But when there is no identification, we are not caught up by these ideas. The meditation becomes easy, experiencing from moment to moment whatever is going on. When the mind becomes composed and collected and concentrated, then only the nature becomes revealed. There will be a lot of things investigated and understood. It is the process of self-discovery.

Munindra continued this process until the end of his life. When Robert Pryor visited him in Calcutta only days before he died, he noticed that Munindra was unable to get out of bed, and remarked to him, "It must be very difficult." Munindra commented evenly, "I never thought it would take this long." Robert reflects, "It was very profound because that was Munindra-ji as a curious observer. He wasn't complaining. I thought, 'Whoa, this is the observing mind. Taking a year to die, he's examining the whole thing.' His body was just wasting away. Other people probably would have been really miserable and barely conscious, but he was still examining everything moment to moment."

Inspiring Others with Zestful Exploration

Munindra's enthusiasm for exploration and discovery was infectious. As Kamala Masters points out, "It wasn't just curiosity for him; it was joyful investigation."

As a result of Munindra's curiosity and joy, Steven V. Smith says he did not feel "pressure to perform" or as if he were trying to pass a test. "It didn't matter what was happening. The question was always: How was I mindful? What was coming up? Everything was interesting, including all the *kilesas* [defilements]. Everything had a place in understanding these things. I think he was the first one to get that across so well, not demonizing certain thoughts and feelings, but understanding them."

Munindra's delight in investigation had a powerful effect on Jack Engler. "He stimulated immense curiosity. He was interested in everything and everyone, whether it was how a particular toy or typewriter worked; why someone had left their family and come halfway around the globe to this dirty, dusty, little village; how you put a rocket or satellite in orbit. His curiosity knew no bounds, and it was all connected, all somehow related to Dharma and to living the life fully." Jack adds, "At that time I had been living my life in a relatively narrow and compulsive way. He opened that up. His energy and enthusiasm gave me permission and sanction to do that."

Munindra was utterly devoted to Dharma, yet not dogmatic. "He always recommended people to investigate, go see other teachers for themselves, read this, and find out that," Uffe Damborg notes. "His attitude to theory was also relaxed. Although he was a very learned man and had studied the Tipiṭaka thoroughly—he was an Abhidhamma *ācariya* [an Abhidhamma teacher] as well—he often said, 'Never mind what the scripture says; never mind what the book says. Try to see for yourself, investigate for yourself.' His Dharma was alive. It was not a tradition; it was a lived life."

Andrew Getz explains, "He was tremendously curious and had a very free way of investigating and exploring life, which I think, in some ways, is the essence of dharma practice. We're all aspiring to understand our minds and the difference between what's wholesome and unwholesome. But it's not necessarily always a simple black-and-white thing. It's not like this is a violation and, therefore, this is the consequence. There needs to be some sort of process to learn what's wholesome, what's not wholesome, and, if mistaken, to explore it. One of the qualities of the enlightened mind is the quality of investigating Dharma and trying to understand."

Jacqueline Schwartz Mandell says she was taken by Munindra's receptive manner in discussing any kind of topic, any kind of dharma point: "He would just dive into a very direct, interested, focused discussion. And, in the quality of that discussion, his only motivation was the discovery of what the truth was. That was extremely inspirational for me, just the dynamic of how he communicated—an investigative, open inquiry."

It was a new experience for Patti Dye Fuller as well. She remembered Munindra talking about love and asking, "What is love? If you see, hear, touch, taste, smell, or think it, what is it?" She said, "I don't know what kind of love he was talking about, whether it was romantic or familial, but it was unique for me to examine the concept in terms of breaking it apart into pieces."

For Howard Cohn, the question was not about love but about happiness. It arose at the end of a joyous day with Munindra, spent laughing and talking.

"His parting remark to me was a springboard into an ongoing inquiry. He said, 'May you truly be happy.' That may not sound like much, but what I got from this was, 'You're a happy guy, but may you *truly* be happy. There's another happiness that you really don't know about yet.' That was a significant moment. It left me with, 'Hmm, you're generally happy. You're maybe a little too busy being happy. May you truly be happy.' There was something humbling about it, and at the same time it inspired a deep inquiry. As the years went on, I understood better what he meant."

Testing and Proving

Munindra's lasting legacy for Akasa Levi is to "question, question, question." According to Akasa, the essential point, as in the *Kālāma Sutta* (AN 3.65), was "Don't believe because it says so in the scriptures, because your family is behind it, or because your guru tells you so. Burn it, test it, scratch it, drop acid on it, weigh it, do everything you can, as you would test gold to see whether it is real or not."

Gregg Galbraith says, "He was like a scientist. He wanted to fully understand the teaching and the alchemy of the teaching and how to apply it to students." That is why he was never satisfied with hearing things secondhand and spent years studying what the Buddha said. "That curiosity and interest was the big motivating factor for him," adds Joseph Goldstein.

Wanting to know things firsthand, Munindra also opted to experience the details of a monk's everyday life, such as alms round in Rangoon. Even before he became a fully ordained monk for a year, he went out as a *sāmaṇera* (novice monk) "with nearly one hundred fifty monks, sometimes two hundred, in the morning, going in a line from door to door." Munindra said, "Oh, it was so interesting for me to see, going with the eyes downcast, with the alms bowl." David Wong says that Munindra was "just full of wonder, his heart bursting out with curiosity, and enjoying everything."

Squeezing Out the Juice

Munindra found the Westerners who came all the way to India to learn about the Buddha's teaching "very sincere and honest." He encouraged them to investigate Dharma with him and was happy that they asked a lot of questions. If anyone was reticent, he would say, "If you don't squeeze the lemon, you won't get any juice." In front of a class of Antioch Education Abroad students, he urged, "You must ask me the hardest question."

Munindra set an example. Ann Shawhan laughs when she remembers being in his first group in California: "He was always asking us questions. It was like having someone from another planet figuring out what we're actually doing and why." Christine Yedica adds, "He was interested in all the different aspects of life in the West, what it was like here and how we did things. There was a lightness and delight in the process of investigation. He would also ask, 'What do you think? What about this?' because he earnestly wanted to hear what people had to say, what they thought, what they felt."

What Steven J. Schwartz most appreciated about Munindra as a teacher was his curiosity about a student's practice: "He was intensely interested in how you practiced, what you experienced, what was happening for you in the moment, in what way he might be able to help. In the same way that he would grill a guy at the Library of Congress about every book they had, he was kind of grilling you about your practice. And it was totally endearing, both generating inspiration to practice and providing very useful guidance, because his questions could determine quite accurately where your practice was and, therefore, what type of instruction or adjustments might be useful."

Munindra's interest in his students, aside from their practice, seemed unique in the world of Theravāda. Jack Engler says, "Most Theravāda teachers are not so interested in the personality or the person's life story, in the different dramas and issues that come up, particularly for Western students. They just give you the straight practice and expect you to do it. But Munindra was intensely curious about individuals. He wanted to know about their families, where they came from, what their interests were, and where they studied. He was interested in their relationships and how they found a way to the Dharma and why they were in India. He would spend hours talking with people about themselves. That was a very special quality he had. And then, gradually, he would talk more and more about the Dharma with them."

Munindra's inquisitiveness was not nosy or prying. He was genuinely attentive because he cared about others and what they experienced. During the period when young Westerners first arrived in Bodh Gaya, one yogi, who had been meditating for years, decided to take LSD and sit under the Bodhi Tree all night. When the acid trip was over and he walked back to his room in the morning, he ran into Munindra, who asked him what was going on. The yogi says, "I had to recount the whole situation to him. He asked me question after question after question about it. He was totally curious about what happened."

Never-Ending Questions

At times, Munindra's never-ending questions could try a person's patience. Steven J. Schwartz describes an incident at the end of a trip to Washington, DC, in the late 1970s. Munindra asked how they were traveling back to Barre, Massachusetts, and Steven replied, "We're going to take the train."

"When are we going?"

"Thursday in the morning."

"What time are we going?"

"Nine o'clock." The questions did not cease, especially because, accustomed to the overcrowded train system in India, Munindra was skeptical and kept reiterating the same queries.

"Finally, I said, 'Munindra, you have asked this question about nine times. You obviously know the answer. What's up?' He said, 'I want to make sure that we can get on the train.'"

"We'll get on the train. Don't worry."

"Well, do you have tickets?"

"No, you get tickets there."

"You can't get tickets there. The tickets may be sold out."

"Well, they don't sell out, because it's an open train."

"That's not possible. The train could get sold out. How many seats are there?"

"I don't know how many seats there are."

"Can't there be more people than there are seats?"

"Well, yes."

"What do they do?"

"They stand."

"Can't there be more people than there's room to stand?"

"Well, yes."

"Then why are you taking the chance? Why don't you get a reservation?"

So Steven called Amtrak to make a reservation. He was on the phone for two hours before he finally got through and made a reservation. "I told Munindra, 'The reservation is set. Are you happy?'"

"Where are the tickets?"

"I don't have the tickets."

"How can you have a reservation without having the tickets?"

"Because we did this on the telephone."

"How can you make a reservation on the telephone?"

"That's the way it works in the United States."

Steven continues, "He doesn't believe me and [says], 'You don't have the reservation, do you? You just didn't want to get the reservation, so you told me you stayed on the phone.'"

"Munindra, I wouldn't do that. I have the reservation. Here's my reservation number."

Steven continues, "He says, 'I don't think this is going to work.' I said, 'It's going to work, believe me. We now have a reservation on a train that you don't really need a reservation for.' The flip side of Munindra's curiosity was his doubting mind, not doubting about the truth, but doubting about whether things will really work in a particular way. It's that doubting that gave rise to the curiosity."

Steven says that when they got to the Amtrak station, he went to a ticket machine, put in his credit card, and out came the tickets. "Munindra looks at the machine, then looks at me and asks, 'Where's the man?'"

"What man?"

"The man who gives the tickets."

"There's no man that gives the tickets; they're in the machine."

"Well, where's the man who takes the money?"

"There's no man who takes the money; it's invisible."

"Invisible money?"

Steven continues, "He sat me down and said, 'You're going to explain this to me because I don't understand how it works.' So I explained to him that I was putting a piece of plastic into a machine and a message was being sent from this machine in Washington, DC, to Tulsa, Oklahoma, which was the center for American Express. The message said, 'Bill Schwartz's card, ninety-five dollars for two tickets.' Once that message was sent, another message was sent to Newark, New Jersey, which was the center of the Amtrak system, to release two tickets. And once that message was sent back to Washington, DC, to this machine, two tickets came out. He was so amazed and kept saying, 'How can people in Tulsa know what people in Washington and Newark are doing instantaneously?' Then suddenly he made the connection: 'That's exactly how the mind works. All of this happens instantaneously, but we don't see it—memories, conditioning, karma, or things that happen over time and space. It is all invisible, but the Dharma makes that visible.'"

Steven explains, "He could sort of intuit how things would work, and what he couldn't intuit, he was very curious about. He would ask a lot of questions and be extremely comfortable with integrating the answers. Clearly, the experiences of technology in America he wasn't used to in Calcutta. But when we got to buy the tickets through the machine, there was something that was not just culture shock. He was really fascinated. He understood that there was a lot happening behind the machine, and he was really curious about what that was. When he found out how fast, broad, spacious, and geographically distant the different systems were that were communicating, he became intrigued with the lesson of it."

And Yet the Mystery

Though Munindra had a passion for inquiry and, in turn, the development of wisdom, there were some aspects of the universe his insight could not fathom. He had vast stores of knowledge, but he felt humbled by how much he did not know, and perhaps could never know. There were some things he simply was unable to penetrate with his faculty of discrimination, and that left him with an increased sense of wonder. One night, gazing at the stars, Munindra looked up and said to Oren Sofer, "The world is full of mystery, so much mystery. There's so much we don't know."

> *Whenever, while dwelling with mindfulness [s]he wisely investigates, examines, and thinks over the law . . . at such a time [s]he has gained and is developing the factor of enlightenment "investigation of the law"* [dhamma-vicaya].
>
> —THE BUDDHA, MN 118

dhamma-vicaya: from *vi* (to take apart) + *ci* (to gather or accumulate). It is translated as "discrimination of dhammas [mental and physical phenomena]" or "discernment of Dhamma"; "analysis of qualities," "investigation," and "examination." This entails discriminating between what is skillful and what is unskillful.

The second of seven factors of awakening (*bojjhaṅga*), *dhamma-vicaya* naturally arises when mindfulness (*sati*) is steadily present. On the Eightfold Path, it is akin to right view (*sammā-diṭṭhi*) and, thus, is associated with understanding, knowledge, or wisdom. Through dynamic inquiry and scrutiny rather than blind faith, one deeply penetrates the nature of a material or mental object. *Dhamma-vicaya* serves to illuminate the field of awareness. Experientially sorting and discerning, one realizes, for example, an object's arising and passing away, its elemental components, its impermanence (*anicca*), not-self (*anattā*), and unsatisfactoriness (*dukkha*), and its wholesome or unwholesome quality. This generally leads to applying one's energy (*viriya*) to choose that which conduces toward freedom and away from suffering.

While examination characterizes *dhamma-vicaya* and exploration or research is its purpose, it manifests as eager curiosity. It is neither rumination nor discursive thought, and it is not restricted to formal meditation. It embraces many kinds of investigation—studying, listening, being in a teacher's presence, testing, and evaluating—in dharma practice and everyday living, challenging beliefs, opinions, judgments, and assumptions to know what is true.

15

No I, No Me, No Mine

Paññā (Wisdom, Discernment)

Just don't identify.
—MUNINDRA

There were many things to value and respect in Munindra, but what inspired some people most was the breadth of his knowledge of Dharma. "He knew what he was talking about," says Gregg Galbraith. "That's why I call him a teacher's teacher."

Joseph Goldstein comments, "I really appreciated the depth of his knowledge. Though I never did a systematic study the way he did, I learned so much of the Pāli Canon and some of the Abhidhamma through the way he taught. I got a very broad understanding of and very good grounding in Dharma because he was such a master of the study aspects as well as the meditation aspects. Those two parts were so well integrated in him that he really gave me an appreciation for both sides, and I see how well they feed each other."

Ways to Grow Wisdom

In Dharma, there are three kinds of wisdom. *Suta-maya-paññā* comes from listening to a teacher and reading the discourses attributed to the Buddha and other texts. *Cintā-maya-paññā* evolves from thinking over what one has heard or read and assessing its value. *Bhāvanā-maya-paññā* arises intuitively from meditative practice. Munindra's resolve to learn what the Buddha knew and his strong investigative interest led him to develop all three. He fulfilled the eight causes and conditions for obtaining the wisdom that is essential to the holy life: (1) He had a teacher whom he listened to and regarded with affection and respect. (2) He asked his teacher questions to clear up any perplexing points. (3) He practiced meditation. (4) He kept *sīla,* for the Buddha counseled, "Wisdom is purified by morality, and morality is purified by wisdom: Where one is, the other is; the moral man has wisdom and the wise man has morality, and the combination of morality and wisdom is called the highest thing in the world" (DN 4.22).

Munindra also learned the teachings: (5) He memorized and recited them, examined and discussed them. (6) He was persistent and energetic in the four efforts (*padhāna*)—avoiding and abandoning the unwholesome and developing and maintaining the wholesome. (7) He did not engage in useless chatter but preferred to speak about Dharma above all or keep noble silence. (8) And he remained focused on the arising and passing away of the five aggregates—form, feeling, perception, volitional formations, and consciousness.

The Pāli Scholar

As a scholar, Munindra offered an important service to students as well as to other teachers. Gita Kedia recalls that whenever she arrived at S. N. Goenka's residence at Dhamma Giri, if she had any question or confusion, he would direct his secretary, "Go and find Munindra-ji." She and others used to see Goenka and Munindra discussing Dharma on their walks or while sitting together. Gita notes, "Munindra only talked about Dhamma, nothing else. And wherever he was, he solved everybody's doubt. People were very much attracted to him because they knew he was such a learned person."

Shyam Sunder Khaddaria was one of them. "I was doing some Bengali translation and recording," he recounts. "Then Goenka-ji told me that I should go tell Munindra-ji what I had done. He [was to] listen to it and comment." After that first meeting, Shyam began visiting Munindra in his room to talk about the Tipiṭaka. "Whenever I used to have any problem regarding *pariyatti* [learning the doctrine], he used to guide me very nicely, give me lots of advice and explanation, and tell me what to read. Any question I put to him, instantly he used to give me the reference: 'That is in such and such *piṭaka* [basket of scripture] and such and such *gāthā* [verse].' It was very valuable that he knew by heart all the *piṭakas, gāthās,* and *suttas.* His way was quite theoretical, scholarly, plus there was his own experience; both combined, it was very authentic."

Peter Martin received similar help. "From time to time," he recalls, "there would be some questions, not about the practice but about the Pāli Canon. I was working with Goenka-ji's chanting and trying to understand more about the Pāli passages. There were some where I wasn't sure of the reference, and [Munindra] helped, 'Yes, this is the story behind that.' And I'd ask him about a particular line: 'What is the translation of that and what is the meaning of that?' He and one other man knew Pāli at a really deep level, not just the translation. Munindra-ji was somebody I could rely on and somebody who, even though I didn't know well, I trusted so much."

Authenticity Inspires Trust

Munindra's authentic wisdom inspired trust in many. Gregory Pai says, "He was certainly a guide in the sense of study and understanding. For example, I'd read the *Visuddhimagga,* but he kept saying, 'Go back and read it again. Read this chapter, you'll like it. Read that chapter, it's good for you.' It was like finding a definitive resource; this was the person who really knew what was going on. So I had a trust in him that was totally implicit. I looked at him as a mentor and certainly as someone who embodied what the teachings meant, not only as a dharma teacher in an intellectual sense of the word, but more as an example to me of how to be in the world."

Wes Nisker adds, "You trusted him because he was carrying a lot of intelligence, history, tradition, and he knew it backward and forward. You also trusted that he was speaking from his own experience. It was very cultured, and he had such a depth, a quiet dignity, and sweetness." Steven V. Smith agrees, "It is one thing to be fired up from feeling someone's love of Dhamma and enthusiasm. It's another for it to be backed up by an encyclopedic hold of practice, theory, instruction, and understanding of the Pāli Canon."

"In that profound knowledge," Uno Svedin comments, "he combined in a very uncommon way the role of scholar and the role of experiencer and practitioner. This is very important for the West because we can recognize ourselves in his way of connecting the intuitive wisdom part and the scholarly part not as two disjunct domains but as a merged wholeness."

Sharing Paññā

As many students have commented, Munindra could speak for long periods of time about Dharma—too long for some. Shaun Hogan says of Munindra's early Western students, "We didn't have a particularly scholarly bent at the time. That's not what attracted us. Yet I think he brought that out in some people. The way he taught made it more and more interesting, and that made it easier for the mind to stay on it. For me, it was just wonderful hearing somebody who obviously wasn't just teaching it because they learned it. He was talking about something that he was most interested in, that he was living." Shaun says Munindra's gift to students was threefold: "the focus on meditation, the joy in doing it, and the scholarly background to back it up." For example, after hearing Munindra talk at length about *paṭiccasamuppāda* (dependent origination), he had a mental construct for understanding what he was experiencing in meditation and a vocabulary for noting.

Pat Masters found Munindra "incredibly intelligent and clearheaded." She respected him for "his knowledge, unbelievable memory, and ability to pull out textual references." While he was the main meditation teacher for some people, she found his lived philosophical approach noteworthy: "It was important to him that people understood the Abhidharma, that people reflected on some of the text, that it wasn't just about sitting on the cushion, and it wasn't just about doing good deeds. It was really having a depth of knowledge. That was part of his gift—his whole intellectual engagement. He was a consummate scholar. In dharma talks, he would always refer back to what the Buddha said. I found that to be a real opportunity for my own deepening, to go back and look at the textual references."

Egoless Wisdom

Despite his experience and scholarship, Munindra was not arrogant and did not seek recognition. David Johnson says he was an example of how someone with great knowledge could be so unpretentious: "It's funny, Munindra comes off as such a sweet, lovable guy that we are taken off guard as to what he really knows and how deep his knowledge runs. I don't think he commanded the respect he really should have received."

"He was so unassuming," Michael Stein remarks. "You knew he knew a lot. But it wasn't like he had to hit you over the head with it. He sat there and listened. If I had problems, he'd tell me how to be gentle and relax in practice. He would go over all of these intellectual, complicated things time and time again from Abhidhamma. If you had questions, he'd explain every little nuance of it."

Fred von Allmen also describes Munindra as an individual who had a great deal to share without tooting his own horn: "You would ask something and then he would start teaching. If you were lucky, your question was answered or you would get a lot of other things. Joseph [Goldstein] called it 'the dharma shower.' In a way, the student's question just pulled the trigger, and then Munindra would go on and on. He would often teach the stages of insight in the Mahāsi [Sayādaw] tradition for three days, from where you start until the first level of enlightenment and then a little further. Still, it took me a while to appreciate him, to realize that he was incredibly learned and realized. When I first met him, he was sitting in his little room and looked funny in his *lungi* and hat—he didn't come across as somebody very impressive. There was never any big deal about this person, about his self. You could feel that sense of ease and an almost tangible no-self with him—it was very light."

David Wong says Munindra imparted wisdom without getting in the way: "What I learned from him is the Dharma; I did not learn him as a lesson. He made himself transparent. He pointed to the moon and I saw the moon; I did not see the finger."

Dhammaruwan Chandrasiri explains one way of understanding wisdom: "I met a senior monk, over eighty, who told me, 'Goodness, son, you must always hide [i.e., not show off]. Very few people will recognize and realize good qualities in you. If you exhibit [i.e., flaunt] your good qualities, you will become famous and people will tend to like you. If you hide your goodness, sometimes you may be misunderstood, but that's what in the end counts and what's right.' Great people in the East, they don't exhibit their goodness; you have to tune in and see it. Munindra-ji was such a person. He didn't have a big name, colorful dress and beads, stuff like that. He never tried to seek fame. But everything that he gained is inner development. Even when others became famous, he did not criticize; he just maintained friendliness and harmony."

Steven V. Smith agrees, "Some of the great teachers, they're invisible. I'm not implying Munindra was fully enlightened—by his own acknowledgment, he was still working on it—but he did have that way of not being someone."

Don't Get Attached to Identity

Munindra demonstrated *anattā* (not-self) by not being overly attached to his sense of personal identity or to his accomplishments. He also encouraged students to let go of their attachment. James Chadderdon recalls such advice: "I can't remember what I said about what was going on for me. All he said was, 'Just remember, don't identify with it.' This really is central to all the teachings and to managing your mind. It has stuck with me ever since, a reminder not to do that [but] to be aware of identification as a process that's habitual. It's hard to get deeper than that teaching. If you're not identified with what's going on around you all the time, your life tends to go a lot better."

Munindra would return to the theme of *anattā* whenever the opportunity arose. Jacqueline Schwartz Mandell says that during question-and-answer periods, "somebody would be very entwined in their own mind about either an emotional or life issue and Munindra would just totally open it up, pull out a karmic story from the Pāli Canon, and tell them how planting positive seeds brings positive results. Since his focus was on liberation, quite naturally his mind would incline toward how to have a conversation with this person to come out of being tied up in their own problems, unlock the grasping, and open the mind to a wider view of understanding impersonality rather than personality."

Yes, There Are Legs

Simply being with Munindra drove home the teaching of *anattā* again and again, sometimes with humor. Kamala Masters recounts such a lesson at a beach on Maui: "He took off his outer robes and had only a light robe underneath to go into the water. That inner robe showed his legs a little more because the outer robes completely covered them, showing only his feet. My eldest daughter exclaimed, 'Oh, you have legs!' He said, 'Yes, there are legs.' For her, it was funny, but really it was a statement of *anattā*."

Years later, in an Indian train station, Kamala recognized the message again: "It was blazing hot. The train was five hours late. There were no restrooms. We had no food. The station agents kept changing the track so we had to keep getting up and moving. I was worried about how Munindra-ji was holding up because he looked so frail. I asked him if he was all right and he replied, 'There is heat here, but I am not hot. There is hunger here, but I am not hungry. There is irritation here, but I am not irritated.' He would always use impersonal speech—*anattā*. Anger, hunger, pain, worry, or tiredness would come and you don't identify with it—'worry is not me.' But if you're not careful, if you're not mindful, it could prompt you to do something that produces unwholesome karma."

Sharon Salzberg reflects on how Munindra taught her about *anattā* early in her meditation practice: "I was very distressed about some nasty thought that had come up in my mind and he said, 'Why are you so upset about this thought that has come up in your mind? Did you invite it? Did you say, this hour, I'd like to be filled with jealousy or greed or whatever it was?' He was pointing to *anattā*—we're not in control of these experiences that come our way."

The Concept of "I"

After intensive practice, Munindra fully understood *anattā* and could explain how contact at the six sense doors gives rise to thoughts, sights, smells, sounds, tastes, and touch and how we misconstrue them with the concept of "I":

> Whatever we see, it is not I, not me, not a man, not a woman. In the eye, there is just color. It arises and passes away. So who is seeing the object? There is no seer in the object. Then how is [the] object seen? On account of certain causes. What are the causes? Eyes are one cause; they must be intact, in good order. Second, object or color must come in front of the eyes, must reflect on the retina of the eyes. Third, there must be light. Fourth, there must be attention, a mental factor. If those four causes are present, then there arises a knowing faculty called eye consciousness. If any one of the causes is missing, there will not be any seeing. If eyes are blind, no seeing. If there is no light, no seeing. If there is no attention, no seeing. But none of the causes can claim, "I am the seer." They're just constantly arising and passing.
>
> As soon as it passes away, we say, "I am seeing." You are not seeing; you are just thinking, "I am seeing." This is called conditioning. Because our mind is conditioned, when [we] hear the sound, [we] say, "I am hearing." But there is no hearer waiting in the ear to hear the sound. Sound creates a wave, and, when it strikes against the eardrum, ear consciousness is the effect. Sound is not a man, not a woman; it is just a sound that arises and passes away. But, according to our conditioning, we say, "That woman is singing and I am hearing." But you're not hearing, you are thinking "I am hearing." Sound is already heard and gone. There is no

"I" who heard the sound; it is the world of concept. Buddha discovered this in the physical level, in the mental level: how everything is happening without [an] actor, without [a] doer—empty phenomena go rolling on.

Munindra elaborated on how identifying with being an actor leads to *dukkha:*

> This "I" is the greatest hindrance on the path of enlightenment. All this greed, hate, and delusion come on account of this ego idea: "My whole body and mind is me" or "There is someone inside the body" or "In the mind, there is *ātman,* a soul exists, someone who is controlling everything, who is seeing." Or there is identifying thought as "me," emotions as "me." For the preservation of "I," all kinds of tension, all kinds of frustration, all kinds of worry take place: "This is me." "This is my mind." "This is my body." "This is my house." "This is my family." "This is my country." Self-illusion from time immemorial. This is wrong view. This is abandoned in the first experience of *nibbāna;* all the *micchā* (wrong views) are cleaned out. As soon as right understanding comes up about this illusive, self-created ego, there comes a different relationship, a friendly, brotherly feeling. It brings harmony and unity between man and man, between nation and nation. When one understands one's process of working, then [one] understands another's. Basic problems are [the] same; basic natures are [the] same.

Munindra also clarified why we refer to "I," "me," and "mine." They are for the convenience of talking:

> Scientists say the sun rises in the east, sets in the west; but the sun never rises, never sets. They know these things, but still they use these terms for understanding. They're concepts—rising or setting, east or west. In reality, there is no east, no west. But for the purpose of communication, it is necessary.

To emphasize the emptiness or impersonality of mental and physical phenomena, Munindra frequently quoted the Buddha's advice to Bahiya on how to train oneself: "In the seen will be merely what is seen; in the heard will be merely what is heard; in the sensed will be merely what is sensed; in the cognized will be merely what is cognized" (Ud 1.10).

Seeing Things as They Are, At the Movies

Larry Rosenberg once took Munindra to a theater in Boston to see a Hollywood movie. He does not remember what it was, but afterward Munindra had a slightly disappointed look on his face and said, "I don't understand all the fuss. Why do people get all excited about these things?" Larry asked him, "What do you mean, Munindra-ji?" Munindra replied, "Well, all I saw was light coming down, hitting the screen, people sitting there in the dark watching, and just a bunch of images moving, one after the other." Larry realized that he had just given a vipassanā description of what was happening; he had not gotten caught up in the theme at all: "It was just a very raw, naked, unadorned description of literally what was happening."

A few months later, they went to see another film, one about World War II. Although the Allies managed to get across a strategic bridge, it was at the cost of great casualties on both sides. When they walked out of the theater this time, Munindra displayed some sadness in his face. Larry asked him, "Munindra-ji, what's the matter?" He responded, "Oh, those people, all those people dying." Larry roared with laughter as he informed him, "Munindra-ji, you have attained movie mind! No one died. Everything you said the first time we went was completely true, but now you understand what a Hollywood film is." Then they both laughed.

Dental Impermanence

Wisdom embraces clear comprehension and acceptance not only of *anattā*, but also of *anicca* and *dukkha*, the other two characteristics of existence. On a walk in Igatpuri, David Brody listened to Munindra talk and laugh about transience: "Everything is impermanent, even my teeth." Then he smiled at David, revealing a mouth that once held many teeth.

As the years went by, Munindra's teeth kept decaying. He declined drilling or extraction because, as he told Joe DiNardo, "I want to see what happens to it by nature." "But it's going to hurt," Joe protested. "That's OK," Munindra said. Joe says, "He was serious about it. He felt that the body decaying was just another experience [of impermanence] for him and he was interested in it. As a result, if you saw him in his last years, his teeth were terrible, rotting."

Munindra once remarked, "In the beginning also, when we are born, there were no teeth. Later on in life, it is like this." By the time he was close to death, he was well prepared to meet it, for he had utilized what helped him understand its inevitability.

Our Mortal Nature

In 2000, Robert Pryor and David Gelles visited Munindra at his family's home in Calcutta. As they leafed through his photo album, they came across one picture after another of dead and decaying bodies. David gasped, then realized that they were a meditation on impermanence: "It was a tool for his practice. He didn't go into a deep sermon about why that was important, just something to the effect that it's a visual reminder of a dead body and that's what people need to see."

After Karen Sirker found a skull while walking along the river in Bodh Gaya, Munindra said, "You should go meditate on that skull so you understand impermanence." Although a skull is a useful reminder, examples of the constantly changing nature of existence are everywhere. Uno Svedin can still hear Munindra repeating, "*anicca, anicca,*" as they stood on the dunes above the beaches facing the North Sea in Holland. "We looked directly out to sea, watching the cold waves rolling in toward the beach just below us. We were standing on top of demolished bunker systems built during World War II by the Nazis. These defenses had been ultrapowerful, and yet less than one-third of a century later, Munindra-ji and I were standing on the remnants of this fortress, now totally useless. I heard him mumble something to himself, to the sea and the dunes, and maybe to the universe. He said, '*Anicca, anicca.* Everything that has come passes away.'"

A few years before he passed away, he expressed the teaching on impermanence in this way,

> Death I don't mind. Every moment we are dying. Everything is impermanent. Who is dying? There is nobody dying. It is just a process. This is [merely a] law of nature.... Everything in nature is arising and vanishing. There is nothing to be afraid of. In death also, smiling you can go. Every moment we are dying. Once you are acquainted with this, then it is simple.

Maggie Ward McGervey took this wisdom to heart when her father died suddenly in a drowning. "Within less than a minute, I went to the truth of impermanence," she recalls. "I was filled with the healing power and the knowing of impermanence that came out of the teachings of Munindra-ji. I suffered more losses in my family before the time in India with the Dharma, and I was just devastated by those. This was difficult—of course, losing a father always is—but it was as natural as breathing to realize the truth of impermanence. It really carried me through the whole grief process and made it a positive experience. I didn't think, 'Oh, Munindra-ji was teaching me about the impermanence of self or body,' but his teachings are very much integrated in my life. It's cellular at this point. The proof is that in the hardest time, the Dharma kicked in almost immediately."

Communicating Wisdom

Munindra employed different ways to impart the wisdom of Dharma. Sometimes it was as simple as penning a one-liner. When Ted Slovin asked him to sign something in a book on the Buddha's teaching, Munindra wrote, "Buddha taught only two things: suffering and the release from suffering." Then he signed his name.

At other times, he followed the Buddha's instruction to keep noble silence and said very little. Bhante Bodhipāla remembers an occasion when they went to the Mahabodhi Society in Calcutta for a one-day meditation course. "During his talk, somebody asked him something regarding the meditation and he did not answer. He just smiled, told the person to practice, and got up to leave. I asked him why he did that. He said, 'There are certain things that should be left silent. Unanswered is a better way to answer that question.' This was a very practical approach for me. There are certain times in which [you] should keep silent instead of answering because once you answer, you keep creating another question."

Marcia Rose had a similar experience on her second visit to Varanasi, where she spent several days by herself, observing the burning ghats, wanting to comprehend that process in a deeper way. Then she went to Munindra to discuss her experience: "I was surprised that what I had seen didn't upset me. I was puzzled that I wasn't reactive about it, but was just there with it, and I wanted to know why this was so. His response to me was, 'Just continue your practice and you'll know.' That's all he said. There was a lot of understanding and wisdom behind it in its succinctness and friendliness."

The First Noble Truth

Munindra's clarity and certainty about Dharma shone through his presence, his actions, and his words. He was not shy about stating what he knew to be true about the nature of reality:

> As one goes higher and deeper, the mind becomes clearer and clearer that everything is suffering—*dukkha*. Buddha says, "Noble truth of suffering." What is the noble truth of suffering? The whole of existence is suffering: Seeing is suffering; hearing is suffering; eating is suffering. When you give attention and come close to it, when you experience it and see it as it is, it is all uselessness. All people are suffering, even if they have enough money, food, power, position. They have everything and still they are suffering. How are they suffering? They have to be separated from their dear and near ones. They have to come into contact with unpleasant ones. What they want that is not fulfilled—this is also suffering. When you come out of your mother, you come with crying. Nobody wants to be old, but whoever is born is destined to get old, to suffer, to have pain and get disease. Nobody wants to die, but death is destined. To live is uncertain, but to die is certain.

When students reported about *dukkha* to Munindra, sometimes his response was surprising. Denise Till comments, "People get caught up in crazy thoughts and emotions. An emotion is just a stirred-up mental state. Munindra-ji would cut right through that and say it's totally deluded, we're creating our own suffering from our own ignorance. He would tell them not to go off on any trips, but just walk. He emphasized walking meditation very much; he found that to be very therapeutic, spacious. People who couldn't sit, who got so caught up in their own stories, Munindra-ji sent them off with 'Keep walking.'"

The Impact of Wise Teaching

Munindra's teaching on the wisdom of Dharma had far-reaching effects, even for students of different schools and disciplines. Derek Ridler says, "One of the things that was very attractive to me was his clarity. I would go to the small group interviews, and I was really taken by his unassuming manner. These teachings on impermanence and suffering came from another culture, another time, yet he was able to express this wisdom in such a way that I could relate it to my own experience. I thought, 'This makes sense to me on a personal level.' There was also an impeccability about his teachings. I can appreciate now his background as a scholar. But that was not the thing that I found most attractive. It was really those immediate teachings that I received from him that stayed in my mindstream."

Although a dedicated practitioner of Tibetan Buddhism, Derek considers the importance of those Theravāda teachings: "What arises for me is a deep sense of appreciation of having had the opportunity to practice vipassanā. It really helped me to learn how to sit in a nonconceptual way. I remember how Nyoshul Khen Rinpoche spoke about the Hīnayāna as a foundational vehicle, not the lesser vehicle, and how crucial that foundation was because, without it, Vajrayāna was like building a beautiful mansion on a frozen lake. And we all know what happens when the lake thaws."

Although following a Zen path since her midtwenties, Wendy Nakao Rōshi also learned from Munindra: "He'd start explaining *nāma-rūpa* [mind-matter] and go on and on in this incredible detail. He was clearly a very intelligent man. I considered myself a new dharma student at the time, and suddenly being exposed to a whole other element of the tradition that I'd never been exposed to was fascinating."

Munindra's wisdom opened many doors for others to gain knowledge. Daniel Goleman remembers Munindra's unexpected and lasting contribution to his life as a psychologist: "He gave me a wonderful book by Mahāsi Sayādaw on the stages of insight, which was one of the few books in those days in English about vipassanā. I was quite fascinated because it was a well-articulated phenomenology of states of awareness, like I'd never seen in the West." Daniel continues, "Munindra helped me find sources. He told me about a book called the *Visuddhimagga*. On a trip to Delhi, I was lucky enough to find it and study it. I used to go and ask him questions, and he would help me clarify points that I wasn't sure I understood. He just knew what I didn't and was extraordinarily precise and clear in his thinking and his teaching style. He was the first one to show me that there was a system of psychology that was quite cogent and robust within Buddhism, which was a shocker for me because I'd been a Harvard graduate student in psychology and I had never been told there was any psychological system outside of Europe and America. That was a major intellectual discovery for me and one that I pursued and, in some ways, continue to pursue. Today I'm involved with the Mind and Life Institute in having neuroscientists look at the outcomes of the methodologies of Abhidharma."

Wisdom without Dogmatism

Munindra's scholarship was not rigid. Peter Skilling comments, "He certainly wasn't dogmatic or I wouldn't have gone back and asked him so many questions." Christina Feldman recognizes this lack of dogmatism in Munindra as well: "He was a person of quite some independence who didn't place as much emphasis on the purity of technique as he placed on people's understanding. That had a big impact on me because it wasn't just about getting the technique right; it was about what kind of wisdom you developed through the technique. Because he had exposure to many different styles of meditation, Munindra-ji wasn't a one-song person. In his own teaching and practice, he found the ability to draw on different styles and techniques and never put them above wisdom. That was a very important transmission because in Asia at that time—and actually still today—monasteries often would have one style that they handed down through generations of teachers without that broader education about the variety of practices that are available. As a teacher, Munindra never lost sight that insight and liberation were the essence, and techniques were in the service of that."

This trait enabled Munindra to guide his students well on their dharma journeys. Steven V. Smith says, "Munindra would know all of these little things. He'd just pull them out of his hat like a magician. I never saw someone who could draw from so many directions at once and make sense of it in the moment as to why a particular method might be appropriate to one person, according to where their practice was at the time."

Manifesting Wisdom

One night in Bodh Gaya, Munindra's talk to the Antioch students was about Abhidharma. John Dunne, who taught philosophy in the program in 1994, remembers that exposition on the roof of the Burmese Vihar. "What Munindra essentially did was go through in very fine detail a number of the mental functions from the Pāli Abhidhamma and the way they related to meditation practice," he notes. "I was really quite amazed and impressed. The only text that was remotely close was the *Visuddhimagga,* but I had never heard a living scholar go through on that level of precise detail and make the connections in such a fine way, and I had never heard a meditation teacher use the categories in such an almost scientific way."

John continues, "Of course, you could tell that he was a serious practitioner of meditation because of his bearing and his calmness—in my experience, he was never perturbed by anything really—but until then I didn't realize the depth of his scholarship. He not only had studied the texts and thought about them, but he'd really connected them to his own personal practice. What he did for me was make a bridge between my scholastic study and my meditation practice."

In the *Lakkhana Sutta*, the Buddha says that it is through the activities of one's life that a person's wisdom shines (AN 3.2). Munindra's discernment was always visible, through his verbal and physical deeds, and available to others. As Ray Lipovsky puts it, "Real teachers, wherever they are at whatever point you're with them, it's all a fantastic lesson because they're just living their life as a manifestation of their wisdom, right? So we get it, if we're lucky enough to be there."

The purpose of wisdom, friend, is direct knowledge, its purpose is full understanding, its purpose is abandoning.

—SĀRIPUTTA, MN 43.12

paññā: from *pa* (rightly) + *ña* (to know); literally, "right knowing." *Paññā* is translated as "wisdom," "discernment," "knowledge," "comprehension," or "insight." In Abhidhamma, it is synonymous with *ñāṇa* (knowledge) and *amoha* (nondelusion). Wisdom discerns between what is wholesome and unwholesome, skillful and unskillful. Thorough attention is its proximate cause, nonconfusion its manifestation.

There are three sources of wisdom: learning; reflecting on

and evaluating what one has learned; and mental development (meditation). The last produces not intellectual understanding but intuitive insight based on direct observation of one's mental and bodily processes, understanding skillful qualities as they are developed through practice. Those qualities include not clinging to concepts but seeing into the true nature of phenomena as ever changing (*anicca*), unsatisfactory (*dukkha*), and not-self (*anattā*), as well as perceiving how things arise conditioned and interdependent (*paṭiccasamuppāda*). Wisdom also means comprehending the Four Noble Truths of suffering, its origin, its cessation, and the path toward ending it.

Paññā appears five times in the thirty-seven requisites of awakening (*bodhipakkhiyā-dhammā*): as *vimaṁsā* (examination), one of four means of accomplishment (*iddhi-pāda*); as *dhamma-vicaya* (investigation of the Truth), one of seven factors of awakening (*bojjhaṅga*); as *sammā-diṭṭhi* (right view) and *sammā-saṅkappa* (right thought), the third part of the Eightfold Path; and as one of five faculties (*indriya*) or powers (*bala*). The fourth of ten perfections (*pāramī*), wisdom purifies the other nine and enables them to fulfill their respective functions. *Paññā* becomes *abhiññā* (supernormal knowledge) through the deepest *samādhi*. Fully matured wisdom leads to *nibbāna*.

16

It's All a Passing Show

Upekkhā (Equanimity)

> *The end of vipassanā is not happiness but equanimity.*
> —MUNINDRA

The American poet Ella Wheeler Wilcox (1850–1919) nicely summed up the quality of equanimity when she wrote the following simple verses.

> It is easy enough to be pleasant,
>   When life flows by like a song,
> But the man worth while is one who will smile,
>   When everything goes dead wrong.

For his students, Munindra was an inspiring model of *upekkhā* in how he handled life's unexpected and undesirable circumstances.

This Is How It Is

Munindra took precise care of his body. Even in his elder years, he could readily jump into yoga āsanas. He was meticulous in his personal hygiene. Whenever possible, he preferred to eat fresh food that was still alive with *prāna* (vital energy). He was someone who maintained a positive attitude in his mind and a smile on his face. Yet, he too suffered what every human being is subject to. Ailments and diseases afflict the body and mind, not to mention the basic pangs of physical and emotional distress—hunger, thirst, heat, cold, fatigue, sorrow, and worry. Diminished strength and faculties accompany aging, eventually leading to death. And we lose those we care about. The difference between how he handled these inevitable conditions and how most people react to adversity is in the fruit of his dharma practice—equanimity.

On a pilgrimage with Munindra to Buddhist sites in India in 2001, Kamala Masters watched how he dealt with knowing he would never again see his old friend, the head monk at a monastery in Sarnath: "There was joy connecting with each other, holding hands. They had tea, walked out down the street. Munindra had tears in his eyes, but he was also calm. Both elderly, they said good-bye to each other. He commented, 'When parting from those we love, there is sadness. This is how it is.' He was balanced inwardly and outwardly."

Kamala saw and experienced this balance on a trip with Munindra to Varanasi. She, Maile Kjargaard (now Ma Vīrañānī), and Norliah Ariyaratne hired a boat to go out with him on the Ganges River before dawn: "As we headed down the river, on the right were the burning ghats. We went close enough to the riverside that you could actually see a body burning and family members crying. I was sitting there with Munindra, holding his hand. I felt a quiet kind of happiness that I could be with my teacher on the Ganges, fulfilling his wishes. I was able to hold the beauty of my connection to my teacher and the rawness of life that was visible on the riverbank, seeing the dead body burning. I was looking at it in a very matter-of-fact way—it wasn't anything special. Then the sun was rising, and there's decrepit Varanasi, one of the oldest continuously occupied cities in the world. When I look back, I reflect on how it took a lot of equanimity to hold the beauty and the sorrow. When I have to give a talk on equanimity, that picture comes to mind. That's how I remember Munindra. He was just looking all around, the mind balanced with all that."

Munindra often said, "If anything happens, it is OK; I accept it." To Westerners, this could easily sound like resignation. But his twinkle and buoyant demeanor always indicated otherwise. Accepting what happens never turned Munindra into a fatalistic doormat; he did not believe in predestination or determinism. He greeted whatever came with equipoise.

Letting It Come and Go

In the winter of 1969, Khanti Moraitis returned a second time to study with Munindra in Bodh Gaya. When she arrived at the Burmese Vihar, she saw that Munindra's right hand was burned from a pot of boiling water and the old monk there had broken one of his legs. When Khanti asked them whether they were in pain, she recalls, "They both had large peaceful smiles on their faces and almost simultaneously said, '*Dukkha*,' in case I had forgotten the teaching."

Shivaya Cain adds, "Munindra was relatively unreactive to almost anything that happened. One of the things that he would always say, which I carried away from being with him, was 'It's all a passing show. Just watch it.' That expression has become very much a part of my life. I find myself using his lines a lot myself, and, of course, now I feel that bond with him any time that I say it. Things will happen and I will naturally say, 'Oh, it's all a passing show.'"

In 1992, Eric Kupers picked up a similar phrase. The other Antioch Education Abroad students had left Bodh Gaya for a weekend in Varanasi, but he stayed behind. Eric says, "I had been sick, and I was having a kind of breakdown. I went and met with Munindra. I told him all my drama and what a hard time I was having emotionally, mentally. He said (I'm paraphrasing), 'All of this is just bubbles. It's going to rise up and pass away. You just need to let it do that.' It really helped, and it's something that I still come back to. I'm sure he had said something like that to us many times when he was teaching us. The one-on-one time I had with him that afternoon, sitting on the porch at the Burmese Vihar, pouring out all the fears I was having and all the confusion, and then having him say, 'It's just bubbles of energy. Just let it come. It just needs to release.' That really helped."

Accepting Pain and Old Age

Sometimes things are short-lived and pass away quickly. At other times, they seem to go on forever. Mustering equanimity for the latter is the greater challenge. Munindra met it again and again as his body struggled to regain and maintain health in his elder years. When he was around seventy years old, he lived with the intense pain of a hernia until he underwent surgery in Calcutta. Although the surgeon he consulted said he would perform the operation himself, in fact, he assigned it to interns and their carelessness cost Munindra dearly. For two years, he endured an ongoing infection. Despite repeated visits to the doctor, pus kept oozing out of the incision. When his students in the West heard about his suffering, several chipped in to bring him to Hawai'i for treatment. On Maui, Kamala arranged for a doctor to open him up a second time. The physician found about a dozen surgical strings that had been left inside during the initial surgery and cleaned out the infected area. Kamala nursed Munindra back to health for more than a month. As painful as the experience was, he said, "I had to accept it. I lived my life that way."

Years later, he also went through an excruciating episode of shingles. The pain was so extreme that he thought he might actually be dying. "It was terrible pain, terrible pain," he said. "For this kind of pain, I was told there is no medicine. It comes by itself and when the time comes, it goes out. But for six months, I suffered it. The mind was OK, but there was pain." Again he stated, "I accepted it; I lived it." Then he added, "Observation is a great medicine as well. So pain is no problem for me. Suffering is a great teacher. I learned much."

In dharma talks, Munindra would explain, "There are two kinds of suffering: physical pain and mental suffering." One is a fact of life; the other is optional. Because of various conditions—climate, food, environment, age, past karma—the body can undergo all manner of discomfort. Yet, whatever the circumstances, as long as we understand, as he put it, "the Law" (Dharma, the truth of reality), the mind can remain undisturbed, unaffected, and equanimous. Once we realize that everything is impermanent, that different phenomena are constantly in a state of flux and they are all "impersonal, universal forces of nature, then we can live well—even enjoy pain—and die well." He remarked, "It's a great help to understand these laws of nature. This whole body is part of nature."

Munindra's general unflappability about body changes that most people would find upsetting impressed his students. James and Jane Baraz remember an incident on Vancouver Island, British Columbia, around 1995: "By that time, Munindra had two teeth left in his mouth; there was a top and a bottom tooth. As we were eating our meal, all of a sudden, one tooth broke, and there he was, no longer able to chew anything. It was amazing—he didn't miss a beat. He just started laughing, 'Ha, ha, impermanence, *anicca.*' It was like the Cat Stevens song 'Moonshadow': 'If I ever lose my mouth, all my teeth, north and south . . .' It was just like that: 'OK, they're gone.' And no *dukkha* at all."

For Sara Schedler, what Munindra taught was in great contrast to what she learned growing up. "He'd lost all his teeth by that time. When somebody asked him about it, he said, all sparkly and with a cute smile, 'Oh, I'm just watching my body decay.' He was so at ease and peaceful about it and just thought the whole thing was really funny. I had never seen a relationship to aging like that. All around me, there's so much tension and violence towards that process (especially in the conservative suburban community where I grew up, where there's all the Botox and this and that to fight against the aging process). It isn't a very graceful process in our society; women in particular suffer a lot about it. So it was just amazing to see this man totally embrace it."

Taking Things In Stride

On another occasion, Sara Schedler found Munindra equally undisturbed when insects swarmed all over him. As a kind of farewell at the end of the Antioch program, the whole student group was meditating at the Mahabodhi Temple. Sara says, "For some reason, the grasshoppers were hatching and I think they were attracted to the white clothes. Munindra-ji's calmly sitting with all the grasshoppers on him, just taking things in stride—'OK, now this is happening.' Just to be so serene. I guess he was one of my first examples of real equanimity—not cold indifference but real equanimity."

In 1993, Stephen and Hazel Strange invited Munindra to travel to Sanchi, India, a small village in the central part of the state of Madhya Pradesh. (A UNESCO World Heritage Site, it contains several Buddhist stupas and monastery ruins dating from as early as the third century B.C.E.) Stephen recalls, "Munindra was so enthusiastic, telling everybody about this trip we were going to make. Although I tried to book tickets on the train, I wasn't able to get a confirmed seat. But people assured me, 'It'll be fine.' So, on the day, we go down to the station, but the ticket inspector looked at my tickets and said, 'Sorry, you're not on the train.' I was incredibly upset because I had told Munindra-ji we were going. Here we'd all come down together, all packed, ready to go, and then right at the last minute we discover that it isn't going to happen. But Munindra-ji was certainly equanimous about it, saying, 'No matter, these things happen.'"

Stephen went to Bombay the next day to get confirmed seats so that they could make the trip several weeks later. This time everything went smoothly, and it turned out for the best. The period when they had originally planned to travel proved to be bitterly cold, but the following month the weather was warm and enjoyable. They had a delightful experience. The lesson for Stephen was: Things happen; there's no reason to agonize over them.

Not Taking Things So Seriously

Like anyone, Munindra had his preferences. He would have preferred to go rather than not go to Sanchi the first time, but he was not attached to when they did go. According to Denise Till, "He never showed too much attachment toward anything. I don't think I ever did see him irritated. He used to say that once you've reached a stage in realization, you still had to live out your old *sankhāras* [karma-formations], and your old body too. It wasn't like you're freed of all your karmas or anything. He would say it's not like that. You've got to work with whatever it is." And he did.

Bhante Vimalaraṃsi remembers that Munindra "was always pretty much balanced. Even in trying situations, he found some humor in it. Being in crowds that were pushing and shoving didn't slow him down; it didn't bother him at all. He was the first example I saw of treating everything lightly, having a different kind of perspective instead of getting caught in your anger and dissatisfactions—seeing that these things start to arise, but not getting overly serious about them."

When Munindra sensed someone else getting overly serious, he cautioned them to pull back. Itamar Sofer recollects Munindra's advice: "One time, I saw in the corner of the room that a spider had made a web and then a fly got caught in it, and the spider started building around him. In my mind I started building the whole drama of this thing, 'Oh, look at this, the spider is creating bad karma. This is so much suffering in *saṃsāra* [endless round of rebirth].' Then we went out for the evening walk and I said to Munindra-ji, 'I feel so much pity for the fly and so much pity for the spider.' He said, 'Just leave these things. Just be equanimous to the whole situation. It is not your karma; you cannot do much about these things. You help the fly, then you disturb the dinner of the spider. Whatever involvement you are doing is against nature. Just observe it in equanimity.' It was such a good, simple lesson, very direct, very strong. Whatever situation you see that you cannot change, just keep equanimity; otherwise, there's too much emotion."

Surrender to the Law

Kamala Masters learned this lesson in her own family life during one of Munindra's visits to Maui. One day, when a struggle ensued between her then husband and their daughter, she was clearly embarrassed by the screaming and door slamming. Munindra reached over, placed a steady hand on her forearm, looked at her with compassion, and said, "Surrender to the Law." She has been grateful for that teaching ever since because accepting how things are in the moment, rather than resisting them, is a means for cultivating nondelusion, or wisdom. "From that wisdom," she adds, "we can let go of our attachment to how we think it should be or how we want it to be. Letting go helps us to cultivate nonattachment, or acceptance and understanding in this case, so that we can take compassionate action from a place of clarity." Once Kamala did "surrender to the Law," to what was actually happening, she noticed that her "reactive and chaotic mind settled" and she was able to draw on equanimity to see clearly and help make peace between father and daughter. "But I also saw with deeper understanding that they had their own stuff to work out," says Kamala. "It wasn't something I could control. Certainly, my desire for it to be perfect, or my aversion to how it was so imperfect, only brought more suffering and confusion to everyone involved. Munindra did not comment much on the event afterward. I imagined that he might judge or criticize us, but he didn't. His behavior showed us that he didn't expect our home to be a heaven or a monastery."[1]

Munindra also helped Kamala comprehend how mindfulness and equanimity supporting each other could change her life. One time, when she asked him why her life had been filled with hardship, he replied:

> This is the Law. What is happening now is the result of actions in the past. But in this moment, depending on how you respond, you can create a different future—one of happiness. That future will eventually become this present moment. And this present moment will become the past. In this way, it is possible for your life to be surrounded by more happiness, in the past, the present, and the future. . . . If you are mindful, you can choose with wisdom how to respond. If you are not mindful, your life is run by reactivity. It's up to you.

The Vicissitudes of Life

Although Munindra honed the quality of equanimity through dharma practice, in some ways, an early experience had already prepared him for the slings and arrows of life. As children, he and his brothers enjoyed favor in their rural community and were especially lauded for their excellence in school. Then their father became a *sāmaṇera*. Out of a sense of responsibility, he continued to live with the family rather than separately in the temple. As a result, the villagers ostracized them, and, overnight, the boys lost their special status. Govinda Barua, the youngest of the three, still remembers that difficult isolation: "We were not allowed to participate in any of the activities of the village. Even the *bhikkhus* who used to come wouldn't enter our house. The local barber wouldn't attend to our haircuts. The *dhobi* [laundrymen] wouldn't come and take our clothes to wash because the village people had forbidden them from providing any kind of help for us. They wouldn't allow anybody to associate with us." The family did not hide in shame, for they knew they had done nothing wrong. They bore the ostracism, and in time, the village dropped it.

Dhammaruwan Chandrasiri talks about Munindra's ability to deal with life's ups and downs, what the Buddha called the eight worldly conditions (*loka-dhamma*) that no one can avoid—praise and blame, gain and loss, honor and disrepute, happiness and misery. "He didn't get carried away by any of those things. When he got praise or blame, he spoke the same way. It didn't change him. Then, when he went through gain and loss, ill repute, he remained the same. People did sometimes say not nice things about him, yet he remained always a steadfast friend, a *kalyāṇamitta,* to so many. He was very sought after in Bodh Gaya; people were coming to look for him, to be his students. Then, all of a sudden, Goenka-ji took over, but it didn't matter to Munindra."

Others also noticed this flexibility to take or leave whatever situation presented itself to Munindra—for example, to enjoy company or solitude. Gregg Galbraith remembers that he was not a big planner but took days as they came: "It seems that everybody's got so many agendas and ambitions. With Munindra, if people came to see him, he made time for them, and that was fine. If they didn't, he had things to do, and that was fine. There was no success or failure in his scenario. Being around Munindra was a lot like being around someone with a nonjudging mind, without this 'I've got to do this or that' or 'This is not good.' He had a lot of equanimity, and being around him helped bring that out in us. You don't have to react to everything. There are times when you need to, as Munindra would say, pay attention and react to the situation, but there're other times when you could just be in passive awareness and not react to everything. He had that ability to be in the world but not get caught up in things, yet be aware and attend to them as they are."

Munindra's equipoise in the face of highs and lows also inspired Erik

Knud-Hansen, who says that, over the years, he has found himself "mostly respecting the teachers who basically didn't lose it when the situation wasn't prime. Munindra had a tremendous ability to just be in balance and not give the outside world that much empowerment. Even when some people couldn't understand his human side, he was graceful in that. I'll always remember what I took as his bottom-line statement: 'Don't judge the Dharma by me. The Dharma is the Dharma. I'm just me.'"

In the same way that he accepted the attacks of illness on his body without creating more pain mentally, Munindra endured verbal attacks without responding negatively. As Gregg Galbraith reiterates, "He was very accepting of things the way they are." And he was able to instill such acceptance in his students, including Naima Shea, who learned how to be with what is, from her first practice session with him: "There are a lot of loud transistor radios in India, and people walked by with music blaring. (There is little that blares quite like Indian pop music!) Someone asked him how to deal with that. He smiled that sweet smile and told us to note, 'listening.' It sounds like nothing, but it is a profound teaching to just be with what is, without reacting or judging, and at the time, it was a bit of a revelation."

Naima continues, "He went on to say that when the mind is on the radio music blaring, just bring the attention back to the breath or the body as gently as a mother with her only child. This is so essential: to be gentle, not to admonish, judge, or blame oneself, which would only make one's practice tight or uptight. That one pithy instruction, in that context, has influenced my whole life in immeasurable ways."

Even If You Are Reclining on a Cloud

Munindra reinforced this teaching for Naima Shea when, a couple of weeks later, having undergone an intensive ten-day retreat with another teacher, she was eagerly sitting in meditation on her own. She says, "I always had a lot of physical pain. It got so bad that I decided to go talk with Munindra-ji about it. I told him I felt like my entire upper body was encased in concrete and that it was splitting in two and that it was terribly painful, hour after hour. He smiled—again, that sweet smile—and told me it was very good for developing concentration! It really struck me, the very idea of not just reacting or worrying or otherwise getting into some concept of what the pain might be—the idea of using the sensation as an ally, so to speak. This has been a very great lesson I have always cherished as well."

Teaching others how to deal with pain is a gift that many have found helpful as they age. Zara Novikoff still remembers Munindra's words from when she first met him by chance in India in 1968: "He gave me instructions to watch my feelings of pain or laughter. Whatever came up in my mind, I had to look at it with equanimity, not to make any comments, not to get angry with myself if I couldn't concentrate or I became restless." Zara recalls, "One day, I was complaining about physical pain, that I could not sit for so many hours on a cement floor. And he said to me, 'Even if you are reclining on a cloud, the pain will still come.' That was really important for me to know. You have to accept whatever comes. Everybody gets pain; you cannot escape it. But the way he said it was with a big smile, like it was a joke. No matter what, he remained peaceful and smiling, bright and alert."

Perfecting Equanimity until the End

While teaching others to cultivate equanimity, Munindra never stopped perfecting it himself. It was a great advantage when he confronted serious health crises. The botched surgery and shingles mentioned earlier were not all he had to deal with. During the second half of 1996, he wrote to Vivian Darst that he had suddenly become seriously ill with bronchitis, fever, and coughing in Calcutta. He was hospitalized and diagnosed with tuberculosis in his left lung, as well as pleurisy. He would need to rest completely and talk less for at least six months while undergoing medical treatment. He told her:

> I do not know how long it will take to fully recover. I am eighty-two years old now, which is an average mature age of man at present. Sooner or later, everyone has to be separated from all dear ones. For this we have to be ready always. This is the law of nature. Suffering is a great teacher. I accept it with equanimity, without reactions, as it is. If I remain alive some more days and everything goes well, I may see you once again in the West. If not, my wholehearted blessings and *mettā* for your health and well-being.

In 2002, Munindra became so frail that he needed support to walk. Robert Pryor remembers that he had a wonderful way of describing his condition: "You'd ask him, 'How are you?' and he'd say, 'The body is very old, but the mind is quite good.' You could tell Munindra was clear; he was right there with you even though he was infirm. And he wasn't a whiner, a grouch, or a grump, which is easy to be when you're sick. I was impressed by that and by that sense of immediacy."

The following year, Munindra was confined to his family's home in Calcutta. Although he was terribly ill and weak, he still received people. Knowing it was probably the last time they would see their beloved teacher, people came from afar to visit him. Kamala Masters arrived at the beginning of 2003. She remembers sitting by his bed and trying to get him to sit up. He had great difficulty moving, but he accepted it with such lightness, even laughing as he said, "The mind is very clear, but the body is not cooperating." Kamala remarks, "It was a great teaching for me, one of those beautiful teachings you could never get sitting in a dharma hall."

When Uno Svedin showed up from Sweden, he noticed that despite Munindra's debilitated condition, "he lit up talking about Dhamma—authority, kindness, and depth streamed from him, as usual. But he was very sick and paid later by needing prolonged periods of rest. In all his ways, he provided us with lessons on how to die slowly in a dignified manner, on what equanimity is when exercised in 'real time.' I have saved this teaching for later parts of my life, when I might need to have the examples of seniors like Munindra-ji as lighthouses."

During the first week of October 2003, Robert Pryor came to see Munindra, accompanied by U Hla Myint, the Burmese teacher who took over for Munindra with the Antioch Education Abroad program when he became too ill to teach, and Phelps Feeley, a teaching assistant. Robert describes that poignant last visit: "As always, his family was very gracious and warmly greeted us. His brother Govinda said, 'He hasn't even been speaking, but you can go in, if you like.' So we went into a lovely corner room that was quiet, with fresh air, and there on the hospital bed was this tiny figure, lying on his side. He was so weak, he couldn't sit up, but they kind of propped his head up and he opened his eyes and looked at us. Gradually, you could see that we came into focus. He spoke to us and was very present. When we told him that the program had gone well, he had a big smile."

Robert continues, "We brought him a *chola* (shoulder bag) with the Mahabodhi Temple embroidered on it. We held it up sideways so that he could see it. He smiled and said, 'Thank you very much.' We only spoke to him for about five or ten minutes. Then, before we left, he gave us a blessing, like he always did—'May you be happy, may you be peaceful . . .'—and it was with his usual intensity of warmth, energy, and spirit. It was extremely profound because it was obvious I wasn't going to see him again."

Robert adds, "That was an amazing teaching because he was projecting *mettā* when he was on his deathbed, literally. And it wasn't like he was this saint that was lying there perpetually in bliss. He was a human being suffering—his body was just wasting away—but he didn't complain about his condition. It was mind-blowing that he could summon the strength to still give a blessing."

Daily, Munindra grew weaker. One day, he said to Dhriti, the wife of his nephew Tridib, "It's time for me to go. I don't have many days. Why are you all buying so many medicines for me? I'll be fine. Don't do anything for me. Don't spend so much on me." Then he refused to take anything more into his body. Dhriti recounts his final hours: "I remember we were all standing together—Subhra, Tridib, my mother-in-law—and tried to convince him to have some food for dinner. He just smiled and said, 'No, no, I don't want to have any. Don't force me today. Tomorrow, I'll be all right. Tomorrow, I'll have whatever you tell me.' Because we kept trying to force him, he said, 'OK, I'll have a little water.' So we gave him two teaspoons of water and he said, 'I've had enough. Whatever you want me to do, I'll do it tomorrow.'"

Dhriti continues, "Around three or three-thirty in the morning, I got up to go to the bathroom and peeked in. I heard him say that he wanted to have some water. So his female attendant gave him some water. Later he asked her, 'Have they sat down for the meditation? Have they started chanting?' That was the last thing he said. That was around five in the morning."

Waiting through the night until the moment he knew his family was engaged in dharma practice, Munindra passed away quietly on October 13, 2003.

Develop a state of mind like the earth. For on the earth people throw clean and unclean things, dung and urine, spittle, pus, blood, and the earth is not troubled or repelled or disgusted. And as you grow like the earth, no contacts with pleasant or unpleasant things will lay hold of your mind or stick to it.

—THE BUDDHA, MN 62.13

upekkhā: from *upa* (upon) + *ikkhati* (seeing). It is generally understood as looking upon all things from a neutral or impartial position. As *tatra-majjhattatā,* it is literally "standing in the middle of all this." Common translations of *upekkhā* include "equanimity," "mental equipoise," "even-mindedness," "nonreactivity," "neutrality," and "impartiality."

As a neutral feeling (*vedāna*), *upekkhā* is neither pain nor pleasure but equidistant between elation and sorrow. As even-mindedness, *upekkhā* becomes the subsiding of attraction and repulsion toward all conditioned things. Insight into *anattā* and *anicca* leads to an unshakable balance of mind. Like the stillness found in an ocean's depths, it is a lack of wavering in the face of life's vicissitudes. Understanding that all beings are heirs of their actions (karma) allows for unprejudiced regard for them. Thus, equanimity is not cold indifference, its near enemy, but disinterestedness, that is, freedom from selfish bias.

Upekkhā is the final of the seven factors of awakening (*bojjhaṅga*), ten perfections (*pāramī*), and four sublime abodes (*brahma-vihāra*). Equanimity guides, stabilizes, and restrains the other three sublime abodes (loving-kindness, compassion, and sympathetic joy) from being squandered in futile pursuits or uncontrolled emotion.

Acknowledgments

A great many people practiced a great deal of *dāna* to make *Living This Life Fully* a reality. I am deeply grateful to all of them for helping me turn a question into an answer. And I apologize if I have inadvertently failed to identify everyone's contribution.

When Robert Pryor agreed to collaborate with me on this project, I became the fortunate recipient of a lot more than his treasured interviews with Munindra. Robert's close relationship with him, his in-depth experience in India over the course of nearly four decades, and his historical knowledge were all essential in discussing the various issues that arose as I dealt with each element of research and writing. I appreciate his feedback on everything I gave him to read and his answers to my endless questions. Robert was also my gracious host at the Burmese Vihar in Bodh Gaya, guiding me around town so I might gain a context for understanding Munindra's life there, as well as introducing me to people for interviews. His continued connection to instructors and Munindra's former students in the Antioch program enabled me to interview many of them. He interviewed six individuals himself, scanned photographs from Munindra's own albums, and spent many hours sharing stories about Munindra. I am deeply grateful for his commitment to honoring Munindra.

Like Robert, Kamala Masters has steadfastly supported this project from the start, including suggesting that I get in touch with Robert when the idea for the book popped into my mind. My dhamma sister since 1983, she provided the opportunities that led to my encountering Munindra during his visits to her on Maui. She, too, read almost every draft I wrote and helped me address various concerns through the perspective of her close relationship with Munindra and considerable experience as a dharma teacher. Despite a heavy retreat schedule, she always made herself available and gave me many interview hours on the phone and in person. Kamala generously accompanied me in Calcutta and Rangoon, where we visited Munindra's old haunts. She also introduced me to Daw Than Myint and Ma Vajirañānī, both of whose kindness, interviews, and careful translations of Munindra's autobiography were an unexpected gift.

Munindra's family in Calcutta offered munificent hospitality. They welcomed a perfect stranger into their home, providing comfortable quarters, delicious meals (for which I especially thank Anita Mondal), warm companionship, and morning meditations. They granted me interviews and access to boxes of Munindra's correspondence (some of which his brother Govinda translated for me), and took me to the Mahabodhi Society, where Munindra had once resided. The family also invited some of Munindra's local students and friends to meet me so I could interview them as well. For all of this and much more, my deep gratitude goes to the entire Barua family, especially Govinda, Subhra, Dhriti, Tridib, and Tapas Kumar.

I want to express my sincere thanks to the many people around the world who generously answered my questions about their experiences with Munindra, whether by phone, postal mail, e-mail, or in person. Without them, there would be no book. Because of space constraints, I was unable to quote every person who was interviewed, but all the stories they shared were vital to my developing an understanding of Munindra's character and influence. The list of contributors identifies those individuals who were quoted. What follows, in alphabetical order, is the more complete list of those who were interviewed. Some of the people listed below made memorabilia (such as photographs, letters, diary excerpts, and class notes) available in addition to their interviews.

In Australia: Martin Barua, Lynne Bousfield, Vivianne Bertelsen McClintock, Danny Taylor, Denise Till, Grahame White. In Switzerland: Ven. Āyukusala Thera (Mirko Frýba), Marie-Claude Badonnem, Matthias Barth, Fred von Allmen. In Sweden: Uno Svedin. In Denmark: Uffe Damborg. In France: Heather Stoddard. In Greece: Khanti Moraitis. In England: Christina Feldman, Urgyen Sangharakshita, Stephen Strange, Christopher Titmuss. In Brazil: Ricardo Sasaki. In India: Dhriti Barua, Dipa Barua, Govinda Barua, Subhra Barua, Tapas Kumar Barua, Tridib Barua, Bhante Bodhipāla, Rajia Devi, Gita Kedia, Shyam Sunder Khaddaria, Ven. Satarakshita, Ram Sevak, Dwarko Sundrani, Manisha Talukbar, Saibal Talukbar, Shuma Talukbar. In Sri Lanka: Dhammaruwan Chandrasiri-Seneviratne. In Burma (Myanmar): Daw Than Myint, Ma Vajirañānī (Ellen Mooney). In Thailand: Peter Skilling. In Canada: Alan Clements, Michael

Gelber, Raymond "Ray" Lipovsky, Luke Matthews, Zara Novikoff, Kristin Penn, George Poland, Derek Ridler. In the U.S.: James Baraz, Jane Baraz, Robert Beatty, Mark Berger, David Berman, Arlene Bernstein, Bhikkhu Bodhi, Roy Bonney, Sylvia Boorstein, David Brody, J. Kenneth Brower, Linda Brower, Ron Browning, Dale "Diinabandhu" Brozosky, John M. Burgess, Robert "Buzz" Bussewitz, Shivaya Cain, James Chadderdon, Paul Choi, Dan Clurman, Howard Cohn, Matthew Daniell, Vivan Darst, Ruth Denison, Sister Shinma Dhammadinna, Joseph "Joe" DiNardo, Tara Doyle, John D. Dunne, Jack Engler, Erica Falkenstein, Phelps Feeley, Patti Dye Fuller, Gregg C. Galbraith, David Gelles, Andrew Getz, Evelyn Goldstein, Joseph Goldstein, Daniel Goleman, Lucinda Green, Tyre Harris, Ed Hauben, Shaun Hogan, David Hopkins, Robert H. Hover, Ella Hurst, Xuan Huynh, David Johnson, Barry Lapping, Akasa Levi, Michael Liebenson Grady, Ven. Khippapañño, Erik Knud-Hansen, Jack Kornfield, Eric Kupers, Rebecca Kushins, Tom and Maggie Lesser, Carla R. Mancari, Jacqueline Schwartz Mandell, Peter Martin, Kamala Masters, Pat Masters, Michele McDonald, Margaret "Maggie" Ward McGervey, Mary Jo Meadow, Peter Meehan, John "Dhamma Dipo" Mills, Maria Monroe, Ginny Morgan, Rōshi Wendy Nakao, Wes Nisker, Philip Novak, Patrick Ophuls, John Orr, Gregory Pai, Robert Pryor, Ram Dass, Rameshwar Das, Bob Ray, Dixie Ray, Caitriona Reed, Sharda Rogell, Marcia Rose, Larry Rosenberg, Ajit Roy, Sharon Salzberg, Dale Samoker, Bill "Chaitanya" Samways, Sara Schedler, Max Schorr, Steven J. Schwartz, Robert H. Sharf, Ann Shawhan, Naima Shea, Karen Sirker, Ted Slovin, Huston Smith, Steven V. Smith, Jeanne Smithfield, Oren Sofer, Marilyn Stablein, Michael Stein, Suil, Robin Sunbeam, Lama Surya Das, Donald Sweetbaum, Jeffrey Tipp, John M. Travis, Bryan Tucker, Stella Valdiviez, Bhante Vimalaraṃsi (Marvel Logan), Wanda Weinberger, Giselle Wiederhielm, Rev. James "Jim" Willems, Spirit Lynn Wiseman, David K. Wong, Sunny Wootton, Christine Yedica, Michael Zucker.

On behalf of Robert Pryor, I would like to thank Bhante Bodhipāla, Erica Falkstein, David Frank, S. N. Goenka, Itamar Sofer, Sara Chalfin, Dwarko Sundrani, Bhante Rastrapal, and Dianeah Wanicek.

Other people contributed in a variety of important ways. My warm thanks to the following: Ajahn Thanissaro (Than Geoff), Steve Armstrong, and Gil Fronsdal were generous either with their scholarly expertise in the Theravāda tradition and Pāli or in reading drafts, or both. David Johnson showered me with audio tapes, videos, and DVDs he made of Munindra as early as 1977. Those talks, given at a retreat and at various dharma centers, along with an interview with the editor of *Yoga Journal,* allowed me to convey Munindra's teachings in his own words. Rishi Barua came to the rescue in carrying out communications for me in India when my own efforts were unsuccessful. Jack Engler suggested Munindra's own words for the original title, "Living the Life Fully," and sent me his writings on Munindra. Jon Kabat-Zinn and Harvey Aronson were kind enough to share information that helped me write the book proposal. Michael Larsen and Toni Burbank were gracious in reading and making comments on my book proposal and recommending publishers. Amy Amita Schmidt was supportive during the search for the right publisher. Tim Lighthiser helped with last-minute etymology.

I am grateful to Dave O'Neal at Shambhala for taking on the project and later passing it on to Eden Steinberg. She was a delight to work with; her skillful editing and easy manner made the process a pleasant rather than onerous task. I also want to thank Katie Keach for her kind assistance during the final editing, Meghan Howard for careful copyediting, and Gopa & Ted2 for design.

Last but far from least, my most heartfelt appreciation is reserved for my loving and generous husband, Larry Jacobs, for the many kinds of support that made it possible for me to fully devote myself to this project.

Notes

Chapter 1: Be Simple and Easy, Just Rest in Awareness

1. Kamala Masters's story is paraphrased and quoted from her essay, "Just Washing Dishes," in Sharon Salzberg, ed., *Voices of Insight* (Boston: Shambhala Publications, 1999), pp. 54–56.
2. Sharon Salzberg, *A Heart as Wide as the World* (Boston: Shambhala Publications, 1997), p. 95.

Chapter 3: It's Really Possible to Wake Up

1. Masters, "Just Washing Dishes," p. 54.

Chapter 4: Give Everything with an Open Heart

1. Masters, "Just Washing Dishes," p. 58.

Chapter 6: Say What You Mean and Mean What You Say

1. Ram Dass, introduction in *The Experience of Insight*, by Joeseph Goldstein (Boston: Shambhala Publications, 1976), p. vii.

Chapter 11: Can I Help You?

1. Masters, "Just Washing Dishes," p. 52.

Chapter 13: Joy Is a Factor of Awakening

1. Sharon Salzberg, "In Memoriam: Anagarika Munindra (1914 [sic]–2003)," *Insight* [IMS Newsletter] (Spring-Summer 2004), p. 8.

Chapter 16: It's All a Passing Show

1. Masters, "Just Washing Dishes," pp. 59–60.

Glossary

Abbreviations Used in Glossary Entries
B   Burmese
H   Hindi
lit.   literally
P   Pāli
S   Sanskrit

Abhidhamma (P; Abhidharma, S): lit., "special teaching"; one of the three *piṭakas*, "baskets" or main divisions, of the Pāli Canon or Tipiṭaka, containing a highly detailed analysis of the fundamental principles that govern the behavior of mental and physical processes and form the foundation of Buddhist psychology and logic. Later versions of Abhidharma vary according to the historical school of Buddhism.

abhiññā (P): higher powers, supernormal knowledge.

anāgāmī (P): lit., "nonreturner"; a disciple of the Buddha who has achieved the third of four stages to *nibbāna* and is never again reborn in the human world but in the Brahma world of Pure Abodes. An *anāgāmī* is free of the first five but not the last five fetters (*saṁyojana*). See also *arahant*, *sakadāgāmī*, and *sotāpanna*.

anāgārika (P): lit., "homeless one"; one who embarks on the homeless life without formally entering the Buddhist monastic order.

anattā (P): lit., "not-self"; impersonality or egolessness, one of the three characteristics of existence. See also *anicca* and *dukkha*.

anicca (P): impermanence, the arising, passing away, and changing of all phenomena, one of the three characteristics of existence. See also *anattā* and *dukkha*.

arahant (P; *arhat*, S): lit., a "worthy one," an "accomplished one"; a disciple of the Buddha who has reached the final of four stages to *nibbāna* and will not be reborn again in any form. An *arahant* has completely uprooted greed, hatred, and delusion, which underlie all ten fetters (*saṁyojana*). See also *anāgāmī*, *sakadāgāmī*, and *sotāpanna*.

bala (P): powers; five strengths (*saddhā, viriya, sati, samādhi,* and *paññā*) that represent unshakable firmness in the five spiritual faculties or *indriya*. See also *indriya*.

Bhante (P): a polite form of address commonly used as a term of respect for Theravādin monks, equivalent to "Reverend Sir."

bhāvanā (P): lit., "calling into existence, producing"; dwelling on something, developing or cultivating by means of thought or meditation.

bhikkhu (P): lit., "beggar"; a Buddhist monk with higher ordination, so-called because he goes on alms rounds for his food.

Bodhi Tree: the particular *Ficus religiosa* (pipal tree with heart-shaped leaves) where Prince Siddhārtha experienced supreme awakening (*bodhi*) and became Gautama Buddha. The alleged direct descendant of this sacred ancient tree grows in the Mahabodhi Temple complex in Bodh Gaya, India, and is a frequent destination of Buddhist pilgrims.

bodhisattva (S; *bodhisatta,* P): lit., "enlightenment being"; in Mahāyana Buddhism, a being who vows to attain Buddhahood through systematic practice of the *pāramīta* and renounces nirvāna until all other sentient beings realize the same path. In Theravāda Buddhism, *bodhisatta* refers only to Prince Siddhārtha in his previous lives before his supreme awakening as Gautama Buddha.

bojjhaṅga (P): the seven factors of awakening—*sati, dhamma-vicaya, viriya, pīti, passaddhi, samādhi,* and *upekkhā*. These are the wholesome states that progressively lead to the experience of enlightenment.

brahma-vihāra (P): lit., "heavenly abodes"; the four "sublime," "noble," or "divine" abodes of *mettā, karunā, muditā,* and *upekkhā*. These are also called the four "illimitables" or "immeasurables" (*appamaññā*).

Buddha (S, P): lit., "Awakened One"; one who has achieved supreme awakening (*bodhi*) and thus attained release from *saṁsāra*.

Buddha-Dhamma (P; Buddha-Dharma, S): The Buddha's teaching or message.

chai (H): tea, often milky and sweet, brewed with aromatic spices. A *chai wallah* is a street vendor of such tea.

dāna (P): gifts, alms, or donations, particularly of robes, food, medicine, and so on, to Buddhist monastics. It also refers to generosity or liberality in general and is the first perfection (*pāramī*).

deva (S, P): lit., "shining one" or "radiant one"; celestial beings or deities who live in various kinds of happy realms.

Dhamma (P; Dharma, S): lit., "the bearer"; the liberating law or doctrine that the Buddha rediscovered and taught as the Four Noble Truths. See also Three Jewels.

dhamma (P; *dharma*, S): phenomenon, thing, object of mind, quality. It is also the adjectival form of Dhamma, as in "dhamma teacher."

dhamma-vicaya (P): investigation, specifically of Dhamma. See also *bojjhaṅga*.

dukkha (P): unsatisfactoriness, the suffering that results because of the unsatisfactory nature and general insecurity of all conditioned phenomena. *Dukkha* is also used to refer to bodily or mental pain, and it is the first of the Four Noble Truths and one of the three characteristics of existence. See also *anattā, anicca,* and Four Noble Truths.

Eightfold Path, the (*aṭṭhaṅgika-magga*, P): the way to liberation from suffering. This is the last of the Four Noble Truths. It is composed of three kinds of training (*sikkhā*), consisting of eight practices or links: (1) Right view and right thought constitute *paññā;* (2) right speech, right bodily action, and right livelihood comprise *sīla;* (3) right effort, right mindfulness, and right concentration are part of *samādhi*. Technically, it is not a path in the sense of sequential steps; rather these links, in part, arise simultaneously, reinforcing each other. See also Four Noble Truths.

Four Noble Truths, the (*ariya-sacca*, P): the basic synthesis of the Buddha's teaching—that there is suffering (*dukkha*), that craving is the cause of all suffering, that there is an end to suffering, and that the Eightfold Path is the way to cease suffering.

gāthā (S, P): brief verses stating a Buddhist teaching, praising the virtue of a Buddha or *bodhisatta,* or relating the struggle with the forces of Māra; for example, the *Theragāthā* (Verses of the Elder Monks) and *Therīgāthā* (Verses of the Elder Nuns).

iddhi (P; *siddhi*, S): supernormal, psychic, or higher spiritual power.

indriya (S, P): lit., "belonging to the ruler Indra"; thus governing. These faculties, in particular, the five spiritual faculties (*saddhā, viriya, sati, samādhi,* and *paññā*), when they become unshakable, are *bala*.

jhāna (P): the state of meditative absorption, a meditative state of profound stillness and concentration, or absorption meditation.

kalyāṇamitta (P; *kalyāṇamitra*, S): lit., "noble friend"; a teacher or mentor who guides a student's meditation. It can also refer to a fellow companion on the Eightfold Path. "Noble" should be understood in the sense of "good" or "admirable."

kamma (P; karma, S): lit., "deed" or "action"; the universal principle of cause and effect; the wholesome and unwholesome volitional actions that cause rebirth and shape a person's life. Only deeds free from desire, hatred, and delusion have no karmic effect.

karuṇā (P): compassion; one of the four *brahma-vihāra*.

khanti (P): patience, forbearance; one of the ten *pāramī*.

kilesa (P): defilements; mental states, such as greed, hate, and delusion, which cloud the mind and result in unskillful actions.

kuṭī (P): simple hermitage hut or meditation cell.

lungi (H): a traditional, informal men's garment in India consisting of a rectangular piece of unstitched cloth, several yards long, wrapped around the waist and the legs, and knotted at the waist.

Māra (S, P): lit., "the killer," "destruction," or "murder." For six years, this tempter-figure unsuccessfully tried to seduce the Buddha (as a bodhisattva) away from his practice to awaken. He sent armies of demons and other obstacles as well as a vision of alluring women to distract the Buddha. Māra is depicted in the texts as both a deity (presiding over the highest heaven of the sensuous sphere) and as the personification of evil and passions.

mettā (P): lit., "friendship" or "kindness"; loving-kindness or loving-friendliness, one of the four *brahma-vihāra*.

Moggallāna (P): the most adept of the Buddha's disciples in the various *siddhis* or *iddhis*, (supernatural or magical powers) that are developed through intensive *samādhi* practice. He used these powers to assist people (deceased or alive) in better understanding their *dukkha*.

muditā (P): appreciative, sympathetic, or altruistic joy; one of the four *brahma-vihāra*.

Nalanda (H): an ancient university in Bihar, India, that was a center of Buddhist learning from the fifth to twelfth centuries and attracted scholars and students from around the world.

nāma-rūpa (P): lit., "name-form." *Nāma* is, literally, "name"; mind, mentality, a collective name for four mental groups (feeling, perception, mental formations, and consciousness). *Rūpa* is form, corporeality, body, and physical phenomenon. Together, they mean mind-body and constitute the fourth link in dependent origination (*paṭiccasamuppāda*).

nekkhamma (P): freedom from craving and desires, renunciation, emancipation from worldliness.

nibbāna (P; nirvāna, S): lit., "to cease blowing," "to become extinguished"; freedom from craving or desire. This is, the highest and ultimate goal of Buddhist aspiration—the extinction of greed, hatred, delusion, and clinging to existence and absolute deliverance from all future rebirth, old age, disease and death, suffering and misery.

nīvarana (P): hindrances or obstacles to full concentration and direct knowledge; specifically, five qualities that blind the mind—sensuous desire, ill will, sloth and torpor, restlessness, and skeptical doubt.

Pāli (P, S): a middle Indo-Aryan language, derived from Sanskrit, in which the earliest Buddhist scriptural corpus, the canon of the Theravāda school, is preserved. The literal Sanskrit translation is "row," indicating a series of Buddhist texts.

paññā (P; *prajñā*, S): understanding, knowledge, wisdom, insight; one of the three kinds of training (*sikkhā*) on the Eightfold Path, the five *indriya*, or *bala*, and the ten *pāramī*.

paramattha (P): that which is true in the highest or ultimate sense versus conventionally or commonly accepted truth.

pāramī (P; *pāramīta*, S): lit., "that which has reached the other shore"; perfection, perfecting qualities that lead to Buddhahood.

paṭiccasamuppāda (P): dependent origination, codependent arising. This is the twelve-linked chain or formulation of causation that describes how the arising of every phenomenon is conditioned by and dependent on the existence of other phenomena, physical or mental.

piṭaka (P): lit., "basket." See Tipiṭaka.

pīti (P): rapture, joy, enthusiasm, one of the seven factors of awakening (*bojjhaṅga*).

prajñā (S): See *paññā*.

sacca (P): lit., "real" or "true"; truthfulness, honesty, integrity; one of the ten *pāramī*.

saddhā (P): conviction, faith, and confidence in the Three Jewels.

sakadāgāmī (P): lit., "once-returner"; a disciple of the Buddha who has reached the second of four stages leading to *nibbāna* having eradicated the first three fetters (*saṁyojana*) and seriously weakened the forth and fifth fetters. See also *anāgāmī*, *arahant*, and *sotāpatti*.

samādhi (P, S): lit., "to establish, make firm"; concentration, the mental state of being firmly fixed on a single object; and the meditative practice of centering the mind. *Samādhi* is one of the *bojjhaṅga*, the last link of the Eightfold Path and the collective term for the last three links, and one of the five *indriya* or *bala*. It is also one of the three divisions of training (*sikkhā*).

sāmaṇera (P): lit., "small renunciate"; a novice monk.

samatha (P): tranquility, serenity; an unperturbed, peaceful, and lucid state of mind achieved through strong mental concentration, synonymous with *samādhi,* one-pointedness of mind, and undistractedness.

sammā (P): perfect, right, properly, thoroughly; the adjective describing each of the steps on the Eightfold Path, for example *sammā-vācā* (right speech).

saṁyojana (P): fetters that bind one to the wheel of existence (*saṁsāra*). There are ten: the lower five (belief in a separate self, skeptical doubt, clinging to rites and

236 · GLOSSARY

rituals, sensuous craving, and ill-will) tie one to the sensuous or material world; the higher five (craving for fine-material existence, craving for immaterial existence, conceit, restlessness, and ignorance) tie one to the higher fine-material and immaterial worlds. See also *anāgāmī, arahant, sakadāgāmī,* and *sotapānna.*

saṁsāra (S): lit., "perpetual wandering"; the endless round of rebirth and suffering.

saṁvega (P): a sense of spiritual urgency.

sangha (P, S): lit., "congregation"; the assembly or community of Buddhist monks, in particular, but all followers (lay and monastic) of the Buddha's teaching, in general. When capitalized, *Sangha* is also the third of the Three Jewels. See also Three Jewels.

Sāriputta (P): one of the Buddha's most important disciples, known especially for his wisdom.

sati (P): mindfulness; a mental factor inseparably associated with all wholesome consciousness.

satsang (S): lit., "true company." In association with others, *satsang* refers to listening to or reading scriptures and engaging in discussion, chanting, or asking questions of a teacher.

sayādaw (B): teacher. When capitalized, *Sayādaw* is a Burmese title for a Buddhist monk, usually the abbot of a monastery, or an honorific form of address for monks in general.

seven factors of awakening: See *bojjhaṅga.*

siddhi (S): See *iddhi.*

sikkhā (P): lit., "training"; the three-fold training that a disciple of the Buddha must undertake in heightened morality (*adhisīla-sikkhā*), heightened mind (*adhicitta-sikkhā*), and heightened wisdom (*adhipaññā-sikkhā*), akin to the tripartite division of the Eightfold Path.

sikkhāpada (P): the steps of training or moral rules. See also *sīla.*

sīla (P; *sīla,* S): morality, virtue; the conscious and intentional restraint from unwholesome verbal and physical actions, and behavioral guidelines for monastics and laypersons. *Sīla* is the first of the three kinds of training (*sikkhā*) and includes right speech, right action, and right livelihood from the Eightfold Path. See also *sikkhā.*

sotāpanna (P): lit., "one who entered the stream" or "stream-winner"; one who has attained the first of four stages to *nibbāna,* having abandoned the first three fetters (*saṁyojana*). See also *sakadāgāmī, anāgāmī,* and *arahant.*

sotāpatti (P): lit., "stream-entry"; the first of four stages leading to nibbāna. See also *anāgāmī, arahant,* and *sakadāgāmī.*

Śrī (S): lit., "diffusing light" or "radiance"; generally, an honorific or title of veneration, but also equivalent to "Mister."

stupa (P, S): lit., "heap"; a moundlike monument containing Buddhist relics.

Sumedha (P): the name of the fourteenth Buddha when he was a bodhisattva during the time of the Dīpankara Buddha. According to legends of Gautama Buddha's life, Sumedha was a young Brahmin who became a diligent ascetic. At one point, out of reverence for Dipānkara Buddha, Sumedha knelt down and spread his hair across a road to keep Dipānkara Buddha from having to step in the mud; and he resolved that he, too, would become a Buddha. Looking into the future, Dipānkara Buddha saw that Sumedha would attain awakening as Siddhārtha Gautama.

sutta (P; sūtra, S): lit., "thread," "that which holds things together"; a discourse or text and, when capitalized, the name for the first division of the Pāli Canon or Tipiṭaka.

Tathāgata (S): lit., "Thus Gone" or "Thus Come"; one who has attained the highest spiritual goal in Buddhism—awakening or enlightenment. The Buddha used this epithet in referring to himself, meaning "Perfectly Awakened One."

Theravāda (P): lit., "Doctrine of the Elders"; the oldest form of the Buddha's teachings, as handed down in the Pāli Canon, sometimes called Southern Buddhism because it predominates in Southeast Asia, or Pāli Buddhism because its scriptures are written in the Pāli language.

Three Jewels: the basic elements of Buddhism—the Buddha, representing awakening; the Dharma (S) or Dhamma (P), the Teaching, Way, or Liberating Law; and the *Sangha,* the Community.

Tipiṭaka (P): lit., "Three Baskets"; the three main divisions (Vinaya, Sutta, and Abhidhamma) of the Pāli Canon, the earliest Buddhist scriptural corpus.

Triple Gem: See Three Jewels.

upekkhā (P): equanimity, one of the four *brahma-vihāra* and seven factors of awakening (*bojjhaṅga*).

vedāna (P, S): feeling, sensation; pleasant, unpleasant, and neutral sensations (mental rather than physical factors) that arise from contact between internal sense organs and objects and their associated consciousness.

vihar (S): a term for a Buddhist monastery, but originally for a temporary shelter used by a wandering monk during the rainy season.

Vinaya (P): discipline; the Buddhist code of behavior for monks and nuns that is the third part of the Pāli Canon or Tipiṭaka.

vipassanā (P): insight; intuitive illumination of the truth of *anicca, dukkha,* and *anattā;* and the meditation practice of observing one's own bodily and mental processes.

viriya (P; *vīrya*, S): energy, effort. It is one of the seven factors of awakening (*bojjhaṅga*) and also known as "right effort" on The Eightfold Path.

yogi (H): a practitioner of spiritual practice; in the context of Buddhist practice, someone on a meditation retreat.

Contributors

Abbreviations used in Contributor Biographies

The following abbreviations and place names appear in the contributor biographies:

Antioch program: Antioch Education Abroad Buddhist Studies Program in Bodh Gaya, India

BCBS: Barre Center for Buddhist Studies in Barre, Massachusetts

Dhamma Giri: a vipassanā meditation center established by S. N. Goenka in Igatpuri, India

IMS: Insight Meditation Society in Barre, Massachusetts

SRMC: Spirit Rock Meditation Center in Woodacre, California

Āyukusala Thera, formerly **Mirko Frýba,** is a retired Czech professor of psychology who became a Buddhist monk in Sri Lanka in 1996. He trained with Munindra in Bodh Gaya in 1967 and thereafter taught vipassanā meditation under his supervision in Switzerland and other German-speaking countries. With Munindra's support, he founded the Swiss Buddhist Union in 1978.

James Baraz has been teaching meditation since 1978 and a course in Awakening Joy since 2003. He is a founding teacher of SRMC, a member of the international advisory council of the Buddhist Peace Fellowship, and coauthor of *Awakening Joy*. He first met Munindra in Bodh Gaya in 1977.

Jane Baraz has been practicing vipassanā since 1976. She served on the SRMC board of directors for its first eight years and helped start the Spirit Rock Family Program. An instructor of English as a second language, she also copresents James Baraz's Awakening Joy courses. She first practiced with Munindra at a California retreat in 1977.

CONTRIBUTORS

Matthias Barth has been practicing meditation since the mid-1970s with Munindra and other eminent dharma teachers. One of the founders of Switzerland's Dhamma Group in 1978, he integrates meditation methods into his work with individuals and groups as a psychotherapist in Bern, Switzerland.

Dhriti Barua came to know Munindra well when she married his nephew Tridib Barua. She teaches English at the International School of Business and Media in Calcutta. Their daughter Pallavi kept Munindra company at the Barua family home at the end of his life.

Dipa Barua is the daughter of meditation master Dipa Ma (Nani Bala Barua). She was born in Burma and practised vipassanā there under the guidance of Mahāsi Sayādaw, Munindra, and Sayādaw U Pandita. She has a master's degree in Pāli and is an employee of the Indian government, a governing member of the Mahabodhi Society of India in Calcutta, and an executive body member of the International Meditation Centre in Bodh Gaya.

Gopendra "Govinda" Prasad Barua was Munindra's youngest brother and a retired employee of Calcutta Telephones. He was first initiated into vipassanā meditation under Munindra's guidance in 1967. He passed away in 2009.

Subhra Barua is the daughter of Munindra's younger brother Sasanka Mohan Barua and his wife Kanak Prova Barua. She is the sister of Tridib and Tapas Kumar. She holds a PhD in Pāli and wrote her doctoral thesis on the Buddhist order of nuns. Starting in 1979, she regularly accompanied Munindra on his vipassanā lectures and attended her first retreat under his guidance in 1990.

Tapas Kumar Barua is the son of Munindra's younger brother Sasanka Mohan Barua and his wife Kanak Prova Barua, and is the brother of Subhra and Tridib. He holds a PhD in chemistry and worked in the Oil and Natural Gas Commission of India before his current job with a foreign oil company in the Sudan.

Tridib Barua is the son of Munindra's younger brother Sasanka Mohan Barua and his wife Kanak Prova Barua, and is the younger brother of Tapas Kumar and Subhra. An engineer in India, he was introduced to vipassanā by Munindra in 1983 in Sarnath.

Robert Beatty is the guiding teacher of the Portland Insight Meditation Community, in Oregon, which he founded in 1979. His meditation training began in India in 1972 with Munindra, and he teaches in the lineage of Ruth Denison.

Mark Berger met Munindra during a 1977 retreat at the Stillpoint Institute in San Jose, California, and remained in contact with him over the next 25 years.

David Berman was a resident staff member at IMS from 1988 to 1999 and also served as Munindra's personal assistant during his 1989 visit. Since 1999, he was on the island of Oahu, sometimes working as administrative assistant to Steven V. Smith and Michele McDonald. He passed away in 2010.

CONTRIBUTORS • 241

Arlene Bernstein is a psychotherapist, gardener, visual artist, and the author of *Growing Season: Life Lessons from the Garden*. She met Munindra in Bodh Gaya in 1978.

Bhante Bodhipāla became a novice monk at the age of seven in Chittagong, Bangladesh. Although he did not meet Munindra until 1993, at the Mahabodhi Society in Calcutta, he knew of him since childhood as they were both members of the same Barua Bengal Buddhist community in neighboring villages. He served as chief monk of the Mahabodhi Temple in Bodh Gaya from 2000 to 2006.

Roy Bonney has been a student of S. N. Goenka since his first retreat in 1972 in Bodh Gaya, where he also met Munindra. He is a photographer and bodyworker in the San Francisco Bay Area.

Sylvia Boorstein is a founding teacher of SRMC, a psychologist, the author of several books on Buddhism and mindfulness practice, and a regular columnist for *Shambhala Sun*. She met Munindra when she began practicing vipassanā meditation in 1977.

David Brody practiced with Munindra while attending the Antioch program in Bodh Gaya in 1997 and also met with him at Dhamma Giri.

Ron Browning began his Buddhist practice with Shunryū Suzuki Rōshi and Kosho Uchiyama Rōshi in the U.S. and Japan. Since 1979, he has practiced in the Theravāda tradition, including five and a half years as a monk. Ron met Munindra at IMS and Yucca Valley in the 1980s. He is founder of Santidhamma Foundation, a nonprofit currently working to reestablish the Buddha-Dhamma in India.

Dale "Diinabandhu" Brozosky brings his extensive training in various contemplative traditions (Hindu, Buddhist, and Jewish) into his teaching and counseling practice based in California. He first met Munindra at IMS in the late 1970s.

John M. Burgess attended retreats with Munindra on the islands of Maui and Hawai'i in the 1980s. Taking Munindra's advice to "seek justice" in his practice of law, he established DharmaLaw. A human rights attorney in San Francisco, he has successfully represented more than two hundred Tibetan asylum cases, including monks and nuns, since 1994.

Robert "Buzz" Bussewitz has been a dharma practitioner since 1978. He first met Munindra while on staff at IMS, visited him in Calcutta in 1985, and also served as his attendant.

Shivaya Cain first met Munindra in Bodh Gaya in 1971 and continues to integrate mindfulness practice into his daily life in the San Francisco Bay Area.

James Chadderdon first met Munindra in Bodh Gaya early in 1977 and several years later drove him from Boulder to Phoenix via the Grand Canyon. He is an attorney in Colorado Springs, Colorado.

CONTRIBUTORS

Dhammaruwan Chandrasiri-Senevīratne, a native of Sri Lanka, spontaneously chanted *suttas* in Pāli at the age of two and was first exposed to meditation teachings at the age of nine, when Munindra visited his family in Kandy, Sri Lanka. He started the Nirodha Trust, a nonprofit that promotes the Buddha's teachings, and he conducts pilgrimage retreat tours to Buddhist sites in his country.

Paul Choi is a psychiatrist, meditation teacher, and father in Oakland, California. He met Munindra at his family's home in Calcutta in 1996 after attending the Antioch program in Bodh Gaya.

Alan Clements met Munindra in Bodh Gaya in 1976 and ordained with his teacher, Mahāsi Sayādaw, in 1979. An internatonal dharma teacher, spiritual activist, and performing artist, he is the author of several books, including *Burma: The Next Killing Fields* and *The Voice of Hope* (conversations with Aung San Suu Kyi). He is also coauthor of *Burma's Revolution of the Spirit*.

Howard Cohn is an original member of the Spirit Rock Teachers Council and has led meditation retreats worldwide since 1985. He first met Munindra in San Jose, California, in the late 1970s and, in the 1980s, served as his attendant at the Yucca Valley retreat center, sat retreats with him in New Mexico and on Maui, and visited him in Calcutta.

Uffe Damborg is a psychologist in Copenhagen, where he integrates mindfulness into psychotherapy and teaches mindfulness meditation. He studied with Munindra in Bodh Gaya from 1968 to 1975, spent some years living in hermitages in Sri Lanka, and cofounded the Northern Light Vipassanā Society in Fredrika, Sweden, in 2008.

Vivian Darst has been practicing in the Theravāda tradition since 1972. She met Munindra at the Mahabodhi Society in Calcutta in 1977 and later traveled extensively with him in North America and Europe. She runs the Flower Lady in Seattle.

Ruth Denison studied in Burma in the early 1960s with the meditation master Sayagi U Ba Khin, met Munindra in Bodh Gaya in the late 1970s, and has been teaching since 1973. She is the founder of Dhamma Dena, a desert retreat center in Joshua Tree, California, and the Center for Buddhism in the West in Germany.

Joseph "Joe" DiNardo, an attorney in Buffalo, New York, first met Munindra in 1978 at a retreat in Yucca Valley and traveled and taught with him in the U.S. and India, remaining close friends with him until his death.

Tara Doyle is a senior lecturer in the Department of Religion at Emory University and serves as director of Emory's Tibetan studies program in Dharamsala, India. As a founding-director and instructor for the Antioch program in Bodh Gaya (1979–94), she worked closely with Munindra.

John D. Dunne is a tenured professor in the Department of Religion at Emory University. He first met Munindra while teaching in the Antioch program in Bodh Gaya in 1994.

Jack Engler is a psychologist on the clinical faculty of Harvard Medical School at the Cambridge Hospital, where he teaches and supervises psychotherapy in the Department of Psychiatry. He first studied with Munindra in India from 1975 to 1977 and remained close to him for the rest of his life. A founding board member of both IMS and BCBS, he now teaches at BCBS.

Erica Falkenstein first met Munindra in 1992 through the Antioch program in Bodh Gaya and received his teachings several times in subsequent years. Based in New York City, she works in international development.

Christina Feldman first met Munindra in Bodh Gaya in 1973 and has been teaching Dharma since 1976 in Europe and North America. Cofounder of Gaia House in England and a guiding teacher at IMS, she is the author of *Compassion, Silence,* and *The Buddhist Path to Simplicity.*

Mirko Frýba (see Āyukusala Thera)

Patti Dye Fuller attended Munindra's first American retreat in San Jose, California, in 1977. She passed away in 2006.

Gregg C. Galbraith began practicing in the Theravāda tradition in 1973 and met Munindra in India in 1974, where he spent a year in residence with him. He also traveled with Munindra in India and the U.S. in the 1970s and 1980s. Gregg runs a business in Carthage, Missouri, and continues his service to Ozark Regional Land Trust, a nonprofit conservation organization he founded in Missouri in 1984.

David Gelles is a reporter for *The Financial Times.* He studied with Munindra in the Antioch program in Bodh Gaya in 2000, visited him in Calcutta, and saw him at Dhamma Giri in 2001.

Andrew Getz has practiced insight meditation since he was a teenager, including a period of monastic training in Asia, and has taught retreats at IMS and SRMC. He met Munindra in Bodh Gaya in the early 1980s. A child and adolescent psychiatric nurse, he cofounded Youth Horizons, which merged with the Mind Body Awareness Project.

S. N. Goenka is a lay teacher of vipassanā meditation in the tradition of the late Sayagi U Ba Khin of Burma. Indian and Hindu by descent, he was born and raised in Burma, where he helped sponsor Munindra's stay, and where the two became close friends. Goenka later settled in India and began teaching vipassanā in 1969, eventually establishing many meditation centers, including Dhamma Giri, Munindra's favorite place to retreat.

Joseph Goldstein first met Munindra in Bodh Gaya in 1967 and spent most of the next seven years studying and practicing under his guidance and inspiration. A cofounder of IMS in 1976, he helped to host Munindra there several times. He is the author of several dharma books, including *One Dharma: The Emerging Western Buddhism* and *Insight Meditation: The Practice of Freedom*.

Daniel Goleman is a psychologist and the author of many books, including *Emotional Intelligence* and *Destructive Emotions: A Dialogue with Scientists and the Dalai Lama*. He first met Munindra in 1970 in Bodh Gaya.

Ed Hauben met Munindra in Cambridge, Massachusetts, and at IMS in the late 1970s. A long-term meditator, he served as president of the IMS board of directors in the early 1980s and assisted with the teen and family retreats. He is now director of Newton Community Education in Massachusetts.

Shaun Hogan attended Munindra's first American retreat in San Jose, California, in 1977.

David Hopkins, a student of S. N. Goenka, met Munindra at Dhamma Dhara in Shelburne Falls, Massachusetts, in the early 1990s, and at Dhamma Giri in 2002.

Xuan Huynh, with her husband Dr. Thanh Huynh, hosted Munindra several times in Honolulu in the 1980s. They are community dharma leaders and teach short retreats on O'ahu.

David Johnson is a business analyst with a technology firm in Silicon Valley and has been practicing meditation on and off since the early 1970s. He met Munindra in 1977 while working as a volunteer at a vipassanā meditation center in San Jose, California.

Gita Kedia is an assistant teacher for S. N. Goenka. She first met Munindra at Dhamma Giri in the 1980s and saw him regularly there and in Calcutta until his death in 2003.

Shyam Sunder Khaddaria has been a student of S. N. Goenka since 1974. He often engaged in scholarly discussion of Dharma with Munindra at Dhamma Giri.

Ven. Khippapañño is a Buddhist monk who ordained in 1949 and practiced in both India and Burma. Munindra was his first vipassanā teacher, in 1967 in Bodh Gaya. He has been teaching insight meditation since 1982 and founded Jetavana Vihāra in Washington, DC, Shākyamuni Meditation Center in California, and helped establish Phu'oá'c So'n Meditation Center in Vietnam.

Erik Knud-Hansen has studied and practiced widely in the various schools of Buddhism as well as in the traditions of Taoism and Advaita Vedanta since 1972, including a year as a Zen monk in South Korea. He has been teaching Dharma since 1984. He spent time with Munindra in the U.S. in the late 1970s.

Jack Kornfield trained as a Buddhist monk in Asia and met Munindra in India in the mid-1970s. A cofounder of IMS and SRMC, he has taught meditation internationally since 1974 and written ten books on dharma practice, including *A Path with Heart; After the Ecstasy, the Laundry;* and *A Wise Heart*. He also holds a PhD in clinical psychology.

Eric Kupers is a director, choreographer, and performer with Dandelion Dancetheater, which he cofounded in San Francisco in 1996. He is a professor of dance and theater at California State University East Bay and a recipient of numerous awards and grants. He studied with Munindra in the Antioch program in 1992.

Rebecca Kushins is a student at the University of Hawai'i and a former staff member of BCBS. She practiced with Munindra through the Antioch program in Bodh Gaya in 2002.

Barry Lapping, one of S. N. Goenka's assistant teachers, has been associated with the vipassanā meditation center Dhamma Dhara in Shelburne Falls, Massachusetts, since it opened in 1982. He first met and briefly practiced with Munindra at the Burmese Vihar in Bodh Gaya in 1970 and later saw him regularly at Dhamma Giri.

Akasa Levi was a Theravāda Buddhist forest monk for six years during the 1970s, trained and ordained by Ven. Balangoda Ānanda Maitreya of Sri Lanka. He met Munindra in Bodh Gaya in 1974. He teaches meditation at the Laughing Buddha Sangha in Santa Monica, California, and leads Zen-Men groups at the Los Angeles Medicine Men's Lodge.

Michael Liebenson Grady has been practicing insight meditation since 1973. He is a guiding teacher at the Cambridge Insight Meditation Center in Cambridge, Massachusetts, and a senior teacher at IMS, where he first met Munindra.

Raymond "Ray" Lipovsky is a metal artist, designer, master goldsmith, engineer, and long-time Buddhist practitioner on the island of Llyndorah in British Columbia. He first met Munindra in British Columbia at a retreat around 1980 and studied with him from 1981 to 1982 in Calcutta and Bodh Gaya.

Marvel Logan (see **Bhante Vimalaraṃsi**)

Carla R. Mancari is cofounder of the Contemplative Invitation Teaching (which includes Christ Centered Prayer) and assists with teaching and retreats. She has studied worldwide with Christian, Hindu, and Buddhist masters, including Munindra, whom she met in 1974 at the Insight Meditation Centre in Bodh Gaya.

Jacqueline Schwartz Mandell is a Buddhist meditation teacher, mother, and the director of Samden Ling in Portland, Oregon. She first studied and practiced with Munindra in Bodh Gaya in 1972 and later cotaught retreats with him during his visits to the West.

Peter Martin teaches English and intercultural communication at Edmonds Community College, near Seattle. He has been practicing vipassanā under S. N. Goenka's guidance since 1980 and conducting courses as a senior assistant teacher since 1984. He spent time with Munindra at Dhamma Giri.

Kamala Masters met Munindra in 1977, when he first came to the U.S., and became one of his most devoted students. She is cofounder of Vipassana Metta Foundation on the island of Maui and offers the teachings of the Buddha in the Theravāda tradition worldwide.

Pat Masters first met Munindra in Honolulu around 1983 and then saw him annually while teaching the anthropology of Buddhism in the Antioch program in Bodh Gaya from 1996 to 1999. She now resides in Honolulu and is an academic dean at the University of Hawai'i.

Luke Matthews, a student and assistant teacher under S. N. Goenka, first met Munindra at the Burmese Vihar in Bodh Gaya in 1971 and saw him there and at Dhamma Giri over a period of thirty-five years.

Margaret "Maggie" Ward McGervey participated in the Antioch program in Bodh Gaya, where she met Munindra in 1986. She later returned to work with the program many times and also assisted and led pilgrimages to the four sacred sites of Buddhism in India.

Peter Meehan is CEO of Newman's Own Organics. He first met Munindra in Bodh Gaya in 1979.

Maria Monroe began practicing insight meditation with Munindra in Bodh Gaya in 1968 and taught vipassanā from 1979 to 1984.

Katerina "Khanti" Moraitis first met Munindra in Bodh Gaya in 1968. She practiced on and off with him from 1969 to 1974, including taking robes for one year, and last saw him when he visited her family in Greece in 1979. She has been a freelance translator for Greek television since 1975.

Ginny Morgan worked as a play therapist for acutely and chronically ill children for many years before becoming the senior teacher for Show Me Dharma Center in Columbia, Missouri. She spent time there with Munindra in the late 1970s and at BCBS in the mid-1990s.

Daw Than Myint first met Munindra at Mahāsi Sayādaw's meditation center in Rangoon, Burma, in 1965, after her mother Hema Prabha Barua and her aunt Dipa Ma (Nani Bala Barua) practiced with him. Now retired, she was a full professor and head of the Department of Zoology at Pathein University.

Rōshi Wendy Egyoku Nakao is abbot and head teacher of the Zen Center of Los Angeles. She met Munindra circa 1980 in California and later practiced with him at IMS and in Calcutta and Bodh Gaya.

Wes Nisker is a member of the Spirit Rock Teachers Council and the author of *Essential Crazy Wisdom, Buddha's Nature,* and other books. He is also a radio commentator, a performer, a founder and coeditor of the Buddhist journal *Inquiring Mind,* and he teaches internationally. He first met Munindra in Bodh Gaya in 1970.

Philip Novak is the Sarlo Distinguished Professor of Religion at Dominican University of California, San Rafael. He studied with Munindra in Bodh Gaya toward the end of 1976. He has been a student of S. N. Goenka since 1977.

Zara Novikoff is a retired nurse on Vancouver Island. She first met Munindra in Bodh Gaya in 1967 while on a pilgrimage with Indians and Sri Lankans, and she practiced with him in 1968. She later saw him several times in the U.S. and Canada.

Patrick Ophuls is the author of *Buddha Takes No Prisoners* and encountered Munindra at IMS in 1978 and on and off between 1981 and 1983.

John Orr received eight years of Theravādin monastic training in Thailand and India. He has been leading meditation retreats in the U.S. since 1980, when he met Munindra at IMS. An instructor of Buddhist studies, meditation, and yoga at Duke University, he is also a teacher and the spiritual director of the New Hope Sangha in Durham, North Carolina.

Gregory Pai considers Munindra his first real mentor in Theravāda Buddhist practice. He met him at the home of Dr. Thanh and Xuan Huynh in Honolulu, in the late 1980s, and corresponded with him for many years. A retired Hawai'i State government employee, Gregory is a community dharma leader on O'ahu.

Robert Pryor is a professor of Buddhist studies and the director of the Antioch program in Bodh Gaya, which he cofounded in 1979. Robert met Munindra in 1972 and remained one of his close students until his death in 2003.

Bob and Dixie Ray cofounded the Southwest Center for Spiritual Living in Las Vegas, New Mexico. They practiced with Munindra on long retreats in the U.S., hosted him in Chicago, and visited him in Calcutta in 1984.

Caitriona Reed first met Munindra in London in 1979. She is a dharma teacher and cofounder of Manzanita Village Retreat in Southern California.

Rajia Devi was the cook for the Antioch program in Bodh Gaya until her death in 2010.

Ram Dass, as Richard Alpert, was a university professor and researcher before traveling to India in 1967 and pursuing various spiritual practices, including Theravāda meditation with Munindra. He is cofounder of the Seva Foundation, an international service organization, and author of such spiritual classics as *Be Here Now.*

Derek Ridler met Munindra on a three-month retreat at IMS and then in India in the early 1980s. A retired marriage and family counselor in British Columbia, he practices in the Vajrayāna tradition.

Sharda Rogell is on the Spirit Rock Teachers Council and has been teaching worldwide since 1987. She began meditating in 1979 and met Munindra two years later, when he was visiting California.

Marcia Rose is the founding and guiding teacher of the Mountain Hermitage in Taos, New Mexico. She has been practicing meditation and studying Dharma since 1970, primarily in the Theravāda tradition, including under Munindra's guidance in Sarnath, India, in 1986.

Larry Rosenberg is the founder and a guiding teacher of the Cambridge Insight Meditation Center in Cambridge, Massachusetts. He is also a senior teacher at IMS and the author of *Breath by Breath* and *Living in the Light of Death*. Munindra was his first teacher of vipassanā.

Ajit Roy spent close time with Munindra in Calcutta and Bodh Gaya before leaving for the U.S. in 1984. He is a jewelry designer.

Sharon Salzberg is a meditation teacher and cofounder of IMS, as well as the author of several dharma books, including *Faith* and *The Kindness Handbook*. She began studying with Munindra in Bodh Gaya in 1971.

Bill "Chaitanya" Samways met Munindra in Bodh Gaya in 1971 and studied with him for several years. He accompanied him on his first trip to Thailand, the Philippines, Hawai'i, and the mainland U.S. in 1977.

Ricardo Sasaki met Munindra at the Mahabodhi Society in Calcutta in 1987 and, a year later, attended his retreats in Sarnath and Bodh Gaya. In 1989, he started the Nalanda Buddhist Center in Belo Horizonte, Brazil, where he is a psychologist and dharma teacher. In 1999, he founded Nalandarama, the first Theravāda center in South America exclusively dedicated to intensive meditation retreats in the forest tradition.

Sara Schedler was a student in the Antioch program in Bodh Gaya in 1999. Munindra was her first dharma teacher, and she continues to practice vipassanā. She works for Friends of the Earth, an environmental policy organization in San Francisco.

Max Schorr is cofounder, publisher, and community director of *GOOD*, a quarterly magazine. He met Munindra as a student in the Antioch program in Bodh Gaya in 2001.

Steven J. Schwartz is a long-term vipassanā practitioner and one of the cofounders of IMS. He first met Munindra in Bodh Gaya in 1972 and for the next decade studied with him there as well as in Calcutta and the U.S. He also accompanied Munindra on trips to New York and Washington, DC.

Ram Sevak met Munindra in Bodh Gaya in 1967, when he was twelve years old. He remained continuously close to Munindra, who mentored him until his death.

Robert H. Sharf is professor and chair of the Center for Buddhist Studies at the University of California, Berkeley. He first met Munindra during his stay in Bodh Gaya from 1972 to 1973.

Ann Shawhan attended Munindra's first American retreat in San Jose, California, in 1977.

Naima Shea began her Buddhist practice with Munindra in Bodh Gaya in late 1972.

Karen Sirker is a senior social development specialist with the World Bank. She met Munindra while attending the Antioch program in Bodh Gaya in 1979 and maintained a correspondence with him thereafter.

Peter Skilling presently heads the Buddhist Studies Group at the École française d'Extrême-Orient (EFEO). He is founder of the Fragile Palm Leaves Foundation in Bangkok, dedicated to preserving, studying, and publishing Southeast Asian Buddhist literature, and he is a founding member of the International Centre for Buddhist Studies, also in Bangkok. He was a monk in Thailand in the early 1970s and met Munindra in India in the late 1970s.

Ted Slovin met Munindra at IMS in 1977 and spent time with him on several subsequent visits to Massachusetts. He is former vice president of the board of directors of IMS.

Steven V. Smith is cofounder of Vipassana Hawai'i and teaches embodied mindfulness and the immeasurables (love, compassion, joy, and equanimity) worldwide. He met Munindra, his first meditation master, in Bodh Gaya in 1976.

Jeanne Smithfield met Munindra at IMS during the late 1970s and early 1980s, where she attended several three-month retreats and was a staff member.

Itamar Sofer first met Munindra during a pilgrimage to Buddhist sites in India conducted by his teacher, S. N. Goenka, in 2001. He saw Munindra thereafter at Dhamma Giri.

Oren Sofer leads a weekly vipassanā group in Berkeley, California, and helps to run the Mind Body Awareness Project, which teaches mindfulness to incarcerated youth. He studied with Munindra in the Antioch program in Bodh Gaya in 1997 and also practiced with him in 2001.

Michael Stein first met Munindra while taking courses with S. N. Goenka in Bodh Gaya in 1972. He later lived next door to him at Samanvaya, the Gandhi ashram in 1973, and saw him numerous times in Massachusetts and at Dhamma Giri.

Heather Stoddard has been head of Tibetan studies at the Institut national des langues et civilisations orientales (INALCO) in Paris since 1977 and established the Shalu Association in 1994 to help protect the cultural heritage of Tibet. A practitioner in the Vajrayāna tradition, she considers Munindra her first spiritual guide, having taken her first retreat with him in Bodh Gaya at the beginning of 1967.

Stephen Strange, a student of S. N. Goenka, first met Munindra around 1987 at Dhamma Giri, where he has attended retreats annually and saw Munindra regularly.

Suil met Munindra while doing courses with S. N. Goenka in Bodh Gaya in 1973. After time as a Buddhist nun in Korea from 1975 to 1981, she met him again at the Lama Foundation in New Mexico in 1982.

Robin Sunbeam is currently a school nurse in northern California. She studied for a year with Munindra in 1972 at Samanvaya, the Gandhi ashram in Bodh Gaya and received his guidance while learning Sanskrit in Rajgir in 1973. She also sat a retreat with him at IMS. Robin taught vipassanā meditation in San Francisco until her first child was born in 1988.

Dwarko Sundrani is one of the last active direct disciples of Mahatma Gandhi and has dedicated his life to working with the poorest of the poor in Bodh Gaya, where he became friends with Munindra in 1954. During the late 1960s, he accommodated Munindra at the Samanvaya Ashram, which he has managed since its establishment by Vinoba Bhave in 1954.

Lama Surya Das studied with Munindra in Bodh Gaya during several winters in the early- and mid-1970s. He is a lama and lineage holder in the Dzogchen tradition of Tibetan Buddhism, founder of the Dzogchen Center in America, and author of *Awakening the Buddha Within* and many other books.

Uno Svedin met Munindra in Bodh Gaya at the end of 1966 and remained continuously close to him until his death in 2003. He holds a PhD in physics and is a senior research fellow at the Stockholm Resilience Centre, Stockholm University, focusing on environmental issues in a social and cultural context. He is also director of international affairs at the Swedish Research Council for Environment, Agricultural Sciences, and Spatial Planning.

Manisha Talukbar, now a retired English teacher, first met Munindra in 1966 at the home of her mother-in-law, who considered him her adopted son. Manisha continued to see him on subsequent visits to Calcutta.

Saibal Talukbar, as a boy, met Munindra on visits with his grandmother to the Mahabodhi Society in Calcutta, beginning in 1991. He also accompanied Munindra to Dhamma Giri and Bodh Gaya and served as his attendant at the Antioch program.

Shuma Talukbar met Munindra through her mother, Manisha Talukbar, and learned vipassanā from him in Calcutta.

Danny Taylor has been practicing vipassanā meditation since 1984. In 1987, he met Munindra at the Mahabodhi Society in Calcutta and then attended his retreat in Sarnath. He currently works as a management consultant in Sydney, Australia, and is a meditation teacher at the Blue Mountains Insight Meditation Centre in the same area.

Denise Till met Munindra in Bodh Gaya in 1975 and they became close friends during the many years she has served as facilities manager and program manager for the Antioch program there.

Jeffrey Tipp is a family and marriage counselor in Vashon, Washington, and the resident teacher at the Blue Heron Zen Community in Seattle. He met Munindra in Seattle in 1978.

Christopher Titmuss, a former Buddhist monk in Thailand and India, is cofounder of Gaia House, an international retreat center in Devon, England. He is also a member of the international advisory council of the Buddhist Peace Fellowship and the author of numerous books. He first met Munindra in 1974 in Bodh Gaya, where he has been teaching annual retreats since 1975.

John M. Travis is the guiding and founding teacher of Mountain Stream Meditation Center, in Auburn, California. He began his studies in vipassanā in 1970, with Munindra, and later studied with a wide variety of other dharma teachers. A meditation counselor and Hakomi body-centered therapist, he leads retreats around the U.S.

Bryan Tucker met Munindra when he began practicing insight meditation in the late 1970s. He later saw him many times both in the U.S. and India. Bryan has taught meditation in India, Europe, Israel, and the U.S., and he currently resides in Boston.

Bhante Vimalaraṃsi (formerly Marvel Logan) practiced with Munindra at the Stillpoint Institute in San Jose, California, in 1977. He became a Buddhist monk in Thailand in 1986 and later studied in Burma and taught in Malaysia. He is presently establishing the Dhamma Sukha Meditation Center near Ironton, Missouri.

Fred von Allmen has been teaching insight meditation worldwide since 1984 and is a cofounder of Meditation Center Beatenberg in Switzerland. He first met Munindra in 1971 in Bodh Gaya and practiced under him in India and at IMS.

Wanda Weinberg was involved in the Antioch program in Bodh Gaya for several years. She studied under Munindra in 2000 and 2001 while serving as the program's teaching assistant and, in 2002, assisted him during his teaching period.

Grahame White is a guiding teacher with Vipassana Hawai'i, and, in Australia, he is a cofounder of the Blue Mountains Insight Meditation Centre, and the director of a wholesale business in Australia. He first met Munindra in Bodh Gaya in 1970 and spent many years there learning Dharma from him.

Giselle Wiederhielm, with her daughter Vivian Darst, hosted Munindra several times in Seattle. She attended a retreat with him in Oregon in 1983.

Reverend James "Jim" Willems has been practicing various forms of Buddhist meditation since 1960 and met Munindra at IMS in the early 1990s. He is an Episcopal priest in San Francisco.

David K. Wong met Munindra at a retreat in San Jose, California, in 1978, took him sightseeing afterward, and last saw him while studying under Taungpulu Sayādaw in 1979.

Sunny Wootton was Munindra's attendant for a three-month retreat at IMS in 1981, spent time with him in India the following year, and cooked for his retreats on Maui in the 1980s.

Christine Yedica began practicing vipassanā in 1974 and met Munindra in Bodh Gaya at the beginning of 1976. She traveled with him and Western dharma teachers in India and the U.S. She was on the board of IMS from 1978 to 1984. As a gerontologist in northern California, she incorporates mindfulness practice in her work with elders and their families.

Michael Zucker, an acupuncturist in Honolulu, studied with Munindra in Bodh Gaya in 1973. He accompanied him during Mahāsi Sayādaw's U.S. visit in 1979 and spent time with him at IMS, where he was a cook on the first staff.

The Munindra Memorial Scholarship and Archives

For anyone who is interested in making a contribution of money, materials, or information to honor Munindra's memory, the following avenues are available:

- A scholarship fund in Munindra's memory has been established at the Barre Center for Buddhist Studies (BCBS). The author's royalties from the sale of this book are dedicated to this scholarship fund.
- A Munindra archive has also been established at BCBS.
- Additional stories and photos may be contributed to www.livingthislifefully.com and www.munindra.com.

For more information, please contact:
Mirka Knaster
P.O. Box 261
The Sea Ranch, CA 95497
Mirka@mcn.org
www.mirkaknaster.com

Robert Pryor
Antioch Education Abroad
150 E. South College St.
Yellow Springs, OH 45387
rpryor@antioch.edu
http://aea.antioch.edu/india